ATTENTION !!!
BARCODE IS ON NEXT PAGE !!

Cheat Sheet

Yardage Needed by Fabric Width

Use this table to easily convert the yardage you need from one fabric width to another. For example, if your pattern calls for 1 yard of 60-inch-wide fabric and the fabric you want to use is only 45 inches wide, the table tells you that you need $1\frac{3}{8}$ yards of the 45-inch width fabric to make the same project.

35 inches	45 inches	50 inches	54 inches	60 inches
$1\frac{3}{4}$	$1\frac{3}{8}$	$1\frac{1}{4}$	$1\frac{1}{8}$	1
2	$1\frac{5}{8}$	$1\frac{1}{2}$	$1\frac{3}{8}$	$1\frac{1}{4}$
$2\frac{1}{4}$	$1\frac{3}{4}$	$1\frac{5}{8}$	$1\frac{1}{2}$	$1\frac{3}{8}$
$2\frac{1}{2}$	$2\frac{1}{8}$	$1\frac{3}{4}$	$1\frac{3}{4}$	$1\frac{5}{8}$
$2\frac{7}{8}$	$2\frac{1}{4}$	2	$1\frac{7}{8}$	$1\frac{3}{4}$
$3\frac{1}{8}$	$2\frac{1}{2}$	$2\frac{1}{4}$	2	$1\frac{7}{8}$
$3\frac{3}{8}$	$2\frac{3}{4}$	$2\frac{3}{8}$	$2\frac{1}{4}$	2
$3\frac{3}{4}$	$2\frac{7}{8}$	$2\frac{5}{8}$	$2\frac{3}{8}$	$2\frac{1}{4}$
$4\frac{1}{4}$	$3\frac{1}{8}$	$2\frac{3}{4}$	$2\frac{5}{8}$	$2\frac{3}{8}$
$4\frac{1}{2}$	$3\frac{3}{8}$	3	$2\frac{3}{4}$	$2\frac{5}{8}$
$4\frac{3}{4}$	$3\frac{5}{8}$	$3\frac{1}{4}$	$2\frac{7}{8}$	$2\frac{3}{4}$
5	$3\frac{7}{8}$	$3\frac{3}{8}$	$3\frac{1}{8}$	$2\frac{7}{8}$

Flat Sheet Sizes

Keep these sizes handy as you prepare to make a dust ruffle for your bed (see Chapter 14):

- Twin: 66 inches by 96 inches
- Full: 81 inches by 96 inches
- Queen: 90 inches by 102 inches
- King: 108 inches by 102 inches

Bed Pillow Sizes

The standard sizes of bed pillows determine how much fabric you need for some of the pillow projects in Chapter 15:

- Standard: 26 inches by 20 inches
- Queen: 30 inches by 20 inches
- King: 36 inches by 20 inches

Decorative Square Pillow Form Sizes

When making one of the pillows I tell you about in Chapter 15, you start with a pillow form of one of the following sizes:

- 12 inches
- 14 inches
- 16 inches
- 18 inches
- 20 inches
- 30 inches

...For Dummies®: Bestselling Book Series for Beginners

Sewing For Dummies

Cheat Sheet

Sewing Machine Needle Size and Fabric Chart

Use this table to help you decide which machine needle size is best for the type of fabric you want to work with. (Chapter 2 tells you more about specific fabric types.)

American Sizing	European Sizing	Suggested Fabrics
8	60	Chiffon, fine cottons, and sheers
9	65	Batiste, voile, blouse-weight silks, georgette, and light-weight microfibers
10	70	Chambray, crepe, tulle, lightweight blouse and dress fabrics, midweight microfibers, and eyelet
11	75	Interlock (T-shirt knit), jersey, satin, tricot, synthetic suede, and velour
12	80	Broadcloth, chintz, midweight corduroy, double knit, duck, gabardine, fleece poplin, velvet, and velveteen
14	90	Canvas, heavy corduroy, denim, real leather or suede, and upholstery fabrics
16	100	Very heavy duck, upholstery, and vinyl

General-Purpose Sewing Machine Needle Point Types

Use this table to match your fabric with the appropriate needle point type. (See Chapter 2 for more information about fabric types.)

Classification	Needle Point Type and Use
15 x 1H (American) 130/705H (European)	Multi-purpose or Universal: Used for most fabrics for general sewing
Blue Tip (American) 130/705HS (European) 130/705HPS (Pfaff) Q Needle (Sears) Singer 2045	Stretch: Used for knits and microfibers and designed to prevent skipped stitches and snagging
15 x 1DE (American) 130/705HJ (European)	Denim or Jeans: A sharp needle designed for sewing tightly woven fabrics such as heavy corduroy, denim, and upholstery fabrics

...For Dummies®: Bestselling Book Series for Beginners

References for the Rest of Us!™

BESTSELLING BOOK SERIES

Do you find that traditional reference books are overloaded with technical details and advice you'll never use? Do you postpone important life decisions because you just don't want to deal with them? Then our *...For Dummies*® business and general reference book series is for you.

...For Dummies business and general reference books are written for those frustrated and hard-working souls who know they aren't dumb, but find that the myriad of personal and business issues and the accompanying horror stories make them feel helpless. *...For Dummies* books use a lighthearted approach, a down-to-earth style, and even cartoons and humorous icons to dispel fears and build confidence. Lighthearted but not lightweight, these books are perfect survival guides to solve your everyday personal and business problems.

> *"More than a publishing phenomenon, 'Dummies' is a sign of the times."*
>
> — The New York Times

> *"...you won't go wrong buying them."*
>
> — Walter Mossberg, Wall Street Journal, on IDG Books' ...For Dummies books

> *"A world of detailed and authoritative information is packed into them..."*
>
> — U.S. News and World Report

Already, millions of satisfied readers agree. They have made *...For Dummies* the #1 introductory level computer book series and a best-selling business book series. They have written asking for more. So, if you're looking for the best and easiest way to learn about business and other general reference topics, look to *...For Dummies* to give you a helping hand.

IDG BOOKS WORLDWIDE®

SEWING

FOR

DUMMIES®

SEWING FOR DUMMIES®

by Jan Saunders

IDG BOOKS WORLDWIDE

IDG Books Worldwide, Inc.
An International Data Group Company

Foster City, CA ◆ Chicago, IL ◆ Indianapolis, IN ◆ New York, NY

Sewing For Dummies®

Published by
IDG Books Worldwide, Inc.
An International Data Group Company
919 E. Hillsdale Blvd.
Suite 400
Foster City, CA 94404
www.idgbooks.com (IDG Books Worldwide Web site)
www.dummies.com (Dummies Press Web site)

Library of Congress Catalog Card No.: 99-63192

ISBN: 0-7645-5137-X

Printed in the United States of America

10 9 8 7 6 5 4 3 2 1

1B/RU/QX/ZZ/IN

Distributed in the United States by IDG Books Worldwide, Inc.

Distributed by CDG Books Canada Inc. for Canada; by Transworld Publishers Limited in the United Kingdom; by IDG Norge Books for Norway; by IDG Sweden Books for Sweden; by IDG Books Australia Publishing Corporation Pty. Ltd. for Australia and New Zealand; by TransQuest Publishers Pte Ltd. for Singapore, Malaysia, Thailand, Indonesia, and Hong Kong; by Gotop Information Inc. for Taiwan; by ICG Muse, Inc. for Japan; by Norma Comunicaciones S.A. for Colombia; by Intersoft for South Africa; by Eyrolles for France; by International Thomson Publishing for Germany, Austria and Switzerland; by Distribuidora Cuspide for Argentina; by Livraria Cultura for Brazil; by Ediciones ZETA S.C.R. Ltda. for Peru; by WS Computer Publishing Corporation, Inc., for the Philippines; by Contemporanea de Ediciones for Venezuela; by Express Computer Distributors for the Caribbean and West Indies; by Micronesia Media Distributor, Inc. for Micronesia; by Grupo Editorial Norma S.A. for Guatemala; by Chips Computadoras S.A. de C.V. for Mexico; by Editorial Norma de Panama S.A. for Panama; by American Bookshops for Finland. Authorized Sales Agent: Anthony Rudkin Associates for the Middle East and North Africa.

For general information on IDG Books Worldwide's books in the U.S., please call our Consumer Customer Service department at 800-762-2974. For reseller information, including discounts and premium sales, please call our Reseller Customer Service department at 800-434-3422.

For information on where to purchase IDG Books Worldwide's books outside the U.S., please contact our International Sales department at 317-596-5530 or fax 317-596-5692.

For consumer information on foreign language translations, please contact our Customer Service department at 1-800-434-3422, fax 317-596-5692, or e-mail rights@idgbooks.com.

For information on licensing foreign or domestic rights, please phone +1-650-655-3109.

For sales inquiries and special prices for bulk quantities, please contact our Sales department at 650-655-3200 or write to the address above.

For information on using IDG Books Worldwide's books in the classroom or for ordering examination copies, please contact our Educational Sales department at 800-434-2086 or fax 317-596-5499.

For press review copies, author interviews, or other publicity information, please contact our Public Relations department at 650-655-3000 or fax 650-655-3299.

For authorization to photocopy items for corporate, personal, or educational use, please contact Copyright Clearance Center, 222 Rosewood Drive, Danvers, MA 01923, or fax 978-750-4470.

About the Author

Jan Saunders is a nationally known sewing and serging journalist and home economist. After graduating from Adrian College in Michigan, she became the Education Director of one of the largest sewing machine companies in the country, and then the Director of Consumer Education for the largest fabric chain in the country. Both professional experiences gave her a solid foundation in the home sewing industry, which she continues to service with her many writing, marketing, and industry consulting projects.

In addition to writing for several home sewing publications, she is a best selling author for several publishers, with 13 books to her credit. Several of her titles have been chosen as main selections for the *Crafters' Choice Collection,* a division of the Book-of-the-Month Club.

To promote her projects, Jan is a frequent guest on several PBS television shows. Jan has also had regular appearances on the Home Shopping Network and the Home & Garden Network. One of her segments has been the most popular with viewers since the series started in 1995.

Jan currently resides in Phoenix, Arizona, with her husband, son, dog, and collection of books, sewing equipment, fabric, and crafting products stashed in every available corner of her home. She and her family will be relocating to the Pacific Northwest.

ABOUT IDG BOOKS WORLDWIDE

Welcome to the world of IDG Books Worldwide.

IDG Books Worldwide, Inc., is a subsidiary of International Data Group, the world's largest publisher of computer-related information and the leading global provider of information services on information technology. IDG was founded more than 30 years ago by Patrick J. McGovern and now employs more than 9,000 people worldwide. IDG publishes more than 290 computer publications in over 75 countries. More than 90 million people read one or more IDG publications each month.

Launched in 1990, IDG Books Worldwide is today the #1 publisher of best-selling computer books in the United States. We are proud to have received eight awards from the Computer Press Association in recognition of editorial excellence and three from Computer Currents' First Annual Readers' Choice Awards. Our best-selling ...For Dummies® series has more than 50 million copies in print with translations in 31 languages. IDG Books Worldwide, through a joint venture with IDG's Hi-Tech Beijing, became the first U.S. publisher to publish a computer book in the People's Republic of China. In record time, IDG Books Worldwide has become the first choice for millions of readers around the world who want to learn how to better manage their businesses.

Our mission is simple: Every one of our books is designed to bring extra value and skill-building instructions to the reader. Our books are written by experts who understand and care about our readers. The knowledge base of our editorial staff comes from years of experience in publishing, education, and journalism — experience we use to produce books to carry us into the new millennium. In short, we care about books, so we attract the best people. We devote special attention to details such as audience, interior design, use of icons, and illustrations. And because we use an efficient process of authoring, editing, and desktop publishing our books electronically, we can spend more time ensuring superior content and less time on the technicalities of making books.

You can count on our commitment to deliver high-quality books at competitive prices on topics you want to read about. At IDG Books Worldwide, we continue in the IDG tradition of delivering quality for more than 30 years. You'll find no better book on a subject than one from IDG Books Worldwide.

John Kilcullen
Chairman and CEO
IDG Books Worldwide, Inc.

Steven Berkowitz
President and Publisher
IDG Books Worldwide, Inc.

Eighth Annual Computer Press Awards ≥ 1992

Ninth Annual Computer Press Awards ≥ 1993

Tenth Annual Computer Press Awards ≥ 1994

Eleventh Annual Computer Press Awards ≥ 1995

IDG is the world's leading IT media, research and exposition company. Founded in 1964, IDG had 1997 revenues of $2.05 billion and has more than 9,000 employees worldwide. IDG offers the widest range of media options that reach IT buyers in 75 countries representing 95% of worldwide IT spending. IDG's diverse product and services portfolio spans six key areas including print publishing, online publishing, expositions and conferences, market research, education and training, and global marketing services. More than 90 million people read one or more of IDG's 290 magazines and newspapers, including IDG's leading global brands — Computerworld, PC World, Network World, Macworld and the Channel World family of publications. IDG Books Worldwide is one of the fastest-growing computer book publishers in the world, with more than 700 titles in 36 languages. The "...For Dummies®" series alone has more than 50 million copies in print. IDG offers online users the largest network of technology-specific Web sites around the world through IDG.net (http://www.idg.net), which comprises more than 225 targeted Web sites in 55 countries worldwide. International Data Corporation (IDC) is the world's largest provider of information technology data, analysis and consulting, with research centers in over 41 countries and more than 400 research analysts worldwide. IDG World Expo is a leading producer of more than 168 globally branded conferences and expositions in 35 countries including E3 (Electronic Entertainment Expo), Macworld Expo, ComNet, Windows World Expo, ICE (Internet Commerce Expo), Agenda, DEMO, and Spotlight. IDG's training subsidiary, ExecuTrain, is the world's largest computer training company, with more than 230 locations worldwide and 785 training courses. IDG Marketing Services helps industry-leading IT companies build international brand recognition by developing global integrated marketing programs via IDG's print, online and exposition products worldwide. Further information about the company can be found at www.idg.com. 1/24/99

Dedication

This book is dedicated to my world of sewing friends — past, present, and future. I am privileged and honored in your presence whether you're holding a needle and thread for the first time or have been sewing longer than I've been alive (and that's a really long time).

Author's Acknowledgments

At age 7, I was learning to sew under the watchful eye of my grandmother. When I had finished hand-stitching the set-in sleeves of a doll jacket, I cried and cried because it didn't look right. Grandma gently grabbed the jacket from me and turned the sleeves "inside out." It was a miracle — the jacket looked just like the one in the store. From that moment on, I was hooked on sewing. It's been an intimate part of who I am ever since. Thank you, Grandma, for being my first teacher.

A big-time thank you also goes to my parents, Ray and Bernice Saunders. Even though I grew up on a strict budget, there was always money for fabric and plenty of praise for my handmade creations.

Thanks also to my most understanding and tolerant husband, Ted Maresh, who hardly mentions the dozens of boxes, packed closets, and my home office overflowing with fabric and sewing paraphernalia. Yes, I will start cooking again now that the book is done. And a big thank you to my wonderfully patient son who has given up a lot of time with me so I could work on this book.

I have the most wonderful network of friends who have influenced what I've done in my life and career. You have provided inspiration, knowledge, encouragement, and expertise, and I thank each of you from the bottom of my heart. Without you, this book would have been written by someone else. Thank you, Robbie Fanning, for teaching me so much about writing, sewing, and keeping life in perspective. Thank you, Jackie Dodson, for your incredible sense of humor, your creative genius, and friendship. Thank you, Gail Brown, for your constant encouragement and market savvy. Thank you, Karyl Garbow, for being a kindred spirit for almost 26 years. Thank you, Sue Hausmann, for your dedication to sewing education in our industry and for always sharing your wisdom with me no matter the time of day. Thank you, Pattie Lloyd, for your incredible attitude, artistic talents, and the enthusiasm for everything you share with me and everyone who touches your life.

Thank you, Andy Chen, for the beautiful photographs and the kind treatment of the projects in this book. Thank you, Chris Hansen, for your wonderful hand and the sensational illustrations that add clarity to my words. Thank you Holly McGuire, Mary Goodwin, Tina Sims, and the team of publishing experts there at IDG. You are all truly amazing at what you do and how you do it.

Publisher's Acknowledgments

We're proud of this book; please register your comments through our IDG Books Worldwide Online Registration Form located at http://my2cents.dummies.com.

Some of the people who helped bring this book to market include the following:

Acquisitions, Editorial, and Media Development

Project Editor: Mary Goodwin

Acquisitions Editor: Holly McGuire

Copy Editors: Tamara Castleman, Brian Kramer, Donna Love, Stacey Mickelbart, Patricia Pan, Rowena Rappaport, Tina Sims, Susan Diane Smith, Linda S. Stark, Janet M. Withers

Technical Editors: Linda Lucas, Melody Schlegel

Editorial Coordinator: Maureen F. Kelly

Acquisitions Coordinator: Jonathan Malysiak

Editorial Manager: Jennifer Ehrlich

Editorial Assistants: Paul E. Kuzmic, Alison Walthall

Production

Project Coordinator: Regina Snyder

Layout and Graphics: Angela F. Hunckler, Brent Savage, Janet Seib, Michael A. Sullivan, Brian Torwelle, Mary Jo Weis, Dan Whetstine

Proofreaders: Mildred Rosenzweig, Marianne Santy, Rebecca Senninger

Indexer: Sherry Massey

Illustrations: Chris Hansen

Color photography: Andy Chen

General and Administrative

IDG Books Worldwide, Inc.: John Kilcullen, CEO; Steven Berkowitz, President and Publisher

IDG Books Technology Publishing Group: Richard Swadley, Senior Vice President and Publisher; Walter Bruce III, Vice President and Associate Publisher; Steven Sayre, Associate Publisher; Joseph Wikert, Associate Publisher; Mary Bednarek, Branded Product Development Director; Mary Corder, Editorial Director

IDG Books Consumer Publishing Group: Roland Elgey, Senior Vice President and Publisher; Kathleen A. Welton, Vice President and Publisher; Kevin Thornton, Acquisitions Manager; Kristin A. Cocks, Editorial Director

IDG Books Internet Publishing Group: Brenda McLaughlin, Senior Vice President and Publisher; Diane Graves Steele, Vice President and Associate Publisher; Sofia Marchant, Online Marketing Manager

IDG Books Production for Dummies Press: Michael R. Britton, Vice President of Production; Debbie Stailey, Associate Director of Production; Cindy L. Phipps, Manager of Project Coordination, Production Proofreading, and Indexing; Shelley Lea, Supervisor of Graphics and Design; Debbie J. Gates, Production Systems Specialist; Robert Springer, Supervisor of Proofreading; Laura Carpenter, Production Control Manager; Tony Augsburger, Supervisor of Reprints and Bluelines

Dummies Packaging and Book Design: Patty Page, Manager, Promotions Marketing

◆

The publisher would like to give special thanks to Patrick J. McGovern, without whom this book would not have been possible.

◆

Contents at a Glance

Cartoons at a Glance

By Rich Tennant

"If it's any consolation, you hemmed the length on this leg perfectly."

page 63

"The intruder was no match for the old woman. She took him down and hand stitched him to the carpet before he knew what was happening. Someone unzip his mouth so we can hear what he has to say."

page 113

"It's a beginner's sewing kit I put together for you. There are scissors, needles, bandages, gauze, antiseptics..."

page 5

"I'm not sure who put the tattoo memory card in my sewing machine, but that's why my pillows are embroidered in serpents coiled around a dagger."

page 277

"Maybe a shower curtain wasn't the best thing to try and make into an evening dress."

page 175

"The black spots? That's where he has holes in his pants. And he has the nerve to call his felt tip marker a 'sewing tool.'"

page 245

Fax: 978-546-7747 • E-mail: the5wave@tiac.net

Table of Contents

Introduction

Sewing is fun, relaxing, and tremendously rewarding. It feels great when you sit down and sew something together (and are tickled with the results)!

Besides the fun and satisfaction you get out of sewing , this wonderful hobby can also save you money. I show you the best ways to stitch up your own hems, repair split seams, and sew on those loose buttons. You can save even more money by making your home decor projects, such as curtains and pillows.

How to Use This Book

Sewing For Dummies is a book for both absolute beginners and experienced sewers. If you're a stone-cold beginner, you'll appreciate that I explain everything necessary to sewing beginning-level projects and that I don't assume that you've ever even picked up a needle and thread before. If you've had some experience with sewing, *Sewing For Dummies* still has something to offer — I tell you tips and tricks that it took me years to pick up. The projects in this book can also be enjoyed by all sewers, no matter what your level of experience.

If you are new to sewing, I suggest that you start by reading the chapters in Parts I and II. There you find some fundamental information on sewing. Besides that, you can skip around from chapter to chapter in the book, reading only about the types of sewing and projects which interest you.

Foolish Assumptions about You

You must have some tools in order to sew — a sewing machine and scissors, for example. For the projects in this book, you need the tools listed in Chapter 1. I call these tools your Sewing Survival Kit, and I ask that you have it handy for just about every one of the projects in this book.

How This Book Is Organized

I organized this book into six parts so that it's easy for you to find exactly the information you need.

Part I: Hardware and "Softwear" for Sewing

In this part, I tell you about the hard and the soft tools you need for sewing and how to work with them, including your sewing machine, fabric, thread, and patterns.

Part II: Sewers! Start Your Engines!

Read the chapters in this part to find out how to do some things fundamental to sewing, including threading a needle, tying a knot, sewing on a button, sewing a seam, and hemming.

Part III: Fashion Fundamentals

When you sew clothes, you usually start out with a pattern and a set of instructions for putting the clothes together. For a beginner, these pattern instructions can sometimes be a little intimidating. The instructions may tell you to do something (like sew a dart or apply a zipper) that you don't know how to do. The chapters in this part help you decipher these sorts of techniques, which are essential to successful fashion sewing.

Part IV: Sewing for the Home

This part of the book lets you turn a little sewing knowledge into untold savings for your home. In this part, I show you how to sew pillows, duvet covers, dust ruffles, drapes and curtains, napkins, place mats, tablecloths, and more. Using the chapters in this part, you can create coordinated looks for almost every room in your home, quickly and inexpensively.

Part V: Alterations and Quick Fixes

Read the chapters in this part when you want creative solutions to fixing what ails your clothes. When clothes get too tight or too loose, too short or too long, you can find out how to fix them here. I also show you how to do some basic repairs on holes, rips, and other mishaps.

Part VI: The Part of Tens

The first chapter in this part is truly the mother lode of project chapters. In it, I give you detailed, step-by-step instructions on creating ten easy projects. Most of the projects in this chapter can be completed in one quick sitting! I also throw in two chapters chock full of tips and hints to help keep you stitching along the straight and narrow.

Icons Used in This Book

Throughout this book, I guide you toward important points by using the following icons.

The information next to this icon tells you how to do something in the quickest and best way possible.

Some sewing tools are essential to sewing, while others are not essential but are still nice to have as you sew. Try out the tools mentioned next to this icon — you may find one that helps you quite a bit with the sort of projects you like to do.

Make sure to read the text next to this icon. It can save you lots of blood, sweat, and tears.

Next to this icon you find information that you should keep in the back of your mind as you sew. These are key points to creative and efficient sewing.

Part I
Hardware and "Softwear" for Sewing

The 5th Wave

By Rich Tennant

"It's a beginner's sewing kit I put together for you. There are scissors, needles, bandages, gauze, antiseptics..."

In this part . . .

To end up with a successful sewing project, you need to start out with good materials. This includes your sewing machine, needles, thread, fabric, and pattern, among other things. I tell you about the very best tools for your sewing projects in this part. In addition, I tell you how to work with those tools once you have them, including how to navigate a sewing machine and how to lay out a pattern.

And just in case you're thinking that there's nothing fun to do in this part, you can think again. I include some low-sew projects that will impress your friends and family with how much you can do with your sewing machine.

Chapter 1

Assembling Your Sewing Kit

• •

• •

*L*ike most hobbies, successful sewing projects begin with a few good tools and a little know-how. Sure, you can collect some of these tools from your household: those old scissors from the garage, the ruler from your desk drawer, and pins scavenged from freshly opened dress shirts, but you'll have a better sewing experience by using the tools intended for the job.

In this chapter, I list and explain the necessities — the tools I use just about every time I sew and that are essential for creating the projects in this book. I also give you some tips about additional tools that come in handy as your skills improve. So you can consider these tools your Sewing Survival Kit.

Keep your Sewing Survival Kit in a small fishing tackle box (other than your sewing machine and pressing tools, of course) or use one of the many sewing or craft organizers available through your local fabric store, craft store, or sewing machine dealer. Choose an organizer that has a handle and a secure latch so that you can easily carry it without dumping stuff all over the place. Use this as a checklist when rounding up the tools for your Sewing Survival Kit; then read the rest of this chapter to understand how each one works.

Making Sure Your Sewing Measures Up

You use a *tape measure* for taking your own measurements, checking measurements on a pattern, and other measuring tasks. (See Chapter 4 for more information on patterns.)

You find all kinds of tape measures on the market. I recommend that you use a paper or plastic-coated fabric tape measure. Neither material stretches, so you always get accurate measurements.

Taking on small tasks with a seam gauge

A tape measure suffices for most measuring jobs, but for measuring small and narrow things, such as hems and buttonholes, use a *seam gauge*. This 6-inch, stiff ruler has an adjustable slide. When you measure a hem, you use the slide to see how deep the hem is as you move the seam gauge all the way around the hemline. When measuring buttonholes, simply set the slide to the correct length and mark away.

Keep your tape handy by draping it around your neck, but remember to take if off when you leave the house, or you end up looking pretty silly.

Cutting Up (Without Cracking Up)

If I could have only two cutting tools, I'd use the following:

- ✔ **8-inch bent dressmaker's shears:** Shears are best for cutting fabric. They have one straight and one bent-angle blade, a round thumb hole, and an oblong finger hole for comfortable, accurate cutting. The bent-angle blade gives your index finger a place to rest when you have a long cutting job. The bend in the blade also prevents you from lifting the fabric off the table, ensuring a more accurate cut.

- ✔ **5-inch trimming scissors:** Scissors have straight blades and two round holes for your finger and thumb. They come in handy for trimming smaller areas on a project and for clipping threads.

When shopping for shears or scissors, make sure that you test the scissors or shears on a variety of fabrics. They should cut all the way to the tips of the blades.

Some brands of scissors and shears are made of lightweight aluminum alloy. The lightweight models are generally more comfortable, can be a little cheaper than other models, and can be resharpened several times. However, with some brands, you may find it tough to cut heavy fabrics or through multiple fabric layers with the lighter-weight blades.

Steel scissors and shears are heavier, which allows them to easily cut through heavier fabrics and more fabric layers. Because the blades are each made of one solid piece of steel, heavy scissors and shears can be resharpened more times than the lightweight variety can, and they often stay sharper longer, too. But they're generally more expensive than their lightweight counterparts.

Keeping your shears and scissors sharp

Shears and scissors must be sharp to be a pleasure to use. After all, cutting is a big part of sewing, and if it's a chore, you won't like to sew.

Most sewing machine dealers sharpen scissors and shears. In addition, many fabric chain stores have a scissors-sharpener who visits the store periodically. After the pro finishes sharpening your shears or scissors, check that they cut to the point.

Regardless of the weight, look for scissors and shears with a screw joining the blades; these models generally cut heavier fabrics and more layers than those that are riveted.

Once you have plunked down money for a good pair of scissors and shears, don't let the family get hold of them and cut plastic, cardboard, wire, or anything you don't normally cut when sewing.

I also often use a pair of 3-inch *embroidery scissors.* The pointed blades are perfect for cutting out unwanted stitches and trimming laces, appliques, and hard-to-reach places.

Making Your Mark

Sewing is an exact science in many ways. When you sew, you must match up the pieces of your project precisely — otherwise you could get the left sleeve in the right armhole and end up feeling like you're walking backwards all the time.

To help you match up pieces exactly the right way, the pattern for a project includes *match points,* called notches and dots, *which are* printed right on the pattern tissue. To use these match points, you lay the pattern tissue down on the fabric, pin the tissue to the fabric, cut out the pattern piece, and clip the notches and mark the dots from the pattern tissue to the fabric. (See Chapter 4 for more information on cutting out and marking patterns.)

Fabric markers made especially for sewing make transferring match points from the pattern to the fabric a quick and easy task. Use one of the following markers, depending on the kind of fabric you want to mark:

✔ **Disappearing dressmaker's chalk:** Excellent for marking dark fabrics. The chalk disappears in about five days or when you wash or iron the fabric.

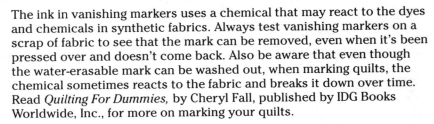

✔ **Wash-out pencil:** Shows up well when marking dark fabrics and erases with a drop of cold water. Looks like a regular pencil with a white, pink, or light blue lead.

✔ **Vanishing marker:** A felt-tipped marker for light-colored fabrics. The ink is usually pink or purple and disappears in 12 to 24 hours, unless you live in a humid climate, and then marks can disappear in minutes.

The ink in vanishing markers uses a chemical that may react to the dyes and chemicals in synthetic fabrics. Always test vanishing markers on a scrap of fabric to see that the mark can be removed, even when it's been pressed over and doesn't come back. Also be aware that even though the water-erasable mark can be washed out, when marking quilts, the chemical sometimes reacts to the fabric and breaks it down over time. Read *Quilting For Dummies,* by Cheryl Fall, published by IDG Books Worldwide, Inc., for more on marking your quilts.

✔ **Water-erasable marker:** A felt-tipped marker for light to medium-colored fabrics. The ink is blue, and marks disappear with clear water or by washing the fabric. This marker works better than the vanishing marker if you sew in a humid environment.

✔ **Invisible or removable transparent tape:** These are useful, but not essential, marking tools. Invisible tape has a cloudy appearance that you can easily see on most fabrics. Removable tape has the same adhesive as sticky notes and doesn't pull off the nap (fuzz) from velvet, corduroy, or velour. I use ½-inch-width invisible or removable tape as a stitching template for sewing in a zipper (see Chapter 9), as a guide for straight stitching, and for lots of other little jobs. Hide it from your family, though, or it may disappear when you really, really need it.

Pinning Down Your Projects

You need pins to sew. Period. You use them to pin the pattern to the fabric, pin the pieces of fabric together before sewing them together, and for several other "pinning" jobs. Because pins are such a constant companion when you sew, buy some that will keep your fingers happy.

I recommend using long, fine, glass-head pins. The glass head is comfortable in your fingers when you pin through multiple layers of fabric, and the extra length makes pinning more secure. Plus, if you accidentally press or iron over the glass heads, they don't melt.

You also need a place to keep your pins. Some pins, like glass-head pins, are packaged in convenient plastic boxes that make great pin holders. But to save time, I wear a wrist pincushion so that my pins stay with me wherever I go.

A magnetic pincushion is handy in your cutting area and at the ironing board. Besides pins, small scissors and a seam ripper also stick to the magnetized surface. It's also wonderful for picking up pins and stray metal objects that fall on the carpet.

 If you have a computerized machine, avoid getting the magnetic pincushion near it because you may wipe out the memory.

Pressing Issues

In sewing, if someone can immediately tell that your project is homemade, it's probably because something just looks . . . wrong. Usually this happens because the project wasn't pressed properly during construction. Using the right tools for pressing is just as important to sewing as using a sharp needle and thread that matches your fabric. Good pressing tools mean the difference between a project that looks good and a project that looks great.

You need a *good* iron. I didn't say an *expensive* one — just a good one. Choose an iron that has a variety of heat settings and the capability to make steam. Also, choose an iron that has a smooth *soleplate* (the soleplate is the part that heats up) and is easy to clean.

 If you use *fusible products,* such as iron-on patches that melt when heated, you can easily gum up the iron. A non-stick surface on the soleplate makes it easy to clean while retaining its smooth, slick surface.

 Several newer brands of irons automatically turn off every few minutes, which is a real pain when you're ready to use the iron, so avoid buying an iron with this feature.

You also need a padded ironing board. Without the padding, seams and edges can shadow through to the right side of the fabric when pressed and look like a pair of ski tracks on either side of the seamline. This gives the finished project a shiny, overpressed look that's tough — if not impossible — to remove.

Also choose a muslin or nonreflective ironing board cover. The silver, reflector-type covers are too slippery and sometimes get too hot, causing unnecessary scorching on some synthetic fabrics.

A *press cloth* is also essential for pressing a variety of fabrics, from fine silks to heavier woolens and wool blends. You place the press cloth between the iron and the fabric to prevent shine and overpressing. Use a clean, white or off-white 100-percent cotton or linen tea towel or napkin, or a purchased press cloth.

If you're considering a print or color-dyed fabric for a press cloth — don't do it. Dyes can bleed through and ruin your project. Terry cloth isn't a good choice either. The napped surface of a terry cloth towel can leave the familiar terry texture on the fabric.

A professional dressmaker friend of mine loves using a cloth diaper for a press cloth. The diaper is white and absorbent, can be doubled or tripled depending on the use, and is a good size for many projects.

After you decide to make sewing a regular hobby and you feel comfortable investing a little extra money into your projects, consider purchasing the following tools:

- **Seam roll:** This fabric cylinder measures about 12 inches long by about 3 inches in diameter. You use the roll to press seams open without causing "tire tracks" on either side of the seam. Because of the shape of the seam roll, the seam allowance falls away from under the iron and won't press through to the right side of the fabric.

- **Tailor's ham:** This stuffed, triangular-shaped cushion has several curves on it that simulate the curves on your body. You use the ham to press and shape darts, side seams, sleeves, and other curved areas on a garment.

Both the seam roll and the ham have a 100-percent cotton cloth side made out of heavy muslin-type fabric for pressing high-temp fabrics such as cotton and linen, and a wool side for pressing lower-temp fabrics such as silks and synthetics.

Needing the Right Needles

Needles come in hand and machine varieties, and within each variety are many shapes, sizes, and types. The needle you select depends on the fabric you use and the project you want to sew.

Generally, the finer the fabric you work with, the finer the needle — the heavier the fabric, the heavier needle.

Selecting needles for hand sewing

When selecting hand needles, choose a variety pack, and you'll have what you need for most basic hand-sewing projects. Variety packs vary from brand to brand but generally have from five to ten needles of various lengths and thicknesses. Some even have different-sized eyes.

The thimble question: To use, or not to use

A thimble protects your finger when pushing the needle through heavy thicknesses of fabric.

Thimbles come in a variety of sizes; choose a thimble that comfortably fits the middle finger on your dominant hand. Try on a variety of thimbles until you find one that's just right — then use it! You will save your fingers a lot of wear and tear.

In a pinch, you can use any hand needle as long as the point can easily penetrate the fabric and the eye doesn't shred the thread.

Selecting needles for sewing machines

For machine needles, size #11 (in American sizing) or #12/80 (in European sizing) works well for general sewing on about 80 percent of today's fabrics.

To make sure that you have the right size needle for the fabric, read your Operating Manual or ask your local sewing machine dealer. Some needles offer different point types designed to handle different stitching techniques and fabric types. For most projects, though, a multipurpose or "Universal" point works beautifully. Buy a package or two of #11 American multipurpose or #12/80 Universal European sewing machine needles, and you should be all set.

When shopping for sewing machine needles, remember to take the make and model number of your machine with you. Some models can use only their brand of needle without causing harm to the machine. When in doubt, ask your local sewing machine dealer what to buy.

During the course of a project, a sewing machine needle gets used and abused, and when the needle becomes bent or burred, the needle skips stitches and can snag the fabric. Unlike hand needles, you need to replace your machine needle frequently. The best machine needle for any project is a new one, so start each project with a new needle.

As ye sew, so shall ye rip

While not a biblical reference, it's a fact of sewing. When you make mistakes, you correct them by ripping out the stitches, or "un-sewing."

Make ripping stitches as pleasant as possible. Buy a sharp *seam ripper,* a little tool with a point that lifts the stitch off the fabric as the blade cuts the thread.

I've put more unwanted holes in a project with a dull ripper simply because I pushed too hard to cut a stitch and the momentum was enough to continue past the stitches into the fabric. For specifics on "un-sewing," see Chapter 5.

Working with a Sewing Machine

Many folks drag out Aunt Millie's 75-year-old clunker from the garage or basement thinking it's good enough for a "beginner." The instruction book for Millie's machine has long since disappeared, and just before completing a project, the machine becomes possessed with demons that sabotage every seam.

Just like your car, you want your sewing machine to be dependable transportation. The machine doesn't have to be a race car, and it doesn't need every modern convenience known to man. It just needs to work well — every time.

Your local sewing machine dealer can show you a wide range of models and prices. Many offer machines on a rental basis, and some dealers let you come into their classrooms and use a machine during open sewing time. You can also take Aunt Millie's machine into a dealer, have an honest assessment made about its general working condition and life span, and see whether you can realistically count on using it.

Finding your way around a sewing machine

Acquainting yourself with the parts of the sewing machine and knowing how it works keep you and your sewing machine out of trouble.

Consider this section of the book your road map to navigating a sewing machine. I tell you all about the parts on a typical machine (shown in Figure 1-1) and what you use them for.

Of course, your sewing machine may look a little different from what you see in Figure 1-1. You may have a newer model, or you may be working on a serger (in which case, you should check out the sidebar "Using a serger," later in this chapter). If things on your machine don't correspond exactly to what I show you, consult the Operating Manual that comes with your machine to see how the parts compare.

The needle

The most important part of the sewing machine is the needle. It's so important that I give the needle its own section, "Selecting needles for sewing machines," earlier in this chapter.

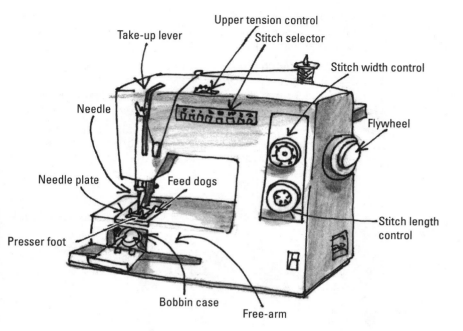

Figure 1-1:
A typical sewing machine and its parts.

Labels (clockwise): Take-up lever · Upper tension control · Stitch selector · Stitch width control · Flywheel · Stitch length control · Free-arm · Bobbin case · Presser foot · Needle plate · Feed dogs · Needle

Always start a new project with a new sewing machine needle.

The presser foot

Sometimes incorrectly referred to as a "pressure foot," the *presser foot* holds the fabric firmly against the feed dogs (keep reading to find out about feed dogs) so that the fabric doesn't flap up and down with each stitch.

For most machines, you can buy different presser feet for specialty jobs. Most machines come with four to five of the most useful variations, including the following (shown in Figure 1-2):

- **All-purpose foot:** This foot, which is usually metal, works well on virtually every kind of fabric. The foot is often available with a Teflon coating for an even smoother sewing experience.

- **Embroidery foot:** Sometimes referred to as the *appliqué foot,* the embroidery foot is often made of a transparent material. The high, wide groove carved out on the underside allows the foot to glide over satin decorative stitches without smashing them into the fabric.

- **Blind hem foot:** This foot helps stitch a truly invisible hem (you can read more about hems in Chapter 7). The blind hem foot usually has a wide toe on the right and a guide (that may or may not be adjustable) and narrow toe on the left.

✔ **Button sewing foot:** This foot usually has very short toes and a nylon or rubber gripper designed to hold a button firmly in place (see Chapter 5 for clever ways to sew on buttons by machine and hand).

✔ **Quilting or edge guide:** This foot slides or screws on behind the ankle of the presser foot. The guide rides over the previous row of stitching for parallel rows of quilting, or next to an edge for perfectly positioned topstitching. (See Chapter 5 for more about topstitching.)

✔ **Zipper foot:** Not surprisingly, you use this foot to sew in a zipper (see Chapter 9 for the details on zippers). The foot has one toe and is adjustable either by sliding the foot over, or by snapping it on the other side of the ankle.

Figure 1-2:
Typical sewing machine presser feet.

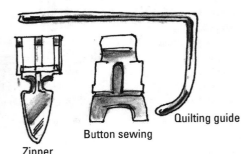

All-purpose Embroidery Blind hem Zipper Button sewing Quilting guide

The presser foot lever

Lift *the presser foot lever* to raise the presser foot. Doing so releases the upper tension so that you can remove the fabric.

Some brands of sewing machines feature a knee lift that allows you to have both hands free when removing the fabric from the presser foot or turning the fabric around.

The feed dogs

Feed dogs, sometimes referred to as "feed teeth," are teeth or pads that move the fabric through the machine. The fabric is sandwiched between the presser foot and the feed dogs, and as the needle stitches up and down, the feed dogs grab the fabric and move it under the foot.

Most machines allow you to sew with the feed dogs up or down. You do most sewing with the feed dogs in the up position; you use the down position mostly for mending or for free-machine embroidery.

The needle plate

Sometimes referred to as a "throat plate," the *needle plate* rests on the bed of the machine and fits over the feed dogs. It also has either a small round hole or an oblong hole that the needle passes through.

The needle plate often includes a series of lines that run in ¼-inch increments from the needle. These lines guide you as you sew a *seam allowance,* which you can read more about in Chapter 6.

For most sewing, you use the needle plate with the oblong hole. This way, the needle has the clearance it needs and won't break when you use a stitch that zigzags from side to side.

The bobbin and company

A *bobbin* is a small spool that holds from about 40 to 70 yards of thread. The machine uses the thread in the bobbin to make a *lock stitch,* the common straight stitch, on today's household sewing machines.

Machines usually come with three to five bobbins that are specially made for the machine's make and model. Bobbins are wound on a *bobbin winder.* Check your Operating Manual for proper bobbin winding and threading instructions. After you wind the thread around a bobbin, the bobbin fits into a *bobbin case,* and the thread is ready to be pulled up through the needle plate, ready for stitching.

If your bobbin has a hole in it, double and twist the thread end, poking the folded end of the thread through the hole from the inside of the bobbin, out. Place the bobbin on the winder, holding the thread end tightly. Start winding until the thread breaks off. This way, when you get to the end of a bobbin, the wrong end of the thread won't accidentally get caught in the stitch.

Bobbin winding does differ with the brand, so check your Operating Manual for bobbin winding instructions. No matter what brand you use, though, don't overfill the bobbin for smooth sewing and the best stitch quality.

The free arm

A *free-arm,* sometimes called an *open arm,* is a squared-off cylinder on the bed of the machine that lets you stitch around tubular areas, such as pant legs, sleeves, cuffs, and armholes, without ripping out a seam.

The flywheel

On the right end of the machine is a *flywheel,* or hand wheel, which turns when you sew. The flywheel can drive the needle up and down, and it coordinates the needle movement with the feed dogs when creating a stitch. On certain machines, this allows you to manually control the needle, which helps you when you want to pivot the fabric under the needle when sewing corners.

To pivot your fabric under the needle, simply turn the flywheel so that the needle is down in the fabric, lift the presser foot, pivot the fabric, lower the presser foot, and then continue sewing.

Depending on the machine model, some flywheels have *a clutch* or button that you must release when winding a bobbin. Consult your Operating Manual for specific instructions on bobbin winding.

The stitch-length control

The stitch-length control determines the distance the feed dogs move the fabric under the needle. When the feed dogs move with shorter strokes, the machine sews shorter stitches. When the feed dogs move with longer strokes, the stitches are longer.

Your stitch-length control gives stitch lengths in one of the following two ways, depending on the make and model of the machine:

- ✔ Millimeters (mm)
- ✔ Stitches per inch (spi)

Throughout *Sewing For Dummies,* I give you stitch length settings in millimeters (mm) and stitches per inch (spi).

The average stitch length for mid-weight fabrics is 2.5 to 3 mm/10 to 12 spi. For fine fabrics, use 1.5 to 2 mm/13 to 20 spi. (Anything shorter is almost impossible to rip out when you make a mistake.) For heavier fabrics, basting, or topstitching, use a 4 to 6 mm/4 to 5 spi. (You can read more about basting and topstitching in Chapter 5.)

The stitch-width control

The stitch-width control sets the distance the needle moves from side to side. This distance is always measured in millimeters (mm).

Some sewing machines have a maximum stitch width of 4 to 5 mm. Others create stitches as wide as 9 mm. A 5-mm width does the trick for most utility sewing. (Throughout *Sewing For Dummies,* I give stitch-width settings in a range that works for most sewing machines.)

The needle position

Needle position refers to the position of the needle in relationship to the hole in the needle plate. In center needle position, the needle is centered over the oblong hole in the needle plate. In left needle position, the needle is to the left of center. In right needle position, the needle is to the right of center.

A few older, less expensive models have either a permanent left needle position or a permanent center needle position. Most newer models (made in the last 20 years or so) have an adjustable needle position. Adjustable needle position comes in handy when you're topstitching, sewing on buttons, and sewing in zippers. Instead of moving the fabric around under the needle, you simply move the needle into position by adjusting the needle position. The needle position control is usually around, near, or a part of the stitch-width control. If you can't locate it, read your Operating Manual.

The stitch selector

If your sewing machine does more than straight stitch and zigzag, there is a way to select a stitch. (See Chapter 5 for more information on basic sewing machine stitches.)

Older machines have dials, levers, buttons, or drop-in cams as *stitch selectors*. Newer, computerized models have keys or touch pads that not only select the stitch but also automatically set the stitch length and width.

The upper tension control

In order to make uniform stitches, your machine requires a certain amount of tension on the thread as it sews. Most machines offer an upper tension control that allows you to adjust this tension.

The upper tension is usually marked in numbers — the higher the number, the tighter the tension; the lower the number, the looser the tension. Some makes have the upper tension marked with a plus sign (+), meaning more tension, and a minus sign (-), meaning less tension.

The old adage "If it ain't broke, don't fix it" definitely applies to the upper tension control. Unless you have major problems with the fabric puckering or the thread looping, leave the tension alone. If you experience these problems, either consult your Operating Manual or a qualified sewing machine dealer for advice on adjusting the tension.

The pressure adjustment

The *pressure adjustment,* which is usually located above the bar that holds the presser foot, controls how much pressure the foot exerts against the fabric.

For most sewing, the pressure is on "full" because you don't want the fabric to slip and slide around under the foot while you sew. For some jobs, like sewing through very heavy fabrics or through multiple thicknesses or stitching complicated embroidery designs, a lighter pressure works better.

The take-up lever

The *take-up lever* is very important in the threading and normal operation of the sewing machine. This lever pulls the thread off the spool, just enough, for the next stitch.

When you stop sewing, make sure that the needle is out of the fabric (you can turn the flywheel to accomplish this) and that the take-up lever is in the highest position. Then you can lift the presser foot and remove the fabric. Otherwise, the next time you take a stitch, the needle comes unthreaded.

Newer machines have a needle-up, needle-down function that lets the needle automatically stop in the up or down position without manually turning the flywheel. Set this function for the up function, and the needle stops out of the fabric — you won't unthread the needle with the next stitch. Set it for the down function, and the needle stops in the fabric for easy pivoting around corners.

The speed control

Many newer machines have a *speed control*. It works like the cruise control in your car or the feature in your computer that controls the speed of your mouse. You adjust the speed control so that you can't sew faster than what feels comfortable.

The reverse button

At the beginning and end of seams, you often want to lock the stitches in some way so that they don't come out. To do this, you can tie off each seam by hand (ugh) or use your *reverse button*. Simply sew three or four stitches, touch the reverse button, and the feed dogs back up the fabric a couple of stitches. Release the button, and the machine resumes stitching forward. The stitches are then locked off and secure.

Maintaining your sewing machine

There's a little-known pest infestation rampant in this country's sewing machines — dust bunnies. These little guys can cause all sorts of problems for you, including the following:

- Skipped stitches
- Needle or bobbin thread looping when it shouldn't
- Noise and lots of vibration
- General sluggish performance

You must keep lint dusted out from under the feed dogs and the area where the bobbin case sits in the sewing machine. When lint gets packed under the feed dogs, it impedes stitch formation.

Using a serger

A *serger* is to sewing as a microwave oven is to cooking. I love my serger because it really speeds up the sewing process by sewing a seam, finishing the edge (like the seams you see in ready-made clothing), and then cutting off the excess fabric in one step. You can use a serger to stitch a wide variety of fabrics, but it can't make buttonholes. A serger is much faster than a standard sewing machine but not as versatile.

Most beginners start off on standard sewing machines. However, if you sew on a serger, I give you special instructions as appropriate throughout *Sewing For Dummies.*

Because removing dust bunnies from your sewing machine sometimes involves taking parts of the machine apart (and then putting them back together), learn how to clean the machine by taking the after-purchase lessons offered by most sewing machine dealers. For really heavy, once-a-year cleaning and tune-up, see your local sewing machine dealer.

Chapter 2

Selecting Fabric, Findings, and Interfacing

. . . .

In This Chapter

▶ Finding fabulous fabric

▶ Deciphering the labels on fabric bolts

▶ Discovering sewing notions

▶ Choosing interfacing

▶ Preshrinking everything in sight

. . . .

*R*ead this chapter to find out about the "softwear" involved with sewing, including fabric, decorative trims, findings, and a mysterious item called *interfacing*.

Choosing the Right Fabric for Your Project

Have you ever bought a good-looking, great-fitting pair of pants on sale, thinking that you were getting a smoking deal — only to find that after the first washing, the pants fell apart, shrank more than a full size, or suffered from terminal wrinkling? Chances are that those bargain pants were plagued with poor fiber content.

You may be wondering what makes a good piece of fabric and how to know whether you're getting the most for your fabric-buying dollar. With that in mind, the following section lists the advantages and disadvantages of common fibers. Note, too, that you can often find a list of recommended fabrics on the back of pattern envelopes. This information about fibers and fabric comes in handy when selecting fabric and also when buying clothes off the rack.

Here's a helpful hint: Don't stray from the advice about the choice of fabric on the back of a pattern envelope — or I promise that the final product won't look as good or fit as well as you intended, even if it is the color you want.

A few words about fiber

Fibers are the raw ingredients used to make up fabric. Fibers are important because they determine the characteristics of fabric, including how comfortable the fabric is to wear, the weight of the fabric, how the fabric holds color after washing or dry cleaning, and how easy the fabric is to care for.

Fibers break down into the following four categories:

- **Natural:** These fibers include cotton, silk, and wool. These natural fibers breathe, take dyes well, and drape beautifully. They also have a tendency to shrink, fade when washed, wrinkle, and stretch out of shape with moderate wear.

- **Man-made:** Acrylic, acetate, and rayon are high-profile members of this man-made fiber group. Acrylic is soft, warm, and resistant to oil and chemical stains, but sometimes acrylic fibers stretch out of shape and pill (form little fuzz balls) with wear. Acetate doesn't shrink, is moth resistant, and has wonderful drapeability; however, acetate can lose its color and shred with wear, perspiration, and dry cleaning. Rayon (which has been referred to as the poor man's silk) breathes, drapes, and dyes well. Rayon also wrinkles and shrinks, so it must be dry cleaned or hand washed and pressed rigorously.

- **Synthetic:** Nylon, polyester, spandex, and microfibers are among the hundreds of synthetic fibers. Nylon is exceptionally strong, elastic when wet, abrasion resistant, lustrous, and easy to wash with low moisture absorbency. Polyester doesn't shrink, wrinkle, stretch, or fade. It's stain- and chemical-resistant, dyes easily, and is easy to wash. But, if you've worn an all-polyester garment, you know that some polyesters don't breathe and are best when blended with natural fibers. Spandex is lightweight, smooth, soft, and is stronger, more durable, and as elastic as rubber. Microfibers take dyes well, are washable and durable, and have incredible strength and drapeability.

- **Blends:** Fibers are blended, so the finished fabric has the advantages of the blended fibers. For example, a cotton/polyester blend washes, wears, and breathes because of the cotton fiber, and it doesn't wrinkle as much as 100-percent cotton because of the polyester fiber.

Fibers should fit your needs and lifestyle. For example, my mom doesn't like ironing or taking things to the dry cleaners. So synthetic, easy-care fibers that are machine washable and dryable and that don't wrinkle are her fabrics of choice. My husband likes the breathable characteristics of cotton, linen, and wool. He doesn't mind going to the dry cleaners and paying the price to have his shirts laundered and his suits cleaned and pressed. So, you guessed it, he's a natural-fiber guy.

A rundown of common fabric types

Woven fabrics are made on a loom similar to the one you may have used as a child to make a pot holder. The lengthwise yarns are called the *warp* and are the strongest yarns in the fabric. Crosswise yarns are called the *woof, weft,* or *filler.* Woven fabrics are stable in the lengthwise and crosswise directions but give a little when pulled on the *bias* — the bias is diagonal to the lengthwise and crosswise grains (see Chapter 4 for more on lengthwise and crosswise grains and the bias).

Knits are constructed with a series of lengthwise loops called *ribs* and crosswise stitches called *courses.* Because of this looped construction, when sewing, you treat knits differently than you treat woven fabrics. Most knits have crosswise stretch and lengthwise stability, so they move and conform to the body. Because the fabric gives, knit projects usually need fewer shaping details — darts, gathers, or seams — than projects made of woven fabrics.

Here is a list of woven fabrics available by the yard:

- **Broadcloth:** A light- to mid-weight evenly woven cotton or silk fabric used in men's shirts. Broadcloth is also made in wool for fine wool suiting.

- **Chambray:** A light- to mid-weight evenly woven cotton or cotton blend used in work clothes, shirts, and pajamas. Chambray is usually made with a colored warp yarn and a white filler yarn. This fabric resembles denim but is lighter in weight.

- **Chintz:** A closely-woven plain weave cotton or cotton/polyester blend used a lot in curtains and draperies. This fabric is printed with figures — most commonly with flowers — and has a smooth shiny or glazed finish.

- **Corduroy:** A mid- to heavy-weight cotton weft-pile fabric that is woven or shorn, creating the distinct ribs on the lengthwise grain. Corduroy comes in various rib widths, solid and printed, and is commonly used in children's clothing and sportswear.

- **Crepe:** A pebbly-surfaced woven or knitted fabric. Because of the pebbly surface, crepes snag more and don't wear as well as even weaves.

- **Denim:** A strong mid- to heavy-weight twill weave fabric in which the warp yarn is a color (usually blue) and the filler yarn is white. Denim is available in many weights depending on the end use and is great for jeans, jackets, skirts, and home decor projects.

- **Double knit:** A mid-weight knitted fabric in which both sides are knitted identically. Keeps its shape and has good recovery. Use double knit to make dresses, tops, skirts, and jackets.

✔ **Duck:** A heavy-weight, tightly-woven cotton or linen fabric available in plain or twill weaves. Duck and canvas are used interchangeably and make great aprons and slipcovers.

✔ **Eyelet:** An embroidered cotton available by the yard for blouses and dresses, or in narrower widths as trim. The distinct embroidery has holes that are overcast with zigzag stitches.

✔ **Flannel:** A light- to mid-weight plain or twill weave cotton or wool fabric. Cotton flannel is often brushed and used for work shirts and pajamas. Wool flannel is not usually brushed and is used as a suiting.

✔ **Fleece:** A light- to heavy-weight hydrophobic ("water-hating") double-sided polyester knit used in pullovers, jackets, mittens, booties, blankets, slippers, and scarves. A common trade name for this type of fleece is Polarfleece. You can also find sweatshirts in fleece made with cotton and cotton/polyester blends.

✔ **Gabardine:** A strong mid- to heavy-weight woven twill fabric made from several fibers or fiber blends. You see it in sportswear, suiting, raincoats, and pants.

✔ **Interlock:** A fine lightweight knit used in T-shirts and other sportswear. Interlock is generally made of cotton and cotton blends and is very stretchy.

✔ **Jersey:** A fine light- to mid-weight knit used in better sportswear, tops, and dresses. Jersey comes in solid colors, stripes, or prints.

✔ **Poplin:** A mid- to heavy-weight, tightly woven fabric with a fine horizontal rib. Poplin is usually made of cotton or a cotton blend and is wonderful for sportswear, children's clothing, and outerwear.

✔ **Satin:** Refers to the weave of the fabric and can be made of cotton, silk, synthetic fibers, and blends. Many types of satin fabrics are used on both clothing and home furnishings, but all of them have a distinct shiny appearance because of the way the fabric is woven.

✔ **Tricot:** A fine, sheer, single knit with vertical ribs on the right side of the fabric and crosswise ribs on the wrong (back) side of the fabric. Stretch the fabric across the grain, and it curls to the right side of the fabric. Use tricot for making lingerie. Tricot is also made into fusible interfacing (see "Interfacing with Interfacing" in this chapter for the details on interfacing).

✔ **Tulle:** An open netting made of knotted, geometrically shaped holes. It's made in several weights, ranging from very fine tulle used in bridal and dance wear to heavy nylon netting used in other crafting projects. Tulle is made of silk or nylon and ranges in width from 45 inches to 120 inches.

✔ **Velour:** A woven or knitted fabric with a thick, short *pile* (little hairs standing up from the fabric) and usually dyed into deep, dark colors. Use the knitted velour for tops and robes. Use the woven velours in home decor projects. Velour is a more casual fabric than velvet (see next bullet). Velour requires a "with nap" layout (see Chapter 4).

✔ **Velvet:** A woven silk or synthetic fabric with a short pile. Use velvet for evening wear, tailored suits, and home decor projects. Velvet requires a "with nap" layout (see Chapter 4).

✔ **Velveteen:** A woven cotton fabric with a short pile, made similarly to corduroy without the ribs. Use velveteen in children's clothing, home decor projects, and evening wear.

✔ **Worsted:** A fine, closely woven wool fabric with a hard, smooth surface. Worsteds make great suiting because they are very closely woven and wear like iron.

Reading Labels and Bolt Ends

In the fabric store, you see fabric on bolts on tables and standing at attention against the wall. At the end of the bolt, you find a label that tells you many important things about the fabric, including the fiber content, care instructions, price per yard, and the manufacturer.

The width of the fabric determines how much fabric to purchase for a particular project. Reading the back of your project's pattern envelope helps determine how much fabric to buy based on the fabric width (see Chapter 4 for more information on reading pattern envelopes).

The two most common fabric widths are as follows:

✔ **45 to 48 inches wide:** Most woven cotton, cotton blends, and novelty prints come in this width.

✔ **54 to 60 inches wide:** Many knits, woolens, and home decor fabrics come in this width.

Occasionally, you find a fabric that is 72 inches wide, and sheer fabrics, such as bridal tulle, can come up to 120 inches wide.

Getting Notions about Findings

Tapes, trimmings, ribbons, piping, laces, elastics, and zippers are all lumped together under the category of *sewing notions* or *findings* — presumably because you need to find and gather them together before making a project.

The back of your pattern envelope tells you exactly which findings and notions you need for a particular project. (Chapter 4 tells you more about pattern envelopes.)

Some pattern envelopes list notions that aren't essential for the completion of the project. If you'd rather not use a notion that's called for, ask the sales associate at the fabric store whether you really need the notion before crossing it off your shopping list.

Bias tape

Bias tape is a long, continuous strip of woven cotton/polyester blend fabric. Bias tape conforms to a straight edge, such as a seam allowance, and can be easily shaped to fit a curve or hem edge.

Bias tape comes in several configurations, including single fold, extra wide, double fold, hem facing, and hem tape. Your project's pattern envelope tells you which type of bias tape you need.

Braid

You use braid to cover an edge or to embellish the surface of the fabric. *Fold-over braid* is used to trim the edges. *Middy* and *soutache braids* are flat, narrow braids often seen on sailor suits and band uniforms. Middy braid has several fine ridges that run the length of the braid, and soutache braid has one deep groove in the center that runs the length of the braid.

Elastic

Elastic comes in many different configurations and widths depending on how it is used:

- ✔ **Elastic thread:** Used for shirring fabric (see Chapter 16), for hemming swimwear, and other decorative applications.

- ✔ **Elastic cord:** This cord is heavier than elastic thread and can be zigzagged over for a soft, stretchy wrist treatment.

- ✔ **Elastic braid:** Looks like middy braid but stretches. Use it in a casing at the wrist or waist (see Chapter 16 for more information on casings). Swimwear elastic is an elastic braid treated to resist wear in salt and chlorinated water.

- ✔ **Knitted elastic:** This elastic is soft and extremely stretchy. When knitted elastic is stretched while sewing, the needle slips through the loops of the knit so that the elastic won't break down or grow larger than the cut length during the sewing process.

✔ **Non-roll waistband elastic:** This elastic works wonderfully through a waistline casing or at the waistline of pull-on shorts, pants, or skirts. The ribs of this elastic keep the elastic rigid so that it won't bend or curl in the casing.

Lace

Lace, which is sold by the yard, comes in the following flavors:

✔ **Chantilly lace:** This very fine lace is often used in lingerie and bridal sewing.

✔ **Lace insertion:** This narrow lace has straight edges so that you can easily insert it between two other pieces of lace or fabric. Insertion lace is most often used on heirloom garments, which are garments with old-fashioned styling.

✔ **Lace edging:** Can have either a straight edge or a scalloped edge. You use lace edging to trim a hem or cuff edge, most often in heirloom sewing. You also use lace edging to trim the edge of tucks. (See Chapter 8 for more information on tucks.)

✔ **Lace eyelet:** This lace features little holes or eyelets. The edges of each eyelet are finished with short, narrow zigzag stitches called *satin stitches.*

✔ **Hem lace:** This lace is flimsy and straight on both edges like lace insertion. Because it's used on the inside of a garment at the hem edge, it doesn't have to be expensive or sensational to do the job.

Piping and cording

Piping and cording have lip edges and are sandwiched between two pieces of fabric at the seamline. (A *lip edge* is a flat flap of fabric or braid that's attached to the edge of the cording for easy application.) The most common types of piping and cording include the following:

✔ **Filler cord:** Fills the center of piping that's wrapped and stitched with fabric. Filler chord comes in a wide range of widths.

✔ **Piping:** Piping is purely decorative. You use it to trim the edges of slip covers, pillows, and cushions. In clothing, use piping at the edge of pockets, cuffs, collars, and yokes in seamlines.

✔ **Cord-edge trim:** You use this trim mostly in home decor projects. One edge of this trim has a twisted cable cord; the other edge is a lip edge. The lip edge is stitched to the cable cord and can be removed by pulling one end of the chain stitch thread. (See Chapter 12 for more information on using cord-edge trim in your home decor projects.)

Ribbons

Ribbons come in hundreds — if not thousands — of configurations, fiber contents, widths, colors, finishes, textures, and edges. Ribbons are used for everything from trimming apparel to decorating floral arrangements. I list three common types of ribbon here, but please be aware that there's a whole world of ribbons to explore out there:

- **Grosgrain (pronounced grow-grain, not gross-grain) ribbon:** Has a ribbed texture and is very easy to sew. Use it on children's clothing because it doesn't snag easily or for trim on something tailored.

- **Satin ribbon:** Has a smooth, shiny texture. Use it on more formal projects and where a dressier look is needed.

- **Silk ribbon for hand and machine embroidery:** Is about ¼ inch wide and a popular ribbon adorning handmade projects.

Rickrack and twill tape

Rickrack comes in many widths and colors. Use it on the surface of a garment to disguise a hem crease that won't press out, or use it to peek out at the edge of a pocket in a seam allowance for extra interest.

Twill tape is made with a twill weave. It comes in narrow, medium, and wider widths and is very stable. Because of its stability, you use twill tape to stabilize shoulder seams and other areas in a garment that may stretch or droop out of shape.

Zippers

Zippers come in a variety of types and configurations, including the following:

- **Conventional nylon coil zipper:** The cool thing about this zipper is that it can heal itself — if the zipper splits, you simply zip the pull up and down, and the split "heals." The zipper can handle only a few such splits, so use a coil zipper in garments for adults in nonstress areas.

- **Molded-tooth zipper:** This zipper has individual zipper teeth made either of metal or nylon. The zipper is quite durable, which makes it great for kid's clothing, outerwear, backpacks, jackets, and sleeping bags.

- **Invisible zipper:** When it is sewn in properly, an invisible zipper ends up looking like a seam.

Interfacing with Interfacing

You apply *interfacing* to fabric to give it more shape than it normally has. Interfacing makes the fabric stiffer, so it holds the shape you want to mold the fabric into. For example, you use interfacing in collars to give them shape and oomph.

Each of the following types of interfacing comes in varying degrees of crispness:

- ✔ **Woven interfacing:** You lay this interfacing out and cut it just like fabric (see Chapter 4 for the details on cutting out patterns).

- ✔ **Knitted interfacing:** Made of nylon tricot, this interfacing is wonderful for use with knit fabrics because it has the same stretchy quality as the fabric.

- ✔ **Nonwoven interfacing:** This interfacing is the easiest to use because you can cut it out any way you please.

You can also choose between *fusible* interfacing, which you iron onto the fabric, and *sew-in* interfacing, which you apply the old-fashioned way — by sewing it onto the garment. (I highly recommend fusible interfacing. Once properly fused, it stays where you want it, and because fusible interfacing is used frequently in ready-to-wear garments, you get a more professional finish on your handmade originals.)

What's the best type of interfacing to use? It depends on the fabric. When selecting interfacing, choose one that has a weight and fiber content similar to your fabric so that the end product is easy to care for. If in doubt, consult the salesperson at the fabric store for help on selecting an interfacing that's compatible with your fabric.

Preshrinking Your Fabric

Before laying and cutting out your project, before sewing a stitch, you must *preshrink* your fabric. Preshrinking allows you to see how your fabric behaves — it shows you how much your fabric shrinks, if the colors run, how much it wrinkles, and other important characteristics of your fabric.

As soon as you get back from the fabric store, preshrink your fabric. Then, if you don't get to the project immediately, you don't have to wonder, "Did I preshrink my fabric already?"

For washable fabrics, preshrink your fabric as you would care for the finished project. For example, if you plan to wash your finished garment in the washing machine with regular-strength detergent and then dry it in the dryer, then wash and dry your fabric in the same way to preshrink it.

After preshrinking, press your fabric smooth and flat. Now the fabric is ready for the layout and cutting process (see Chapter 4).

Also preshrink any trims, tapes, and piping you plan to use with your project. Wrap them around your hand, remove your hand from the trim, creating a *hank*. Put a rubber band around the hank and wash the hank along with the project's fabric.

For dry-clean-only fabrics and zippers, set your steam iron for high steam. Hold the iron above the surface of the fabric, letting the steam penetrate the fibers, but without soaking the fabric or zipper. Line dry the fabric and then press the fabric with a dry iron (not set on the steam setting).

Fusible interfacing can be tricky — unless you preshrink it

If fusible interfacing is not fused according to the manufacturer's instructions, it can shrink after you wash the project, causing a rippled, bubbly appearance. It can also detach from or become too crisp for the fabric, resulting in a stiff, boardy look that screams H-O-M-E-M-A-D-E.

Preshrinking woven or knitted fusible interfacing reduces the chances of such disasters. I preshrink these types of interfacings by soaking them in hot tap water until they are completely wet and then letting them air dry.

Fusible tricot, which is a wonderful lightweight knitted interfacing, curls terribly when you preshrink it. So I cut out my pattern pieces on the bias, and the tricot behaves beautifully in the finished project without preshrinking. Other fusible interfacings that work well without preshrinking are the nonwoven variety, provided that you follow the manufacturer's instructions for application printed on the plastic interleafing wrapped around the interfacing. These directions tell you everything you need to know about using the product, including important information such as how to cut out the pattern pieces, how hot to set your iron, and how long to leave the iron on the fabric.

Chapter 3

Threads and Other Closers

. . . .

In This Chapter

▶ Picking out the right thread

▶ Acquainting yourself with sewing doo-dads that close things

▶ Making three very easy projects: the button hair clip, the button gift box, and the low-sew greeting card

. . . .

In this chapter, you deal with issues of closure — closures in sewing that is. Besides finding out about threads that close seams, you take a closer look at buttons, snaps, snap tape, hooks and eyes, and hook and loop fasteners.

Selecting the Thread for Your Project

All-purpose sewing thread is the type and weight of thread that works well for most fabrics. You can find several all-purpose brands at your local fabric store that may or may not have the thread weight marked on the spool. Ask your sewing machine dealer what thread brand is recommended for your sewing machine.

Some all-purpose threads are a cotton-covered polyester; other all-purpose threads are 100-percent polyester. A good rule to remember when selecting thread is to match the fiber of the thread to the fiber of the fabric (see Chapter 2 for more information on fibers). Then unwrap a little of the thread from the spool and take a close look at it. It should have a smooth, even appearance. Take that unwrapped strand of thread and place it on your fabric. The thread color should be slightly darker than your fabric for a good match.

If you see five spools of thread for only one dollar, run the other way. It's promotional thread made with short fibers, which get lumpy and fuzzy very quickly. The lumps cause uneven thread tension, creating puckered seams that you can't press flat. The extra fuss may also cause skipped stitches because it packs into and under the feed dogs (see Chapter 1 for more on feed dogs), impeding proper stitch formation. So use good thread and clean out lint frequently for smooth sewing.

Serger thread

All-purpose polyester, all-cotton, or cotton-covered polyester serger threads are fine, 2-ply threads available in a few basic colors on cones that can hold up to 1,000 yards of thread. (A *ply* is a finer, slightly twisted strand used to make the thread.) When three, four, or five separate threads are used to serge a stitch, the finer serger thread creates a smoother seam finish than the 3-ply all-purpose sewing thread used on a conventional sewing machine. Because it is a finer thread, serger thread should be used only on the serger and not for all-purpose sewing with your sewing machine.

Fast and Fabulous Fasteners

Without the fasteners described in this section (and shown in Figure 3-1), you couldn't keep your pants up or shirt closed!

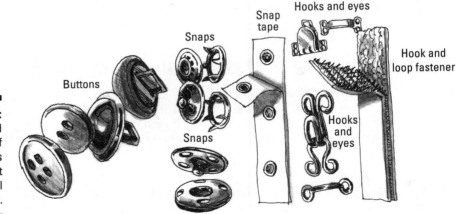

Figure 3-1:
You find fasteners of all shapes and sizes at your local fabric store.

Here, I give you a brief introduction to these closers. You find the specific use and application of many of the fasteners I list here in the projects throughout the book.

The following fasteners all come in a variety of sizes, shapes, and colors. The back of your pattern envelope tells you which (if any) of these fasteners you need and exactly which type and size fastener to use.

Without further ado, I give you some fabulous fasteners:

✔ **Buttons:** Buttons (and their corresponding buttonholes) close a garment, and they may have a decorative function as well. (See Chapter 5 for tips on sewing on buttons.) When selecting them, decide whether you want a bold statement or a subtle one to guide your color choices. Also remember basic design principles by using contrasting buttons to draw the eye vertically or horizontally. Tone-on-tone buttons usually don't draw the eye anywhere, which may be exactly what you want for a particular project.

When selecting buttons, stick to the size guidelines suggested on the back of the pattern envelope. This way, the buttonhole position and spacing correspond to the button size for an easy, proportional application. The easiest buttons to make buttonholes for are flat 2- or 4-hole buttons (refer to Chapter 9 for specific instructions on making buttonholes to fit your buttons).

✔ **Snaps:** You use sew-on snaps to close necklines on dresses, blouses, and baby clothes, among other uses. You use the "gripper-type" sport snaps on active sportswear and outerwear (see Chapter 9 for more on sport snap application).

✔ **Snap tape:** Snap tape is a soft twill tape with a row of snaps running the length of it. Snap tape is as fast to undo as hook and loop fastener and much more flexible. You use snap tape on baby clothes and home decor projects.

✔ **Hooks and eyes:** You use hooks and eyes at the top of a zipper to keep the neckline closed and in shape. You can also use a specially designed skirt hook and loop at a waistband.

✔ **Hook and loop fastener:** Better known by the trade name Velcro, hook and loop fastener comes in many weights, colors, and widths. Some types of this fastener are fusible; others have a peel-and-stick backing.

Making Three Projects That Use Buttons

I think of buttons as the jewelry on a project. You can get some practice handling these little gems and ease into sewing by creating the three easy-to-make projects in this section. Check out the finished projects in the color pages of this book.

The button hair clip

To make this great no-sew hair clip, you need the following materials in addition to your Sewing Survival Kit (see Chapter 1):

✔ One medium to large hair clip. (If you don't need a hair clip, decorate a pin instead. Pin and hair clip bases are available at your local craft store.)

> ✔ 20 to 30 buttons. (Three to four of them should be flat, 2- or 4-hole buttons; the rest are buttons with shanks. *Shank buttons* have a loop or bar found under the button where the thread attaches the button to the fabric. Find buttons by the bag at your local craft store.)
>
> ✔ E-6000 or Goop glue (available at a craft or hardware store).
>
> ✔ A piece of cardboard approximately 8½ by 11 inches.
>
> ✔ (Optional) Rubber gloves to protect your hands from the glue.
>
> ✔ Wire cutters.

Just follow these steps to get some great experience working with buttons:

1. **Using the cardboard to protect your working surface from glue, generously glue three or four flat, nondescript buttons to the top of the hair clip.**

   This button base provides the platform for the rest of the buttons. The larger the base buttons, the better (and they don't have to be very interesting, either, because you're going to cover them with other buttons).

   Make shank buttons flat by cutting off the shanks with a wire cutter (for metal buttons) or scissors (for plastic buttons).

2. **Saving your prettiest buttons for last, start gluing buttons around the perimeter of the platform; then glue toward the center until you have a pleasing arrangement.**

   The glue doesn't set up immediately, so move the buttons around until you like what you see.

3. **Glue on your remaining buttons. While the glue is still wet, cup and press your hand over the buttons on the hair clip or pin so that the buttons form a dome.**

4. **Set the hair clip or pin on the cardboard to dry overnight.**

The button gift box

Make a fabric-covered gift box where buttons frame the lid. Choose a fabric to color-coordinate with a room or special outfit, and voilà! — you have a lovely, one-of-a-kind heirloom in less time than it takes to shop for one. To make this great box, you need the following supplies in addition to the Sewing Survival Kit described in Chapter 1 of this book:

- 18 to 20 flat buttons (these won't show, so it doesn't matter what they look like).
- 40 to 50 pretty buttons of varying sizes and shapes.
- E-6000 or Goop glue (available through your local craft or hardware store), or Cool Gloo (see the appendix).
- A piece of cardboard approximately 8½ by 11 inches.
- (Optional) Rubber gloves to protect your hands from the glue.

> ✔ One papier-maché box with lid, 4 to 6 inches by about 3 inches (available through your local craft store).
>
> ✔ ¼ yard of mid-weight woven fabric to cover the box that coordinates with the buttons, the room, or a special outfit.
>
> ✔ Thread that matches the fabric.
>
> ✔ Sewing machine threaded and ready to go (refer to your Operating Manual for threading and bobbin winding instructions).
>
> ✔ Fabric glue, such as Fabri-Tac (available at your local craft or fabric store).

Follow these steps to create a one-of-a-kind decorative box:

1. **Take the following measurements from your box (you need these measurements to cut the fabric to cover the box and lid):**

   - Box length: _____
   - Box width: _____
   - Box side height: _____
   - Box circumference: _____
   - Lid circumference: _____
   - Lid lip height: _____

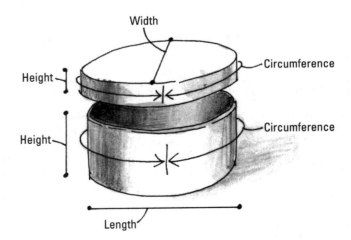

2. **Cut a piece of fabric the size of the box circumference plus 1½ inches; also cut the fabric 1 inch wider than the sides.**

3. **Cut a second strip of fabric the length of the lid circumference plus 1½ inches; also cut the fabric the width of the lid lip height plus ½ inch.**

4. On the wider fabric strip, fold up and press each long edge ½ inch.

5. On the narrower strip, fold up and press each long edge ¼ inch.

6. Edgestitch both top and bottom edges of both strips to add a crisp edge to the fabric and make it easier to glue.

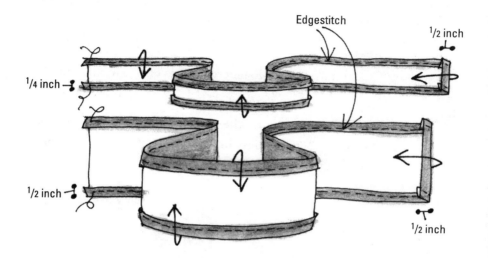

(*Edgestitching* means that you stitch next to the folded edge of the fabric. See Chapter 5 for more information on edgestitching.)

7. On both strips, fold up one short end ½ inch and press it.

8. Using the gloves to protect your hands and the cardboard to protect the table, glue the wide fabric strip to the bottom part of the box.

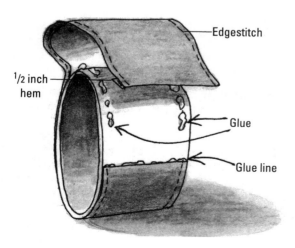

Lay the box on its side. Starting at one end, run a bead of the fabric glue the height of the box. With the glue bead toward you, glue down the short, unhemmed end of the fabric. Run short beads of glue on the box at both the top and bottom edges, pressing on the fabric as you go.

The glue dries quickly, so glue only a little bit at a time.

9. **Using the box lid as a pattern, cut a piece of fabric the shape and size of the lid.**

   Buttons are glued over the fabric edges, so it doesn't need to be a perfect fit.

   Note that you use two different types of glue in the project. One is for fabric; the other is for the other project materials. Remember to use the glue specified for best results.

10. **Using the *fabric glue*, glue the fabric to the top of the lid.**

11. **Using the *E-6000, Goop, or Cool Gloo*, glue the flat, nondescript buttons around the perimeter of the box lid.**

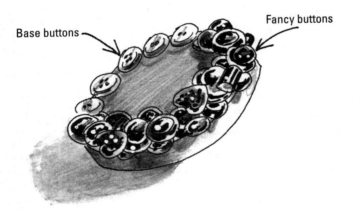

Base buttons

Fancy buttons

This procedure forms a platform for the rest of the buttons that frame the lid.

12. **Glue the prettier buttons around the perimeter of the lid, creating a frame by stacking and arranging the buttons for the look you want.**

13. **Let the glue dry for a couple hours.**

14. **Finish the box lid by using the fabric glue and gluing the narrow fabric strip to the lip edge of the lid as you did in Step 8.**

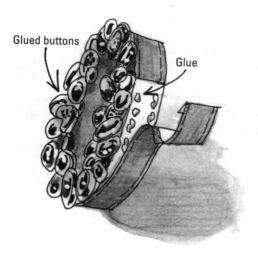

Glued buttons

Glue

The low-sew greeting card

Want to wow your friends and family? Sew a card. This one was designed by my long-time friend and coauthor, Jackie Dodson. Jackie crafts these one-of-a kind treasures by using ribbons, buttons, stamps, old postcards, plus other odds and ends collected from garage sales and flea markets. She even photo-copies old photographs of friends and family members and adds them to her cards. So dig through that trunk, find that box of mementos in the attic, or clean out your closets and drawers. You'll find a lot of material and inspiration from stuff you already have on hand. You also need the following supplies:

- One blank card and envelope
- Red, green, and gold tissue paper (or three colors that match the button gift box fabric)
- (Optional) Threads that contrast with the papers
- A 4-inch-by-8-inch piece of tracing paper
- A pencil
- A pair of sharp scissors
- A glue stick (available at your local craft store)

You can find special papers and blank cards with matching envelopes at art supply stores and craft stores. Papers are available by the 8½-by-11-inch sheet, in a package (if you're doing all of the same color scheme or more than one of the same card), and in different textures and colors. Some papers are different colors on each side. Also, don't overlook designer tissue papers!

To create the card, just follow these steps:

1. **To form a sort of frame for the front of the card, cut the red paper into a rectangle slightly smaller than the face of the card. Then glue-stick the rectangle to the front of the card, positioning the rectangle so that the margin at the bottom is a little wider than at the top.**

   Don't overglue. When you add stitching to the card, the glue can gum up the needle, causing it to skip stitches.

2. **Cut a rectangle out of the green paper that's slightly smaller than the red rectangle.**

   The green rectangle fits inside the red rectangle, so be sure that you have the border you want.

3. **Make the tree pattern; then trace it onto the green paper.**

   Using your tracing paper, trace the half-tree pattern, shown in the following figure. Cut out the pattern. Center the foldline of the pattern down the length of the green rectangle. Trace around only the branch side of the pattern (the branches are cut on one side of the tree in the next step; then the tree is folded open to make the whole tree).

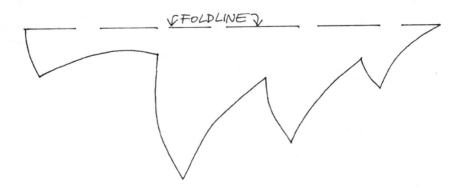

4. **Using your sharp scissors, cut the half-tree pattern out of the green paper and fold it back at the foldline.**

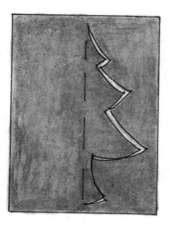

5. Glue the green rectangle over the red rectangle so that the border is even all the way around.

6. (Optional) Sew decorative borders around the inside of the rectangles.

Thread your sewing machine with thread that contrasts with the paper (gold thread often makes a nice contrast). Set your sewing machine for a 3 mm/9 spi straight stitch and sew ⅛ inch inside the edges of each rectangle without sewing through the tree. Pull the threads to the back of the card and tie them off. (Chapter 5 tells you more about straight stitching, and Chapter 6 explains tying off threads.)

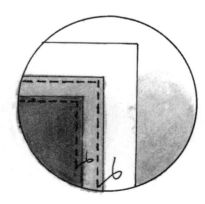

Chapter 4
Working with Patterns

- -

In This Chapter

▶ Selecting the right pattern

▶ Reading the pattern and the pattern envelope

▶ Laying out and cutting the pattern

▶ Marking why-fors and how-tos

- -

*B*esides starting with a good piece of fabric and a pattern that fits your figure type, the business of laying out, cutting, and marking the pattern pieces correctly, as you see in this chapter, are the foundations to your sewing success. After you understand these important steps, you'll find yourself zooming toward a finished project.

Shopping for Patterns

Patterns are marketed through pattern magazines that are available on the newsstands at your local bookstore or grocery store. You can also find them in pattern catalogs at fabric stores that carry fashion fabrics (fabrics that are made into clothing as opposed to fabrics that are made into home decor, craft, or quilting projects). Besides catalogs, some brands that have specially priced or promotional patterns are also displayed on spinner racks for easy access.

Stores that specialize in home decorating fabrics often don't carry clothing patterns. However, regional and national fabric chain stores often carry both types of fabric, plus quilting fabrics and supplies, and everything else you need to complete clothing, home decor projects, crafting projects, quilting projects, and more.

What comes first, the pattern or the fabric?

For me, it's either. Sometimes, I'm inspired by a design I see in a department store, boutique, or movie, and I look for a pattern to match that design. Other times, the fabric "speaks to me," and I look for a pattern that works well with the fabric. Even if you're just starting out with sewing, feel free to let your creative juices flow in either direction.

In addition to commercial patterns made by companies such as Burda, Kwik Sew, McCalls, Simplicity, Stretch & Sew, and Vogue/Butterick, independent pattern companies may or may not have a catalog. You'll find their patterns in specialty sewing and fabric stores, craft and quilt stores, and sewing machine dealerships. If you can't find what you're looking for in your local fabric chain store, take a creative field trip and find these other retailers. They may have just the pattern you're looking for.

In most pattern catalogs, sections identify projects by categories, which range from dresses and children's clothing to crafts and home decor projects. Within those categories, you often find patterns categorized by degree of difficulty, usually placing emphasis on those projects that are easy to sew.

Even though a pattern might be labeled "easy" or "quick," the pattern instruction writers sometimes assume that you have a certain amount of general sewing knowledge. If you're a real beginner, look for patterns with few seams and simple lines. If you're in a quandary about a particular pattern, have a sales associate at the fabric store help you.

Sizing Things Up for Fashion Sewing

Determining your pattern size for a garment can be a humbling experience. Patterns for adults usually run small — sad but true (patterns for children have the opposite problem and run larger than ready-made sizes).

That means, for example, that if you usually wear a size 10 dress, you may find yourself buying a size 12 pattern!

And there's more bad news. For measurement accuracy, someone else must take and record your measurements. You just can't get accurate measurements by yourself, so don't even try it. Find someone you trust, swear them to secrecy, and start measuring. (See Chapter 1 if you're in the market for a measuring tape to take your vital statistics.)

Dressed in your underwear or a leotard, tie a piece of narrow ribbon or elastic around your waist. Don't cinch the ribbon too tight. Wiggle around until the ribbon or elastic finds your natural waistline. If you don't have a waistline, put the elastic where you wear a belt. It's important to locate your waist to take your measurements and decide your figure type.

Have your helper take the following six measurements. Figure 4-1 shows you the exact placement of each measurement:

- ✔ Height: _____
- ✔ Full bust circumference: _____
- ✔ High bust circumference: _____
- ✔ Waist circumference: _____
- ✔ Back waist length: _____
- ✔ Hip circumference: _____

Next, take these measurements to the catalog counter. Somewhere in the front or back of the pattern catalog, you'll find measurement charts. Using your height and back waist length, determine your figure type (Junior, Misses/Miss petite, Unisex, and so on).

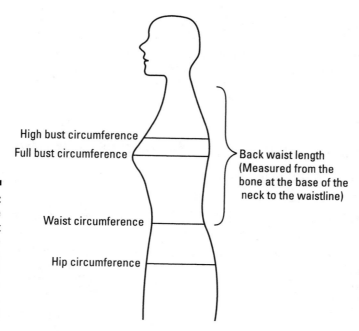

Figure 4-1:
Determine the correct pattern size by taking these measurements.

High bust circumference

Full bust circumference

Back waist length
(Measured from the bone at the base of the neck to the waistline)

Waist circumference

Hip circumference

Next, compare your other measurements with the charts in the catalog, finding a size that comes closest to your measurements. This is your pattern size. Write your size, the brand name of the pattern, and the pattern number (usually a four-digit number) on a piece of paper and walk over to the pattern drawer.

Patterns are filed in the drawers numerically by brand. So, once you find the brand, the pattern number, and your size, pull out the pattern from the drawer. Find your size on the chart on the back of the pattern envelope to see how much fabric you need to buy for your size.

The Pattern and All Its Parts

Nothing can be more intimidating than trying to figure out what all the hieroglyphics are on the various parts of a pattern. I tell you just what you need to know about pattern parts in this section.

Reading the front of the pattern envelope

On the front of the pattern envelope, you often see several style variations of the same project. In the world of sewing, these style variations are called *views*. One view may have a collar, long sleeves, and cuffs. Another view may have a V-neck and short sleeves.

In home decor patterns, you may have several views in one pattern for a basic window treatment. Another pattern may have several pillow views. A third has several options for slipcovers. Views simply give you style options on creating the same basic project.

Reading the back of the pattern envelope

The back of a pattern envelope contains the following information about your project:

- ✔ **The back of the project in detail:** The front of the pattern usually just shows the front of your project.
- ✔ **A description of the project by view:** Always read the description of a project on the back of the pattern envelope. Drawings and photographs can be deceiving, but this written description tells you exactly what you're getting.

↙ **How much fabric to buy:** This information is based on the width of the fabric you choose, the view you're making, your size, and whether your fabric has nap or not. (See Chapter 2 for more information on fabric widths.)

If your fabric has nap, the pattern requires you to buy a little more fabric. Your fabric has nap if it falls into any of these categories:

- **Contains a one-way design:** For example, your fabric shows dancing elephants printed in the same direction. If you cut out some of the pattern pieces in one direction and other pattern pieces in the opposite direction, you'll find elephants dancing right side up on part of the project and upside down on another part of the same project. You need extra fabric so that you can get all your elephants going in the right direction.

- **Has a fuzzy texture:** Such as velvet, corduroy, Polarfleece, and some sweatshirt fleeces. When brushed in one direction, the fabric is smooth; when brushed in the other direction, it's rough. This texture difference translates into a color difference. You need more fabric to cut out the pattern pieces in the same direction.

- **Contains an uneven stripe:** For example, the fabric has three colored stripes — red, blue, and yellow. To match the stripes at the seams, you need extra fabric because the pattern must be laid out in the same direction. If the front and back pattern pieces are laid out in opposite directions, the stripes are cut on the front, going from red, to blue, to yellow. The stripes on the back would be cut so that they go from yellow, to blue, to red. When you sew the seam together, the stripes don't match at the side seams. See "Laying out plaids, stripes, and one-way designs," later in this chapter, for more information.

- **Contains an even or uneven plaid:** The color bars in a plaid must match both vertically and horizontally. If the plaid is not symmetrical in one or both directions, you need to lay out the pattern pieces all going in the same direction. This technique requires more fabric — for making the plaid match. See "Laying out plaids, stripes, and one-way designs," later in this chapter, for more information.

↙ **List of notions needed for specific views:** These notions include items such as the number and size of buttons, the zipper length and type, elastic width and length, shoulder pad style and size, hooks and eyes, and so on.

It's what's inside that counts

Inside your pattern envelope, you find the following items necessary for your project:

- **Pattern pieces:** Some pattern pieces are printed on large pieces of tissue paper. Others are printed on sturdy pieces of white paper called *master patterns.*

  To preserve the master pattern for reuse, simply trace the size you need onto a piece of pattern tracing material. (This material is available through sewing mail-order catalogs and specialty fabric stores. Look for Trace-A-Pattern and Do-Sew brands.)

  This way, you can trace off another view or cut out a project for someone else who is a different size without destroying the master pattern.

- **Key and glossary:** Help you decipher the markings on the pattern pieces.

- **Pattern layout:** Shows you how to lay out the pattern pieces on the fabric yardage for each view.

- **Step-by-step instructions on how to put the project together:** Written in various degrees of clarity depending on your knowledge of sewing. Don't worry — this book tells you what you need to know to decipher the instructions.

The project instructions may run more than one page. If they do, staple the pages together in the upper-left corner and post them in front of you as you sew. Then you can easily check off each step as you finish it. If you don't have a place to post the sheet, set it next to your sewing machine, folded to the section you're working on, for a handy reference.

Decoding the Pattern Pieces

All pattern pieces have the following information printed on or near the center of each pattern piece:

- **Pattern number:** If you accidentally mix together pattern pieces of different projects, these numbers can help you figure out which pieces belong to which projects.

- **Name of the pattern piece:** These names are pretty straightforward — for example, sleeve, front pant, and so on.

- **Letter or number of the pattern piece:** These help you find all the pattern pieces for the view you're making.

- **Size:** Many pattern pieces show several sizes; each size is marked clearly, so you shouldn't have too much trouble keeping them straight.

- **Number of pieces you need to cut:** Often you need to cut more than one of each pattern piece.

These pattern markings appear around the periphery of the pattern pieces:

- ✔ **Cutting line:** This is the heavy, outer line on the pattern piece that guides you when cutting out the pattern piece. Sometimes you see scissors symbols on this line.

- ✔ **Seamline or stitching line:** You usually find this broken line ¼ to ⅝ inch inside the cutting line. Multiple-sized patterns may not have a seamline printed on the pattern. Read the pattern guide sheet to determine the width of the seam allowance. (Chapter 6 tells you more about seams.)

- ✔ **Notches:** You use these diamond-shaped match points on the cutting line for accurately joining pattern pieces together. There may be single notches, double notches, or triple notches all on one pattern.

- ✔ **Circles, dots, triangles, or squares:** No, this isn't a geometry lesson — these indicate additional match points that aid in the construction, fit, and ease in putting the project together. For example, your guide sheet instructions may tell you to gather the waistline of a skirt between the large dots before putting on the waistband, meaning that the gathering stitches are stitched and pulled up between the large dots printed on the seamline.

- ✔ **Place on fold (center front) or (center back) brackets or symbols:** These indicate that the pattern piece is laid out exactly on the fold, which is also the lengthwise grain of the fabric. When the pattern piece is cut out and the paper pattern is removed, the fabric opens into a full piece.

- ✔ **Lengthen or shorten here directives:** Based on your measurements, your body may be longer or shorter than the paper pattern piece. These double lines show where you can cut the pattern apart to lengthen it or fold up the pattern piece to shorten it.

- ✔ **Darts:** Broken stitching lines meet at a point to create the dart. Some patterns also have a solid line that runs the length of the dart showing where you fold the fabric to create the dart. (See Chapter 8 for more information on darts.)

- ✔ **Center back and center front:** You find these clearly labeled with a solid cutting line or "place on fold" symbol. If there is a solid cutting line, there is a seam down the center front or center back. If the center front or center back is placed on the fold and cut out, there is not a seam down the center front or the center back.

- ✔ **Zipper position:** Shows the zipper placement. The top and bottom markings (usually by dots) show you the length of the zipper. (See Chapter 9 on specifics for putting in a zipper.)

- ✔ **Grainline:** The most important pattern marking, this symbol has a straight line, and most of the time, arrow heads are at each end of the line. The grainline parallels the *selvages* (finished edges) of the fabric. See "Placing the pattern pieces on-grain," later in this chapter, to find out why this marking is critical for your sewing success.

✔ **Directional stitching symbols:** These symbols, which often look like small arrows or presser feet symbols, indicate the direction you sew when sewing the seam.

✔ **The hemline:** Shows the recommended finished length of the project, which may vary from person to person. But, even though the hemline may vary, the *hem allowance* (the recommended distance from the hemline to the cut edge) never varies. See Chapter 7 for more information on hem depths.

Figure 4-2 shows the full gambit of markings you may find on a pattern piece.

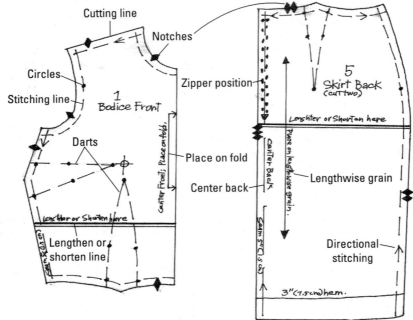

Figure 4-2: These pattern pieces have typical pattern markings.

Laying Out the Pattern

Before laying out the pattern on the fabric, you need to understand some basic fabric terminology. Why? Let me put it to you this way: Understanding the parts of the fabric and cutting your pattern pieces on-grain means that seams stay pressed and straight, pant legs and sleeves won't twist when you wear them, and the creases in your pants stay perpendicular to the ground.

What happened to the other half of the pattern?

Look at your pattern pieces. You have only one sleeve, half of a front top, half of a back top pattern, half of a facing, half of a collar, and so on. Did the company forget to print the whole pattern?

Because the fabric is folded in half the long way (usually with the right side of the fabric to the inside), the pattern pieces are laid out and cut on a double fabric layer. So, most of the time, you need only half of the pattern to make a complete garment.

The fabric and its parts

As you take a closer look at the fabric, you need to become familiar with certain terms that are used throughout this book, as shown in Figure 4-3:

- ✔ **Selvages:** The finished edges where the fabric comes off the looms. The selvages are parallel to the lengthwise grain.

- ✔ **Lengthwise grain or grainline:** Runs the length of the fabric, parallel to the selvages. On knit fabrics, the lengthwise grain is usually more stable and less stretchy than the crosswise grain.

- ✔ **Crosswise grain:** Runs across the width of the fabric, from selvage to selvage and perpendicular to the lengthwise grain. On knit fabrics, most of the stretch is usually across the grain.

- ✔ **Bias:** Is 45 degrees between the lengthwise and crosswise grains.

Preparing the fabric

After preshrinking your fabric, press it flat. (See Chapter 2 for more information on preshrinking.)

Even after preshrinking and pressing your fabric, you may notice a crease running down the center of the goods — that's where the fabric was folded on the bolt. You can press this pesky crease out of most fabrics by sprinkling equal parts of white vinegar and water on a press cloth and then laying the press cloth on the crease between the iron and the fabric, pressing until the fabric is dry.

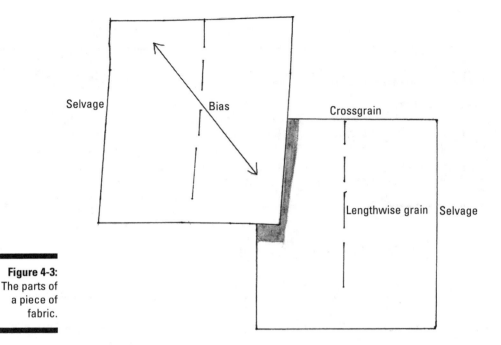

Figure 4-3:
The parts of a piece of fabric.

After you press the fabric, refold it as it was when it came off the bolt so that the selvages are even.

Then take a look at the fabric. Is it even? If not, then you need to pull the fabric back on grain. To do so, unfold the fabric again, pull it on the bias (as shown in Figure 4-3), and straighten it. If it's a large piece of fabric, get a helper to pull the yardage from one corner, while you pull on the yardage from the opposite corner.

Knowing right from wrong

The *right side* of the fabric is the pretty side that everyone sees. Many fabrics are on the bolt with the right side folded to the inside to keep it clean. The *wrong side* of the fabric is the inside you don't see when you're wearing the project. When you lay out the pattern for cutting, be sure that all the pattern pieces are laid out as shown in your pattern guide sheet instructions.

The pattern guide sheet shows the right side of the fabric shaded in a darker color than the wrong side of the fabric, so you can see what's going on in the step-by-step illustrations.

Placing the pattern pieces on-grain

Each pattern piece shows a *grainline* or "place on fold" symbol (which is also the lengthwise grain). (See "Decoding the Pattern Pieces," earlier in this chapter, for more information on the chicken scratches you find on pattern pieces.) The grainline allows you to cut the piece *on-grain*, meaning that the pattern piece lines up with the lengthwise grain of the fabric.

Lay out and cut your fabric on a large table or counter. If you don't have a large table to cut on, buy a foldable cutting board available through your local fabric store. This cutting board is made of corrugated cardboard, usually has an inch and a metric grid printed on it, and opens to extend a small table into a workable cutting space. When you're finished with the board, simply fold it up and slide it under your bed or behind your dresser. Even though you can lay out and cut on the floor, your back will thank you for using a cutting board, table, or counter.

Follow these steps to lay the pattern pieces on the fabric:

1. **Find and cut apart the paper pattern pieces you need to make your project view; then set them aside.**

   When you cut the paper pattern pieces apart, don't cut them out right on the cutting line; leave a little of the paper past the cutting line. Leaving the extra paper makes cutting out the paper pieces faster and easier.

2. **Fold and then lay the fabric on a table or cutting board, as shown in the pattern guide sheet instructions.**

   If the fabric is longer than your table or cutting board, prevent the excess fabric weight from stretching and pulling on your fabric by folding it and laying it on the end of the table.

3. **Locate the lengthwise grain or "place on fold" symbols on the paper pattern pieces. Mark over these symbols, using a highlighter for easy reference.**

4. **Following the layout suggested on the pattern guide sheet, lay out the pattern on-grain, making sure that the grainline is parallel to the selvages.**

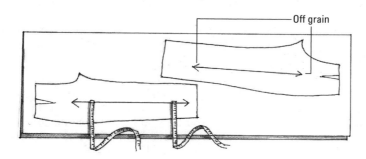

You can check that each pattern piece is placed precisely on-grain by poking a pin straight down into one end of the grainline, measuring the distance from the top of the grainline to the selvage, and then measuring the distance from the bottom of the grainline to the selvage. Be sure to pivot the paper pattern so that each end of the pattern piece is equidistant from the selvage. However, do this only if you have the table top protected with a cutting board or table pad.

Now you're ready for pinning and cutting. See "Pinning and Cutting Out the Pieces," later in this chapter, for more information.

Laying out plaids, stripes, and one-way designs

You don't often see perfectly matched plaids and stripes in ready-to-wear garments — unless you're willing to pay for it. It's tough for garment manufacturers to match designs because they stack fabrics 10 to 12 inches high and cut each pattern piece with a jigsaw.

As a home sewer, though, you're cutting one garment at a time, so it's much easier to get a perfect match with a one-way design, stripe, or plaid.

If you plan to use fabric that contains a plaid, stripe, or one-way design, avoid patterns that say "not suitable for plaids, stripes, or one-way designs." Princess lines and patterns with long vertical darts are also hard to match if you use this kind of fabric. Because you need more fabric when working with these fabrics, remember to use the "with nap" yardage requirements found on the back of the pattern envelope.

One-way designs

Your fabric contains a one-way design if the pattern makes sense only when viewed from one direction. For example, fabric printed with dancing elephants makes sense only if all the elephants are dancing right side up. To make all the elephants dance right side up all over the project, the pattern pieces are laid out all in the same direction.

When working with a one-way design, consider the following factors:

- ✔ **Size of each design in the print:** If the fabric has a small-scale, all-over print, you don't need to worry so much whether the design matches. If the scale of the print is large, you want the design to match across the front, over to the sleeves, and to the back of the garment.

    Placement is important when working with a large-scale print. For example, you don't want a print with big red balloons to end up with a balloon at both bust points. You also don't want sailing ships positioned over your derriere because they may look like they're sailing over the ocean blue when you walk — so think before cutting.

> ## Pattern piece storage made easy
>
> Trying to put the pattern pieces back into the envelope once they're out is like putting toothpaste back into the tube. Instead, tape a gallon-sized plastic freezer bag to your sewing machine. Put the pattern envelope, extra pattern pieces, and the guide sheet into this bag — it's much easier than using the pattern envelope, and everything fits.
>
> Then, when you finish with each pattern piece, fold it so that the pattern number, name, and company name show. This way, if you forget to mark something, you can see it though the freezer bag and locate it easily without unfolding and shuffling through multiple paper pattern pieces.

✔ **Size of the repeat of the pattern:** This is the distance between each design that is repeated on the fabric. If the repeat is ½ inch, it's small and may not matter too much if it is not matched. If the repeat is 4 inches, the repeat is large and should be matched.

Even and uneven stripes

Stripes have bars of color printed, knitted, or woven either horizontally or vertically in the fabric. Stripes come in two varieties:

✔ **Even stripe:** Has an even number of stripes, and all the color bars are the same width. An example is a T-shirt knit with a 1-inch white stripe and a 1-inch blue stripe. When working with an even stripe, pattern pieces can be laid out in either direction (with the top edge of the pattern at the top of the fabric or the top edge of the pattern at the bottom of the fabric), and the stripes will match.

✔ **Uneven stripe:** Has the same- or different-width stripes and an odd number of color bars. An example is a T-shirt knit with horizontal stripes with a 1-inch red stripe, a ½-inch white stripe, and a 1-inch blue stripe. If the pattern pieces are cut in opposite directions, the stripes won't match because one pattern piece has the color bars lined up as red, white, and then blue; the other pattern piece is cut so that the color bars line up as blue, white, and then red.

As a beginning sewer, you need to be aware of uneven stripes and steer clear of them. If you're unsure whether the fabric you chose is an uneven stripe, ask the fabric store sales associate to identify it for you.

Even and uneven plaids

Plaid fabrics have color bars printed or woven into the fabric both horizontally and vertically. Plaids come in two different flavors:

✔ **Even plaid:** Has color bars that match in the lengthwise and crosswise directions. To check this, fold the fabric in half the long way (as when you're laying out the pattern ready for cutting). Then turn back a corner, folding it on the bias (see "The fabric and its parts" in this chapter for information on the bias). If the top layer of plaid forms a mirror image of the bottom layer, it's an even plaid. Even plaids are easier to match than uneven plaids.

✔ **Uneven plaid:** May or may not match in one or both directions and so is more difficult to work with. Do the same test as for even plaids to determine whether you have an uneven plaid on your hands. If, by folding down a corner, the plaid is not a mirror image, you may want to choose another plaid. Until you have considerable experience in laying out and cutting fabric, avoid uneven plaids.

As a beginning sewer, you need to be aware of uneven plaids, and steer clear of them. If you're unsure whether the fabric you chose is an uneven plaid, ask the fabric store sales associate to identify it for you. As your skills improve, start with a small, even plaid and gain some confidence before tackling the uneven plaids.

Laying out twice and cutting once

The following tips help in laying out a pattern for large, one-way designs, stripes, and even plaids:

✔ **Centering:** Decide what you want in the center of the project and fold the fabric there, matching the stripes, plaid, or one-way designs across the width and length of the fabric. Doing so may mean that the selvages are not even. You may also have to pin the fabric together every few inches or so — so that the fabric won't shift when you lay it out and cut it according to the pattern.

✔ **Placement:** Generally, the dominant stripe or color bar in a project is placed directly on, or as close as possible to, the hemline edge. This arrangement means placing the hemline marked on the pattern tissue along the dominant color bar of the fabric. Avoid the dominant stripe, color bar, or big red balloons across the bust or at the fullest part of the hips.

✔ **Crosswise matching:** You accomplish this by watching where the notches are on the pattern pieces. For example, to match the design at the shoulder seams, notice where the notches fall on a particular color bar and within the plaid itself.

To help you do this, center the first pattern piece on the fabric where you want it. Take the pattern piece you want to match the fabric to and place it over the first, matching the notches.

Using an air-soluble marker, draw the design onto the paper pattern tissue, following the dominant color bars. Remove the pattern piece that has been drawn over and place it on the fabric so that the color bars on the pattern paper match those on the fabric. (See Chapter 1 for more information on air-soluble markers.)

Pinning and Cutting Out the Pieces

Pin the pattern piece to the doubled layer of fabric so that the pins go through both fabric layers and are parallel and to the inside of the cutting line. (See "Laying Out the Pattern," earlier in this chapter, for more information on folding your fabric to create a double layer.)

You don't need to pin every inch. Just pin at the notches and everywhere the pattern changes direction. On long, straight edges, such as pant legs and sleeve seams, place pins every 4 inches or so.

Cut out your pattern pieces by using a pair of sharp dressmaker's shears. (See Chapter 1 for more information on choosing the right scissors for cutting.) For accuracy, cut in the middle of the solid cutting line marked on the pattern tissue, trying not to lift the fabric off the table too much when cutting.

Rather than cutting around each individual notch, save time by cutting straight across the notches on the cutting line. Then, after the pattern piece is completely cut out, go back and, with the tips of your sharp scissors, snip into the notch about ¼ inch. A single notch gets one snip in the center of the notch; a double notch gets two snips, one in the center of each notch; a triple notch gets three snips. When you go to match up the pattern pieces at the notches, just match up the snips — it's fast and accurate.

On Your Mark!

After you cut out the pattern pieces and you fuse on any necessary interfacing, you're ready for marking. (See Chapter 2 for more information on interfacing.)

You find many marking tools on the market, but using pins, disappearing dressmaking chalk, and an air- or water-soluble marking pen is the easiest way to go. (See Chapter 1 for more information on these tools.)

When marking with a chalk, I prefer marking the wrong side of the fabric. It's easier to see and won't show on the right side of the fabric. When marking with a water- or air-soluble marker, the ink often bleeds through the fabric, and the marks from either marker are easily removed with clear water.

You need to mark the following things from your pattern pieces onto your fabric:

✔ Darts (see Chapter 8)

✔ Tucks (see Chapter 8)

✔ Pleats (see Chapter 8)

✔ Dots, circles, triangles, and squares (see "Decoding the Pattern Pieces," earlier in this chapter)

When you begin constructing the project, you transfer the marks to form darts, tucks, pleats, and the other symbols on your fabric pattern pieces for very good reasons: so that you can see and understand what the drawings and text in the pattern guide sheet instructions mean for you to do. For example, when marking a pleat, tuck, or dart, instead of marking the entire stitching line, simply mark the dots on the stitching lines. When you put the right sides together for sewing, pin the project together by matching the dots; then sew from dot to dot (pin to pin). For specific instructions on marking and sewing darts, tucks, and pleats, see your pattern guide sheet instructions.

The following marking techniques are what I do depending on the type of fabric used in a project:

✔ **Mark light-colored fabrics by using your air- or water-soluble marker.** Do this by placing the point of the marker on the tissue pattern at the dot or circle, as shown in Figure 4-4.

The ink bleeds through the pattern tissue, the first layer of fabric, and then to the second layer of fabric for an accurate mark.

✔ **Mark dark fabrics by using your disappearing dressmaker's chalk.** Push pins through the pattern paper and both fabric layers at the dots, as shown in Figure 4-5. Open the fabric between the layers and mark both layers where the pins enter the fabric.

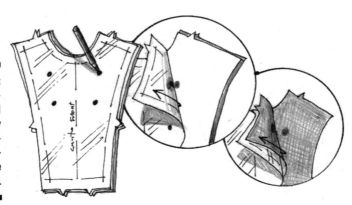

Figure 4-4:
Mark light-colored fabrics by using an air- or water-soluble marker.

✔ **Mark hard-to-mark fabrics by pin-marking.** Push the pins straight through the fabric on both fabric layers. Carefully remove the pattern paper by tearing it over the pin heads. Then pull apart the fabric layers. The pins pull right up to the heads and accurately mark the fabric, as shown in Figure 4-6.

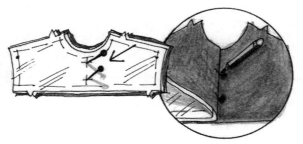

Figure 4-5:
Marking layers of dark fabric.

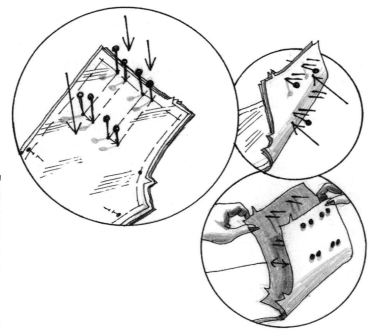

Figure 4-6:
Mark pattern pieces by pushing pins straight through both fabric layers.

Why is marking important?

There's nothing worse than getting halfway through a project, noticing that the pattern guide sheet tells you to sew "from this mark to that mark," and realizing that you forgot to mark something (or thought it wasn't important). You have to stop what you're doing and rifle through your paper pattern pieces to locate the appropriate one. Next, you have to look for that pesky little mark and transfer the mark to your fabric before going any further. Save yourself time and frustration — mark the dots, circles, squares, or triangles, even if you think that you won't need them later. Trust me, you will.

Part II

Sewers! Start Your Engines!

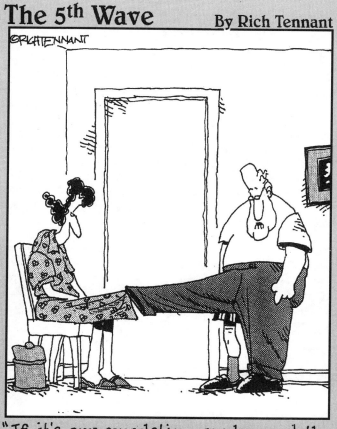

The 5th Wave

By Rich Tennant

@RICHTENNANT

"If it's any consolation, you hemmed the length on this leg perfectly."

In this part . . .

The chapters in this part focus on the fundamentals of sewing. If you are a stone-cold beginner to sewing, you'll definitely appreciate the step-by-step information in this part about threading a needle, sewing many common types of hand stitches, using an iron effectively, finishing fabric edges, sewing seams, and hemming, among other fun sewing fundamentals. If you have sewn before, you may be tempted to skip over the chapters in this part — don't! In each of the chapters, I include several tips and hints that help even a more experienced sewer. Plus, this part contains some really great sewing projects — don't miss them!

Chapter 5

Sewing 101

*W*hether you're quilting, embroidering, mending, or constructing a project, you need to know some sewing basics to get you through your projects. This chapter covers the important sewing fundamentals.

Threading the Needle

When a motorist "threads the needle" on the freeway, she's weaving in and out of traffic, almost hitting other cars in the process. Although threading the needle in sewing is much less dangerous, it does require some know-how to maneuver efficiently.

Hand needles

To begin threading a hand needle, reel off a strand of thread about 18 to 24 inches long. Longer threads tend to tangle and wear out before you use them up.

Starting with the end of the thread that came off the spool first, cut the thread cleanly and at an angle with a sharp pair of scissors. Doing so puts a little point on the thread so that it slips easily through the eye.

The cheapest sewing notion on the market is your own saliva. Moisten the thread end to help it glide right through the needle's eye.

Some needles have very small eyes; some people have very poor eyesight. A *needle threader,* which you can find at your local sewing supply store, can help with tight threading situations. To use a needle threader, poke the fine wire through the eye of the needle, push the thread end through the wire loop, and then pull. The wire grabs the thread and pulls it through the needle's eye, as shown in Figure 5-1.

Self-threading hand needles make threading even easier. To use a self-threading needle, hold the needle and a length of thread in one hand. Pull the thread end across the self-threading eye so that the thread lies in the notch. Snap the thread into the notch until it clips into place, as shown in Figure 5-2.

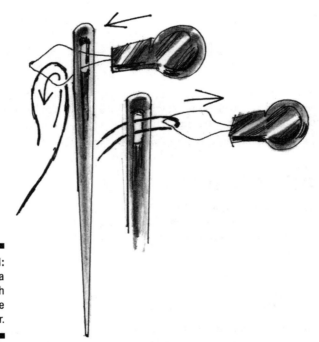

Figure 5-1:
Threading a needle with a needle threader.

Figure 5-2:
Threading a
self-thread-
ing needle.

No amount of spit helps thread a tapestry needle because the end of the
embroidery floss or yarn commonly used with these needles tends to get
frizzy at the end. Just fold over the end of the floss or yarn and poke it
through the larger eye, as shown in Figure 5-3.

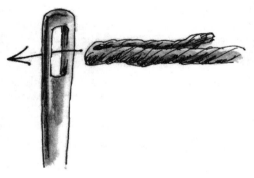

Figure 5-3:
Getting
yarn or
embroidery
floss
through a
tapestry
needle.

Machine needles

A machine needle, meaning a needle for a standard sewing machine or serger,
has both a round and flat side, as shown in Figure 5-4. (See Chapter 1 for
more information on sewing machines and sergers.)

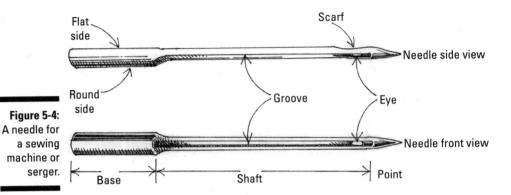

Figure 5-4:
A needle for
a sewing
machine or
serger.

For sewing machines with a side-loading bobbin (meaning that the bobbin goes in the left side of the machine), the flat side of the needle base faces to the right. For most sergers and sewing machines with top- and front-loading loading bobbins (meaning that the bobbin goes in the front or drops into the top of the machine's bed where the fabric rests on the machine when sewing), the flat side of the needle base faces to the back.

Make sure that the needle is positioned properly for your kind of machine. The long groove running the length of the shaft protects the thread as it stitches up and down through the fabric. The scarf, the little indentation behind the eye, creates a loop that enables the bobbin thread to lock with the top thread, making a stitch. If the needle is in the machine backwards, nothing works right.

The anatomy of a machine needle makes threading it easier than threading a hand needle. Instead of spitting on the thread, just follow these steps:

1. **Lick your finger and then rub it behind the eye of the needle.**

2. **Cut the end of the thread cleanly and at an angle.**

3. **Starting just above the eye, run the end of the thread down the shaft in the front groove until the thread pokes through the eye.**

   When the thread hits the eye, the moisture pulls the thread through it, and you're ready to sew.

Tying the Knot

You might think that having a knot in your thread is a bad thing. It is if you didn't put it there and the thread tangles when you don't want it to. It's not when the knot stops the thread from pulling completely through the fabric when you're sewing on a button and at other times where you want to anchor the end of the thread. The following instructions explain how to tie a sewing knot.

When preparing to write this book, I took an unofficial poll of my sewing buddies to discover whether right-handed sewers tie a sewing knot with their right hand. (I'm right-handed and I do.) I found out that how you tie a knot doesn't seem to have a thing to do with the dominant hand; what feels natural when it comes to knot tying depends on the way you were taught.

I don't want to leave anyone out! The following steps tell both lefties and righties how to tie a sewing knot:

1. **Hold the thread between your thumb and index finger and wrap a loop of thread around the tip of your opposite index finger.**

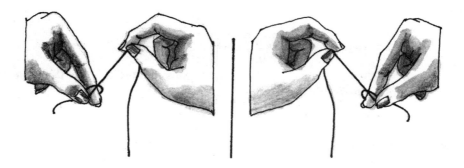

2. **Roll the loop between your finger and against your thumb so that the loop twists.**

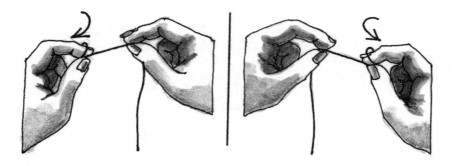

3. **Slide your index finger back while rolling the thread until the loop is almost off your finger.**

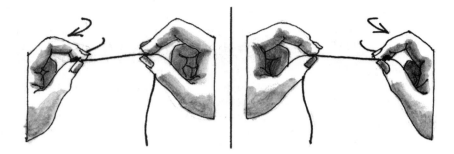

4. **Bring your middle finger to the twisted end of the loop, remove your index finger, and firmly place the middle finger in front of the twisted thread against the thumb.**

5. **Pull on the thread with the opposite hand to close the loop and form the knot.**

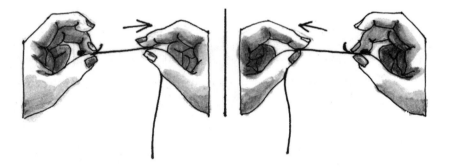

Straight Talk on Hand Stitches

Any given sewing job may entail several types of stitches, and you definitely need the right stitch for the job. For example, you shouldn't use a hand-basting stitch to permanently sew together a pair of overalls; the stitches are too far apart, and your overalls will fall apart the first time you attempt to lift that bale or tote that barge. In this section, I familiarize you with the basic hand stitches and their uses.

The securing stitch

In hand sewing, you secure the end of a stitch by sewing a knot — regardless of the stitch. To sew a knot, take a small backstitch and form a loop over the point of the needle. When you pull the thread through the loop, it cinches the thread and secures a knot at the base of the fabric (see Figure 5-5). When securing a high-stress area, sew two knots.

Figure 5-5: Use this technique to securely "fasten" a hand-sewn stitch.

The hand-basting stitch

You use hand-basting stitches to temporarily hold two or more layers of fabric together. (See "Basting: The Key to Faster Sewing," later in this chapter, for more information.)

Each basting stitch should be about ¼ inch long with less than ¼ inch in between each stitch. When you use stitches with thread that contrasts with the fabric, the stitches are easier to pull out after you sew the permanent stitches.

Working from right to left (for right-handers) or from left to right (for left-handers), weave the point of the needle in and out of the fabric, working it through the fabric (see Figure 5-6).

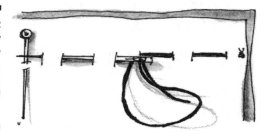

Figure 5-6: You baste by simply weaving the needle in and out of the fabric.

The running stitch

You use this very short, even stitch for fine seaming, tucking, mending, and gathering. Because the stitch is so short and tight, this stitch is usually permanent.

To make a running stitch, weave the point of the needle in and out of the fabric by using very short (⅟₁₆-inch), even stitches before pulling the needle through the fabric (see Figure 5-7).

Figure 5-7:
Use short, even stitches when fashioning running stitches.

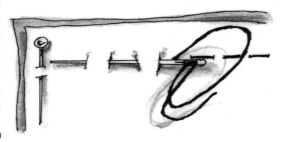

The even backstitch

The even backstitch is the strongest hand stitch. Because of its durability, you use this stitch most often when repairing a seam.

To create the even backstitch, pull the needle up through the fabric, and poke the needle back into the fabric half a stitch behind where the thread first emerged. Bring the needle up half a stitch in front of where the thread first emerged (see Figure 5-8). Repeat for the length of the seam.

Figure 5-8:
Here's the way to make the even backstitch.

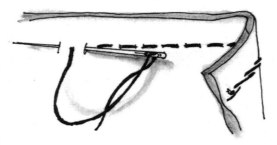

The blind hemming stitch

These stitches are taken inside the hem allowance between the hem and the garment (see Chapter 7 for more information on the fine points of hemming). With a little practice, a fine needle, and fine thread, good blind hemming stitches don't show on the right side — hence the name "blind."

Because the blind hemming stitch is used for hemming, you will have already turned up the hem allowance and pressed it into place. The edge of the hem should also be finished by pinking the edge or overcasting (see Chapter 6 for more on edge finishes).

Fold the hem allowance back — ⅜ inch — and take the first short stitch ¼ inch from the hem edge. Take the next short stitch by catching only a thread of the fabric. Continue with stitches spaced about ½ inch apart, catching the hem allowance in a stitch and taking as fine a stitch as possible into the garment. Stitch back and forth between the hem allowance and the garment around the hemline until the blind hemming is complete (see Figure 5-9).

Figure 5-9: Blind hems require fine stitches about ½ inch apart.

The slant hemming stitch

This stitch is the fastest — but least durable — of the hemming stitches because so much thread is on the surface of the hem edge. (If you've ever caught your heel in your hem and pulled it out, you may be the victim of a slant hemming stitch.) So, if you're in a hurry and you're hemming the bottom of a blouse you tuck in, use the slant hemming stitch.

Take a stitch around the hem edge and then up through the garment, catching only a thread of the garment fabric (see Figure 5-10).

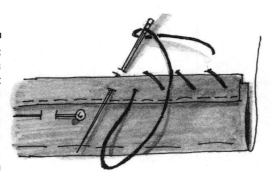

Figure 5-10: Though it's the least durable, the slant stitch is quick and easy to stitch.

The hemming slipstitch

You use the hemming slipstitch when working with (guess what?) a folded hem edge. This stitch is very durable and almost invisible. (See Chapter 7 for more information about hemming.)

Fasten the thread to the hem allowance by poking the needle through the fold of the hem edge and bringing it up through the fabric. With the point of the needle, pick up one thread from the garment and work the needle back into the fold of the hem edge (see Figure 5-11). Then repeat the process.

Figure 5-11:
Here's how
to make the
nearly
invisible
hemming
slipstitch.

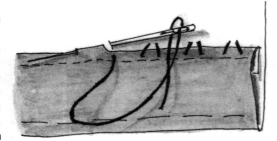

The even slipstitch

You can join two folded edges by using the even slipstitch. Most often this stitch comes into play when you want to repair a seam from the right side because the seam is difficult to reach from the wrong side.

Fasten the thread and bring it out at the edge of the fold. Taking fine stitches, work the needle, slipping it through the fold on one edge and drawing the thread taut. Take another stitch, slipping the needle through the opposite, folded edge (see Figure 5-12).

Figure 5-12:
Use the
slipstitch to
join two
folded
edges or
seamlines
together.

Making Machine Stitches Work for You

My parents gave me a sewing machine for my high-school graduation. After threading the machine, the first thing I did was to try all the stitches. I had no idea what they did and thought I wouldn't use most of them. Then, during a class from my sewing machine dealer, I discovered that the various stitches save time and produce more professional results.

The basic machine stitches

Figure 5-13 shows the very basic machine stitches. Of course, your machine may offer more, or fewer, of these stitches. Compare them with what's available on your sewing machine. I bet you'll find a good selection.

- **Straight:** You use the straight stitch for basting, seaming, and topstitching.

- **Zigzag:** The machine adds width to the straight stitch to make the zigzag stitch. You use the zigzag stitch for stitching around appliqués, making buttonholes, sewing on buttons, and embroidering. The zigzag stitch is as practical as it is fun.

- **Three-step zigzag:** When used on the widest width, the ordinary zigzag stitch pulls the fabric into a tunnel and the fabric rolls under the stitch — not very desirable. To eliminate this problem, the three-step zigzag stitch was invented. The needle takes three stitches to one side and then three stitches to the other side, keeping the fabric flat and tunnel-free. Use the three-step zigzag for finishing raw edges, sewing on elastic, mending tears, and making decorative effects.

- **Blind hem and stretch blind hem:** The blind hem stitch is designed to hem woven fabrics so that the stitches are almost invisible when looking at the right side of the garment. The stretch blind hem stitch has an extra zigzag or two that stretches to invisibly hem knit fabrics. Both stitches have decorative applications, too.

- **Overlock:** Many of the overlock-type stitches on today's sewing machines are designed to stitch and finish seams in one step, simulating the serger stitches that you see on ready-to-wear garments. Some of these stitches work well on woven fabrics; some work better on knits.

- **Decorative:** Decorative stitches fall into two basic categories: closed, satin-type stitches (such as the ball and diamond) and open, tracery-type stitches (such as the daisy and honeycomb). The stitch sampler belt in the color pages in this book is decorated with both types of stitches (see Chapter 17 for instructions on how to make this belt). Many newer machines can be programmed to combine these stitches with other stitches, elongate the designs for a bolder decorative effect, and even stitch someone's name.

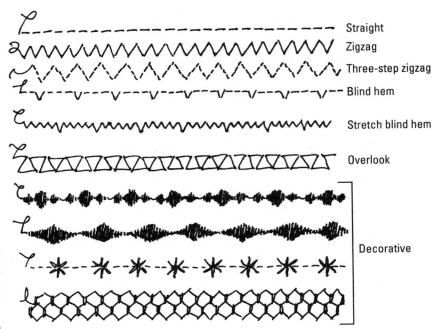

Straight

Zigzag

Three-step zigzag

Blind hem

Stretch blind hem

Overlook

Decorative

Figure 5-13:
Basic
machine
stitches.

The newest high-end sewing machines can also create intricate embroidery designs (like those you see on ready-to-wear garments) by using *embroidery cards.* Embroidery cards are smaller than computer discs and can store several large, intricate motifs. Some machines also offer scanners, which allow you to add additional patterns to the machine's stitch library. You can contact machine manufacturers to find out about all the options (see the appendix).

Throughout this book, I tell you about the uses of these stitches. However, before taking your machine through its paces, you need to know how to select a stitch, set the stitch length, and set the stitch width.

Selecting a stitch type

If your sewing machine does more than straight stitch and zigzag, the machine must give you some way to select the stitch you want to use.

Older machines have dials, levers, buttons, or drop-in cams as *stitch selectors.* Newer, computerized models have keys or touch pads that not only select the stitch but also can automatically set the stitch length and width. You must consult the Operating Manual that comes with your sewing machine to get the specifics on how to select a stitch type.

Selecting the length of the stitch

The length of the stitch determines the stitch's durability. Short stitches (1 to 3 mm, 13 to 60 spi) are very strong and are meant to be permanent. Longer stitches are usually temporary or are used as a decorative topstitch (see Chapter 6 for more details on topstitching).

Stitch length is determined by the distance the feed dogs move the fabric under the needle. When the feed dogs move with shorter strokes, stitches are short. When they move with longer strokes, stitches are longer. (See Chapter 1 for more information on feed dogs.)

Stitch length is measured two different ways — in millimeters (mm) and in stitches per inch (spi). The setting used depends on the brand and model of your machine.

Throughout this book, I give you the necessary stitch length settings both ways. Check out Table 5-1 if you want to compare stitch length in millimeters to stitch length in inches.

Table 5-1	Converting Stitch Lengths
Stitch Length in Millimeters	*Stitch Length in Stitches per Inch*
0.5	60 (fine setting)
1	24
2	13
3	9
4	6
5	5
6	4

Use the following as a general rule for stitch lengths:

- ✔ The average stitch length for mid-weight fabrics is 2.5 to 3 mm/10 to 12 spi.
- ✔ The average stitch length for fine fabrics is 2 mm/13 to 20 spi.
- ✔ For heavier fabrics, basting, or topstitching, use 4 to 5 mm/5 to 6 spi.

Setting the stitch width

The *stitch-width* control sets the distance the needle moves from side to side while creating a stitch. You don't need to worry about the stitch width when sewing straight stitches — just set it to 0 (zero).

All machines measure the stitch width in millimeters (mm). Some makes and models have a maximum stitch width of 4 to 6 mm. Others create stitches as wide as 9 mm.

Is wider better? When it comes to decorative stitches, it usually is. A 5- to 6-mm width is sufficient for most stitches where you're overcasting the raw edge, blind hemming, or making buttonholes.

Throughout this book, I give machine stitch-width settings in a range that works for most makes and models.

Stitching-in-the-ditch

You use this simple technique to tack down facings and to tack up a quick cuff or hem. All you do is follow these steps:

1. **Place the crack of the seam right side up and perpendicular to the presser foot so that the needle is poised over the seamline.**

2. **Using a straight stitch, sew so that the stitches bury themselves in the crack of the seam.**

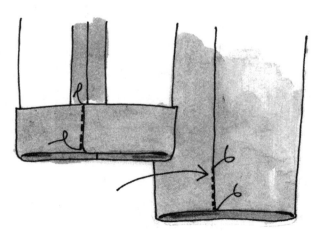

Instead of backstitching, pull threads to the wrong side of the project and tie them off (see Chapter 6 for more on tying off threads).

Topstitching

Topstitching is an extra line of stitching sewn on the right side of the fabric that parallels a seamline or is used to sew a hem. Topstitching is usually visible on a project, so it needs to look good.

Your pattern instructions tell you exactly where on the project to topstitch. To topstitch, simply place the project under the needle, right side up, and stitch at the specified location. Because topstitching is usually an important part of the overall garment design, you usually want to tie off the threads (see Chapter 6) rather than backstitch.

Starting and Stopping

For smooth and easy sewing, follow these techniques for starting and stopping stitches on your sewing machine and serger.

. . . with your sewing machine

Lower the presser foot onto the fabric before sewing a stitch. If you don't, the fabric flops all over the place as the needle goes up and down, and you don't get anywhere. You may even jam up the machine . . . bummer. After a few seams, lowering the foot becomes second nature.

Also, pull the top and bobbin threads to the right or to the left of the needle before lowering the foot. This way the foot pressure holds the threads firmly, and they won't tangle or jam at the beginning of a row of stitching.

Stop sewing at the end of the fabric, stopping with the take-up lever at the highest position (see Chapter 1). If you don't, you may unthread the needle with the next stitch. Next, lift the presser foot, pulling out several inches of thread. To remove the fabric from the machine, cut the threads, leaving a 6- to 7-inch thread tail on the fabric and 2 to 3 inches of thread behind the foot. Most machines have a thread cutter located near the needle, or you can cut threads with a pair of scissors.

. . . with your serger

Starting and stopping with sergers is easier than with sewing machines because sergers are designed for speed and durability. Leaving the presser foot down and with a short thread chain coming off the back of the foot, simply butt the fabric edges under the toe of the foot and step on the foot pedal. When the serger starts, it grabs the fabric — and you're off and running.

To stop, gently pull the fabric as it comes out of the serger behind the foot, keeping constant, gentle tautness. Serge off the edge, creating a thread chain behind the foot. Stop serging and cut the thread chain, leaving enough on the fabric to tie off threads or to weave back under the stitches.

Basting: The Key to Faster Sewing

Basting in sewing is nothing like basting a turkey in the kitchen. In sewing, *basting* means to temporarily hold pieces of a project together. You can hold them together with your hands (called *finger-basting*), with long-hand or machine stitches (called *hand-basting* or *machine-basting*), or with pins (called *pin-basting*). The long stitches and pins are easily removed to check and adjust the fit before permanently sewing the seam together.

My seventh-grade home economics teacher made me hand-baste an entire project together before machine stitching. It took forever, and I thought that it was a real waste of time. Now that I don't have that girlish figure of old, I don't baste the whole project together, but I do pin- or machine-baste in the following circumstances and suggest that you do, too:

- When you're not sure how one pattern piece fits into another
- When you need to check and adjust the fit of the project

Using a contrasting thread color makes locating and tearing out your basting much easier. If you're machine-basting, use contrasting thread in the bobbin case. (See Chapter 1 for more information on the bobbin case.)

To baste two pattern pieces together, start by placing and pinning the right sides together and then use either of the following methods:

- **Pin-basting:** Pin parallel to and ⅝ inch from the cut edge. For small areas such as a shoulder seam, pin every 1 to 2 inches. For larger areas, such as the side seam on a pair of pants, pin every 3 to 4 inches.

- **Hand-basting:** As I just described, thread your hand needle and run a row of hand-basting stitches along the seamline.

- **Machine-basting:** Set the stitch length to a long 4 mm/6 spi straight stitch and slightly loosen the upper thread tension. Then simply stitch along the seamlines. Remember to put the tension back to normal when you finish basting.

To prevent needle breakage when machine-basting or sewing, remove the pins before the foot reaches them, as shown in Figure 5-14.

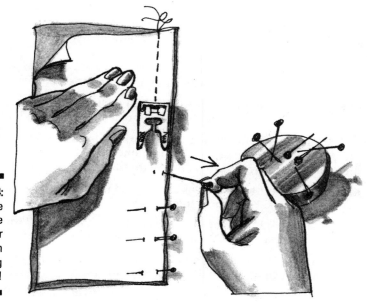

Figure 5-14:
Remove
pins before
running over
them with
your sewing
machine!

If something is fairly close-fitting, add all elements that affect the fit of the project before basting. (If you don't, your basting won't give you an accurate picture of what the project will look like.) For example, you may be working on a dress bodice that includes darts and shoulder pads. You should first sew and gently press the darts as shown in the pattern guide sheet. Next, pin in the shoulder pads and then baste the side seams together. You can then try on the bodice and get a fairly good idea of what the final product will look like.

Sewing on Buttons

For many people, sewing on a button is their introduction into the world of sewing. Sewing on buttons is a great way to start with sewing because it shows you that technique is very important when doing anything with a needle and thread — even something small.

Yes, there is a right way to sew on a button, which you can do either by hand or on the sewing machine. If I am replacing or moving one button, I sew it on by hand. If I make something that requires sewing on several buttons at once (like down the front of a shirt), I do use my machine. Here's how.

By hand

Follow these steps to sew on a button of any size by hand:

1. **Mark the spot on the fabric where you want the button to go, using a fabric marker or dressmaker's chalk from your Sewing Survival Kit.**

2. **Pull off a strand of thread from 18 to 24 inches long. If it's any longer, the thread tangles and may break before you sew on the button.**

3. **Thread the needle (as shown and described in the section "Hand needles," earlier in this chapter), pulling one end of the thread to meet the other so that you have a double thread.**

4. **Knot the ends of the thread as shown and described in the section "Tying the Knot," earlier in this chapter.**

5. **From the top right side of the project, stab the needle all the way through the fabric so that the knot ends up on the mark.**

6. **Bring the needle back up and all the way through the fabric, a short stitch (not more than ⅛ inch) away from the knot.**

7. **Thread the button on the needle, pushing it firmly against the surface of the fabric, and then pull the thread up through the left hole.**

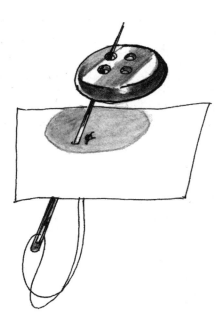

8. **Create a *spacer* by placing a toothpick, matchstick, or hand-tapestry needle on top of the button between the holes.**

This technique gives you enough thread to raise the button off the fabric's surface so that you have room to button the buttonhole. The extra room created by the spacer is called a *thread shank*.

9. **Push the needle down through the hole on the right (the one directly opposite the hole you started with). Pull the thread tight.**

Repeat this process, stitching up through the left hole and down through the right hole one more time for each set of holes so that you secure the button with two passes of the needle.

10. **After you stitch the button on, remove the toothpick.**

11. **Poke the needle through a hole in the button (it doesn't matter which one) so that the needle comes out between the button and the fabric.**

This step gives you a chance to examine what's going on between the button and the fabric. Those connecting threads running out the back of the button into the fabric are the base of the thread shank.

12. **Wrap the thread around these connecting threads three times to secure the thread shank.**

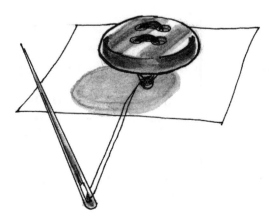

13. **Push the needle through a thread loop as it goes around the shank, pulling the thread tight. This ties a knot.**

14. **Repeat Step 13 and clip the thread close to the shank.**

By machine

If you have several buttons to sew on at one time, consider using your machine to help you with the job. To use this technique, you need a glue stick and a button-sewing foot for your machine.

Just follow these steps:

1. **Mark the spot on the fabric where you want the button to go, using a fabric marker or dressmaker's chalk from your Sewing Survival Kit.**

2. **Dab the back of the button with a glue stick and place the button over the place you marked.**

3. **Prepare your machine with the following settings:**
   - **Stitch:** Zigzag
   - **Length:** 0 mm
   - **Width:** 4 mm
   - **Foot:** Button-sewing, all-purpose, or foot shank without the sole
   - **Feed dogs:** Down
   - **Needle position:** Left (see Chapter 1)

4. **With the presser foot up, turn the flywheel by hand, stabbing the needle through the left hole in the button, and then lower the presser foot.**

   For a four-hole button, start with the holes farthest away from you.

5. **Slide a toothpick, matchstick, or tapestry needle over the button, between the holes and perpendicular to the foot.**

   Adding this spacer raises the button off the fabric's surface so that you have room to button the buttonhole.

   Sometimes the foot has a helpful little groove that holds the spacer in place.

6. **Check that the needle clears each of the holes in the button by taking a couple of zigzag stitches, moving the flywheel by hand.**

7. **Slowly step on the foot control and stitch, counting five stitches — zig left, zag right, zig left, zag right, zig left.**

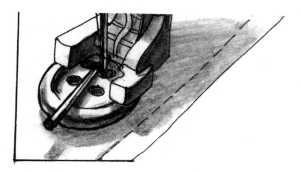

For a four-hole button, lift the foot and move the project so that the needle is over the front two holes and then sew five more zigzags to secure the front of the button.

8. **Move the stitch width to 0, place the needle over one of the holes, and step on the foot control again, taking four to five stitches in the same hole.**

   This step helps to secure and knot the stitches.

9. **Lift the foot and remove the project, reeling off a 7-inch tail of thread.**

10. **Remove the spacer so that you can use it to sew on the other buttons, if necessary.**

11. **Proceed to the rest of the buttons, repeating Steps 4 through 10 until all the buttons are sewn on.**

12. **Pull the needle and bobbin threads between the button and the fabric so that you are ready to create a thread shank, as follows:**

    • Thread a large-eye tapestry needle with the 7-inch thread tail from the needle and, between the button and the fabric, pull the tail through any hole in the button.

    • Thread a large-eye tapestry needle with the 7-inch thread tail from the bobbin and pull the tail through the fabric between the button and the fabric.

    • Thread both tails through the needle's eye and wrap the thread tails around the connecting threads three times, creating a thread shank to secure the button.

13. **Push the needle through a thread loop as it goes around the shank, pulling the thread tight. This ties a knot.**

14. **Repeat Step 13 and then clip the thread close to the connecting threads.**

Creating a Button Collage Greeting Card

Practice your hand and machine button-sewing technique by making this very decorative greeting card (see the photo in the color section). You'll not only get more bang for your gift-card buck, but you'll also impress the heck out of the lucky recipient.

To make this great greeting card, you need the following tools (in addition to the tools in your Sewing Survival Kit, which I tell you about in Chapter 1):

- 4 to 5 inches of 2-inch to 2 ½-inch-wide ribbon, trim, or belting. (I used Guatemalan belting, which you can usually find at craft and fabric stores, to create the card you see in the photo.)
- Handmade paper (available at craft, art supply, or scrapbook stores) that complements the colors in the belting.
- 1 3-inch length of rickrack buttons that complement the colors in the belting.
- 1 5-inch length of rickrack buttons that complement the colors in the belting.
- 3 four-hole buttons that complement the colors in the belting.
- 1 color of all-purpose thread that contrasts to the colors of the papers.
- 1 blank card and envelope (available at your local craft store).
- A ruler.
- A glue stick.
- FrayCheck (see the appendix).
- A pencil.

After assembling your tools, follow these steps to create a card that makes a lasting impression:

1. **On the handmade paper, lightly pencil-mark a rectangle slightly smaller than the front of the blank card.**

2. **Rip a rectangle out of the handmade paper.**

   Lay the paper and ruler on the table. Lay the edge of the ruler along one of the pencil lines of the paper. Holding the ruler down with one hand, pull up on the paper with the other hand, ripping the paper against the edge of the ruler. Repeat this process for the other three sides of the paper. Because you're using handmade paper, the edges should look rough.

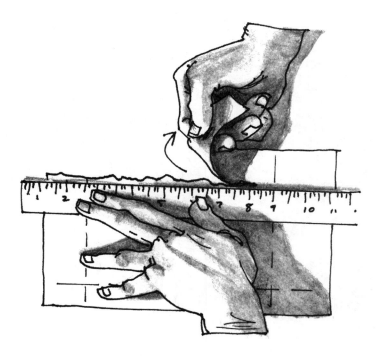

3. Center and glue the ripped paper rectangle on the front of the card by using the glue stick.

4. Cut and FrayCheck the ends of the rickrack and belting. Let the ends dry.

5. Center the belting strip on the rectangle and glue the strip in place over the handmade paper rectangle.

6. Glue the rickrack to the edges at the top and the bottom, covering the raw edges of the belting.

7. Set up your machine like this:

   - **Stitch:** Straight
   - **Length:** 3 mm/9 spi
   - **Width:** 0 mm
   - **Foot:** All-purpose

8. Stitch the rickrack trim on the card by following the shape of the zigzags on the rickrack.

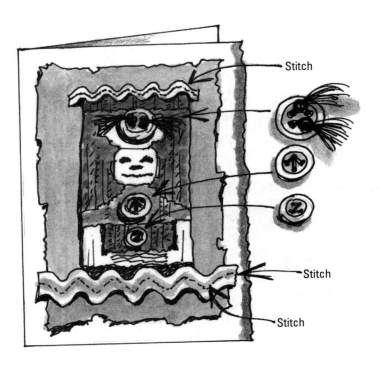

9. Sew on three buttons either by hand or with your machine.

If you use Guatemalan belting, stitch one button at the top of the head and the other two centered down the belting. This is a creative process, so if you would rather sew the buttons on somewhere else, go ahead and have fun.

Pressing Matters

What's the difference between ironing and pressing?

- You *iron* by pushing and pulling a hot iron across the fabric in a side-to-side motion.
- You press by using an up-and-down motion as you firmly push down on an area of the fabric with an iron.

When making the projects in *Sewing For Dummies,* you are asked to either press or iron. Now you know the difference (read more about pressing tools in Chapter 1).

Why press and iron as you sew?

Sewing changes the texture of the fabric wherever stitching occurs. Pressing sets the stitches so that they become part of the fabric, and ironing puts the fabric back as close to its prestitched state as possible. If you don't press and iron while constructing a project, the seams stay as they are coming out of the sewing machine or serger, and the project has a rough, unfinished look.

In addition to the seam roll and pressing ham (see Chapter 1), a tool I use a lot is a Seam Stick. It's made of a very smooth, hard wood and is curved like a seam roll (see Chapter 1 for more on pressing tools), though it's much longer and narrower. Its size and shape allow you to easily slip it in a sleeve or pant leg. This tool enables you to press the fabric easily — much more easily than with a seam roll. A wool sleeve is also available for the tool, which makes it perfect for pressing lower-temperature fabrics such as synthetics and blends. Although it's not a replacement for a seam roll, the Seam Stick is a wonderful addition to your pressing tools. You can order a Seam Stick by contacting Belva Barrick, CFSC, 5643 W. Townley Ave., Glendale, AZ 85302.

When and where to press

Press every seam right after you sew it and every time the pattern guide sheet tells you to.

Use a hotter steam setting for natural fibers such as silk, cotton, wool, and linen. Use lower synthetic-temperature settings for man-made and synthetic fiber fabrics. Depending on your iron, you may or may not be able to use steam at these cooler settings. If you're in doubt about what works best on your fabric, do a test-press on a fabric scrap by using the iron with and without steam.

Press the seam flat and together, setting the stitches in the fabric. Press the iron over the seamline from the wrong side of the fabric. This step sets or *blends* the stitches in the fabric. Then position the iron so that you press the seam allowance together from the seamline out toward the edge (see Figure 5-15).

Then press a ⅝-inch seam open over a seam roll, and a ¼-inch seam to one side.

Your pattern guide sheet may instruct you to press other items throughout the course of a project. Don't try to cut corners by skipping these instructions. To encourage this "pressing" habit, try the following tip.

Set up your pressing area close to your sewing area. If your chair is on wheels, lower the ironing board to a comfortable height so that you can use your iron and ironing board from a seated position.

Figure 5-15:
Iron along the seamline to set the stitches. Press seams open over a seam roll or to one side in an up-and-down pressing motion.

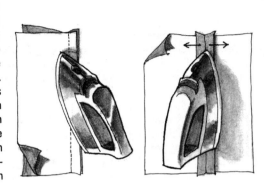

Pressing napped fabrics

Napped fabrics like velvet, velour, corduroy, and Polarfleece all have a fuzzy texture that can crush when iron pressure is put on them. Follow these tips when pressing napped fabrics:

- ✔ Don't press Polarfleece.

- ✔ Lightly press velour by using a good deal of steam and pressing from the wrong side.

- ✔ Press and iron corduroy from the wrong side of the fabric.

- ✔ Upholstery velvet is designed to be sat on, so the nap doesn't crush as easily as it does with dressmaking velvet. Also press upholstery velvet from the wrong side.

- ✔ Velvet almost crushes when you look at it. Lay a large scrap of velvet or a terry cloth towel on the ironing board, nap side up. Then lay the napped side of the velvet against the napped side of the towel and carefully press the garment from the wrong side. Be careful to set your iron for the appropriate temperature for the fiber content of your fabric (see Chapter 2 to read about fiber content). An iron that's too hot melts the fiber and creates unwanted shine that never presses out.

Chapter 6

Sewing Sensational Seams

Simply put, you form a seam every time you sew two pieces of fabric together. You need straight seams, curved seams, and corner seams to build a project. Then, once a seam is sewn, you beat a seam into submission with the iron, scissors, and the sewing machine to keep its shape.

Before you sew two pieces of fabric together, though, you must do a little preparation work. Strangely enough, you finish a seam before you begin it!

You Finish the Edges First!

Seam finishing is what you do to the fabric edges to prevent them from raveling. Finishing the seams also gives the project a neat, polished look.

The following seam finishes are for woven fabrics. If you are working on a knit, skip ahead to the section "Sewing straight seams," where the seams of knit fabrics are stitched and finished at once.

Pinking

Pinking the raw fabric edges is a quick way to finish a seam. You do pinking by trimming the raw edge of a single layer of fabric with a pair of pinking shears, which are shears with a funny-looking zigzag pattern on the blades. Woven fabrics are suitable for pinking because the blades cut clean little zigzags into the fabric, thereby preventing the raw edges from raveling.

Don't use pinking shears on a knit fabric. The blades chew up and snag the fabric beyond recognition. Skip ahead to the section "Sewing straight seams" for information on sewing seams on knits.

Don't cut out a project with pinking shears and think that you are saving a step — a pinked cutting line is not accurate. Instead, cut out your pattern pieces by using your dressmaker's shears. Then remove the paper pattern and pink the raw edges of each pattern piece, pinking one layer of fabric at a time.

Finishing (overcasting) edges with your sewing machine or serger

You finish the raw edges on a fabric so that the seam allowance doesn't ravel up to the seamline — the line of stitches that joins the fabric pieces together to make a seam. Woven fabrics ravel, so you can finish the edges by using stitches on your sewing machine or your serger. Knits don't ravel, but the edges on a knit sometimes curl and are hard to press flat, so the seams are handled a bit differently (see "Seaming Fabrics," later in this chapter).

Just follow these steps to finish woven fabric edges:

1. **Set your sewing machine like this:**

   • **Stitch:** Three-step zigzag

   • **Length:** 1 to 1.5 mm/20 spi or fine

   • **Width:** 5 to 6 mm

   • **Foot:** All-purpose

   If you are using a serger, set your serger like this:

   • **Stitch:** Three-thread overlock

   • **Length:** 3 mm

   • **Width:** 5 mm

   • **Foot:** All-purpose

2. **With either the right or the wrong side up, start sewing or serging the raw edge, guiding the fabric so that the stitches catch the fabric on the left and sewing just off the edge at the right.**

   Because you use these stitches to finish (or *overcast*) the edge of the fabric rather than to construct a seam, you don't need to backstitch.

Securing Your Seams

When sewing a seam with a straight stitch, you want to secure the stitches at the beginning and end so that the stitches don't pull out during construction. You can prevent stitches from coming unstitched two ways:

- ✔ By backstitching at the beginning and end of the seam
- ✔ By tying off the threads

Backstitching or not

Most machines have a backstitch or reverse button (see Chapter 1). To secure a seam with backstitching, simply take the first two or three stitches and then touch the reverse button. The machine automatically sews backward until you release the reverse button. Backstitch at the beginning and at the end of a seamline (see Figure 6-1), and you have all the stitch security that you need!

Figure 6-1:
Keeping your seams in place with backstitching.

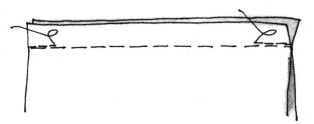

Don't backstitch when using a stitch other than a straight stitch. It's not necessary, and doing so may damage your sewing machine.

Sometimes you don't know how something fits until you sew it together and try it on. When you aren't sure that you want a seam to be permanent, just sew the seam without backstitching and leave the thread tails free at both ends of the seam. It's easier to remove stitches that have not been backstitched.

Tying off threads

You may want to tie off threads rather than backstitching at the point of a dart or at the beginning and end of a line of topstitching — like topstitching around a sleeve hem, for example. Tying off the threads is less bulky — important at the point of a dart — and it just plain looks better than backstitching.

The standard in seam allowances

The seam allowance on a pattern piece is a line that shows you where to stitch the pattern pieces together. As a rule, you can count on the following seam allowances as industry standards:

✔ ⅝ inch for woven garments

✔ ½ inch for home decorating projects

✔ ¼ inch for knit fabrics

Look on your project's pattern guide sheet if you're unsure about the seam allowances for your project.

When tying off threads, lift the presser foot and remove the fabric, pulling off and cutting a length of thread at least 8 inches long. Then, from the wrong side of the stitching line, pull up on the bobbin thread. The pulled thread brings a loop to the wrong side. Now grab the loop and pull it through until both threads are on the same side of the fabric. Tie off the threads as follows:

1. **Starting with thread tails at least 8 inches long, hold the threads together and form a loop.**

2. **Bring both threads around and through the loop, working the loop to the base of the stitch.**

3. **Holding the threads with your thumb, pull them taut so that the loop forms a knot at the base of the fabric at the stitching line.**

Seaming Fabrics

Sewing a seam is kind of like driving a car. In fact, in school I passed my driver's test on the sewing machine before I could sew a stitch (or drive a car). I had to prove that I could control the sewing machine — that I could start, stop, maneuver both inside and outside curves, and turn corners safely. Thank goodness I didn't have to parallel park!

Consider this next section your driving test and put the pedal to the metal and sew some seams.

Sewing straight seams

For straight seams every time, follow these steps:

1. **Set your machine like this for woven fabrics:**
   - **Stitch:** Straight
   - **Length:** 2.5 to 3 mm/10 to 12 spi
   - **Width:** 0 mm
   - **Foot:** All-purpose

   Set your machine like this for knit fabrics:
   - **Stitch:** Zigzag
   - **Length:** 1 to 2 mm/13 to 24 spi
   - **Width:** 1.5 to 2 mm
   - **Foot:** All-purpose

This seaming technique works great on wool double knits and Polarfleece because the seams are pressed open. For all other knits, skip ahead to the section "Sewing ¼-Inch Seams."

2. **Place and pin your pattern pieces so that the right sides of the fabric are together.**

   From now on when you see the words "place the right sides together," you'll know what they mean. Use as many pins as it takes to hold the edges together so that they don't slide around. The more you sew, the closer you can estimate how many pins you need for a particular job.

   For easy pin removal, pin perpendicular to the seamline so that the pin heads are toward your dominant hand and the pins either enter or exit the fabric about ¼ inch from the edge of the fabric. (See Chapter 5 for more on using pins when sewing.)

3. **Place the seam under the presser foot and line up the edge of the fabric with the appropriate seamline marked on the needle plate.**

   On the needle plate, you should see a set of lines to the right of the needle. Depending on your machine, sometimes they are marked as ⅝, ½, and so on; sometimes you see just plain old lines. Placing the bulk of the fabric to the left, line up the raw edges of your fabric along the ⅝-inch line. If you have everything lined up properly, the needle should be poised to hit the fabric right on the ⅝-inch seamline.

   If your needle plate has plain old lines, place your sewing tape measure under the needle so that the long length of the tape is to the left. Poke the needle into the tape at the ⅝-inch mark and lower the foot. The short end of the tape should line up with the ⅝-inch line in the needle plate. Either remember which line is needed for the ⅝-inch seamline or place a strip of tape, aligning the edge of the tape with the ⅝-inch line.

4. **Lower the presser foot onto the fabric and stitch, backstitching at the top and bottom of the seam. (See "Backstitching or not," earlier in this chapter, for more information.)**

If the needle hits a pin, the needle, the pin, or both can break, sending shards all over the place. Unless you plan on wearing safety goggles when you sew, pull out the pins before sewing over them.

Slow down when you seam a curve. Using the line in your needle plate, guide the edges along the appropriate line for an even sewing distance along the length of the curve.

5. **Press the seam flat and together. Then, from the wrong side, press the seam open. (See Chapter 5 for more information on pressing.)**

Turning corners

When turning a corner in the car, you slow down and stop, look both ways, and then turn. You do the same when turning a corner in sewing. Follow these steps, and you'll have good-looking corners every time:

1. **Mark the corner on the wrong side of the fabric with a dot so that you know exactly where to stop and pivot.**

   Once you stitch several corners, you'll have a good idea where to stop sewing to turn a corner without marking the corner first.

2. **As you approach the corner, slow down and stop, with the needle all the way into the fabric.**

3. **Leaving the needle in the fabric, lift the presser foot and pivot the fabric around the needle so that the other edge of the fabric lines up with the appropriate line in the needle plate.**

4. **Lower the presser foot and start sewing again.**

Sewing ¼-Inch Seams

When seaming a T-shirt, sweatshirt, and other active knit sportswear fabrics, a ¼-inch seam is usually stitched and pressed to one side.

Some patterns call for ¼-inch seam allowances; others call for ⅝-inch seam allowances. If the pattern you're working with calls for the wider seam allowances, instead of trimming them to ¼ inch, leave them wider to allow for fitting and then trim them off later. Exceptions are those areas where ribbing is applied at the neck edge and cuffs — trim those to ¼ inch before sewing. Depending on the capabilities of your sewing machine, ¼-inch seams are made in one or two steps.

This technique for seaming knits is called the two-step method because the seam is sewn with two separate passes through the sewing machine:

1. **Set your sewing machine like this:**

   - **Stitch:** Zigzag

   - **Length:** 2.5 to 3 mm/10 to 12 spi

   - **Width:** 1.5 to 2 mm

   - **Foot:** All-purpose

2. **Place and pin your pattern pieces so that the right sides of the fabric are together. Place the seam under the presser foot so that the needle sews ⅝ inch from the raw edge.**

3. **Set your sewing machine like this:**

   - **Stitch:** Three-step zigzag

   - **Length:** 1 to 1.5 mm/13 to 24 spi

   - **Width:** 4 to 5 mm

   - **Foot:** All-purpose

4. **Guiding to the immediate right of the tiny zigzag stitches, sew the second row of stitching with the three-step zigzag stitch. Repeat Steps 4 and 5 in the section "Sewing straight seams," earlier in this chapter, to finish and press the seam.**

Let 'Er Rip

You may think that if you're a careful sewer you won't make mistakes that need to be ripped out . . .WRONG. Ripping is part of sewing, no matter how experienced you are. But I do have a rule: Don't rip it out, if you can live with it. I say this because the mistake may look worse after you fix it than it did before you ripped it out. So sleep on it, look at your project with new eyes in the morning, and then decide if it's worth doing it over.

Now that you know when to rip, look at the easy ways to do it. My two favorite methods are using a seam ripper (see Chapter 1 to read more about a seam ripper) and pulling the needle and bobbin threads.

A *seam ripper* has a very sharp point that lifts a stitch away from the fabric and a knife edge that cuts the thread in one smooth motion.

Simply work the point of the ripper under the stitch and cut through the thread. After you cut the stitch, gently tug open the seam until another stitch holds the seam closed. Cut this stitch with the ripper and pull the seam open as before until you have "unsewn" the distance you want to open (see Figure 6-2).

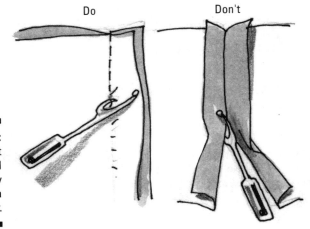

Figure 6-2:
Ripping out
unwanted
stitches by
using a
seam ripper.

This little tool is sharp enough to cut fabric. Don't push the ripper and cut through a whole line of stitching at once or you may cut a slit in the fabric, right next to the seamline — an almost impossible place to fix.

If you prefer to rip out stitches without the aid of a seam ripper, follow these steps:

1. **Loosen the stitches enough to have about a 2-inch thread tail.**

2. **Holding the project in one hand, jerk the thread tail back toward the stitching line, against the stitches, with the other hand.**

   This action breaks four to six stitches at once.

3. **Turn the project over and pull out the bobbin thread tail. Jerk on that thread tail, pulling against the stitches and breaking another four to six stitches.**

4. **Keep pulling the top thread and then the bobbin thread until you have unsewn as much stitching as needed.**

Shaping Up Those Curved Seams

Have you ever heard someone say, "The devil's in the details"? When it comes to sewing, nothing is truer. Sewing would be wonderful (but very boring) if all the seams were straight. They're not. In this section, you see how to take curved seams and whip them into shape by using your sewing machine and scissors. You'll use these techniques time and time again in many aspects of sewing, so mark this spot in the book with a sticky note and refer to it often.

. . . *with your sewing machine*

Staystitching is a technique that you can use on a single layer of fabric inside the seam allowance to "stay" or prevent curved fabric edges from stretching out of shape while you work on a project.

Staystitch neckline curves, armhole curves, and those edges cut on the bias (see Chapter 4 to read more about the bias), as shown in Figure 6-3.

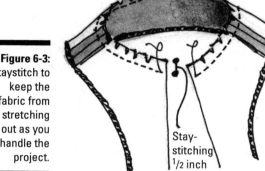

Figure 6-3: Staystitch to keep the fabric from stretching out as you handle the project.

Stay-stitching ¹/₂ inch

To staystitch an edge, use a regular straight stitch and sew a row of stitching ½ inch from the raw edge. If you're not sure whether to staystitch an area or not, see where your pattern guide sheet recommends it.

Understitching is a line of stitching found *under* or on the inside of a project close to the seamline. Collars and facings are understitched so they stay in shape and conform to the opening they're sewn into. Even though you don't see it, without understitching, armhole and neckline facings pull out of their openings, collar seams roll and look . . . well . . . tacky.

Curved seams, like those found on an armhole or neckline, are finished with another piece of fabric called a *facing*. Once the facing is sewn to the neckline or armhole, the seam allowance is pressed to one side, toward the facing. Then the seam allowance is understitched to compress the bulk created by the extra thickness of the seam allowance, to conform to the shape of the curve.

Understitching can be done with a straight stitch, but the stitch doesn't really do a whole lot to compress all that bulk. This method uses one of the most practical stitches on the sewing machine — the three-step zigzag stitch — that really flattens the seam allowance and gives you beautifully finished edges.

To understanch, do the following:

1. **After sewing the seam in question, press the entire seam allowance to one side.**

   For a neckline or armhole that has a facing stitched to the opening, press the seam allowance toward the facing.

2. **Set your machine like this:**

   - **Stitch:** Three-step zigzag
   - **Length:** 1 to 1.5 mm/20 to 24 spi
   - **Width:** 4 to 5 mm
   - **Foot:** All-purpose

3. **With the fabric right side up, place it under the presser foot so that the crack of the seam allowance is to one side of the needle or the other.**

   Which side? The side where the seam allowance is pressed. When the right side of the project is up and the seam is pressed to the right, the needle should be to the right side of the seamline. When it's pressed to the left, the needle should be to the left side of the seamline.

4. **Sew, guiding the needle so that when it travels over to the left side of the stitch, it comes to within ¹⁄₁₆ inch from the seamline.**

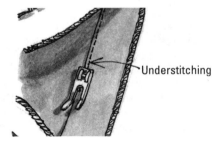

Understitching

TIP

As you are sewing, grasp the facing and seam allowance in your right hand with your thumb under the facing. Then, by periodically peeking under the fabric, check that the seam allowance is pushed toward the facing side of the seam. This way, all the bulk of the seam allowance is caught in the understitching.

Edgestitching is topstitching (stitching sewn on top of or on the right side of the fabric) that is very close to the finished edge. You find edgestitching on the edge of collars, cuffs, pockets, waistbands, front shirt plackets, and other edges where you want a crisp, tailored look. Even though you can edgestitch with an all-purpose presser foot, it's tricky to sew straight because you're sewing so close to the edge.

This technique uses the blind hem foot as a guide, enabling you to edgestitch quickly, accurately, and professionally:

1. **Set your machine like this:**

   - **Stitch:** Straight
   - **Length:** 2 to 3 mm/9 to 13 spi
   - **Width:** 0 mm
   - **Foot:** Blind hem or edgestitch
   - **Optional:** Near left needle position (check your Operating Manual)

2. **Place the guide in the foot along the finished edge and sew.**

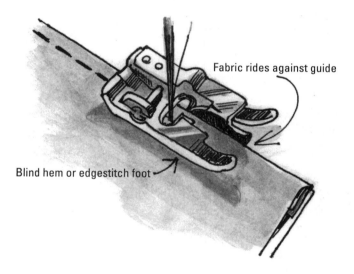

Fabric rides against guide

Blind hem or edgestitch foot

Using this foot makes edgestitching a lot easier to sew an even distance from the edge. Instead of backstitching, pull the threads to the back and tie them off (see "Tying off threads" in this chapter for more information).

If you don't have a blind hem foot and a variable needle position, place the fabric under the foot so that when the needle is in the fabric, the edge of the fabric is about $\frac{1}{16}$ inch from the needle. Notice where the edge of the fabric is in relationship to the foot (this spot could be at the edge of the needle hole, where there's a line in the foot, or where the foot changes direction). Sewing slowly, guide the edge of the fabric by that spot on the foot.

. . . with your scissors

Clipping a seam to the staystitching or seamline releases the seam allowance on an inside curve so that it's flexible enough to spread open. This way, after stitching the armhole or neckline facing, for example, the facing turns smoothly to the inside of the garment. If you didn't clip the seam, when you turn the facing to the inside of the armhole or neck edge, the seam is stiff and bunchy and the facings pop out of the opening.

Clipping is done with the very sharp scissor tips. Clips in the fabric are cut perpendicular to the seamline and come to within $\frac{1}{16}$ inch of the staystitching or seamline. Rather than holding the seam allowance closed and clipping both seam allowances simultaneously, clip each seam allowance separately, alternating the clips across the seamline from one another. This sure-fire clipping technique pads the seam allowance, creating the smoothest curved seam ever, as shown in Figure 6-4.

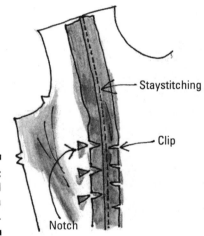

Figure 6-4:
Clipping and notching a seam.

Notching a seam to the staystitching or seamline is just the opposite of clipping. It's done to reduce bulk in the seam allowance of an outside curve, such as the outside edge of a collar or princess seam line (refer to Figure 6-4).

Notch a seam allowance by cutting away little triangular-shaped pieces of fabric. Using your scissor tips, rather than holding the seam allowance closed and notching both seam allowances simultaneously, cut one notch out of a seam allowance separately, alternating notches across the seamline from one another. Cut away each notch up to within $\frac{1}{8}$ inch of the seamline.

Cut away small notches from small curves that are spaced about ¼ to ½ inch apart. Cut away larger notches from larger curves spaced from about ½ to ¾ inch apart.

After some experience, you find that cutting away more notches is usually better than cutting fewer, bigger ones. This way, when an affected area is stitched, notched, turned, and pressed, the seam allowance fits and presses smoothly — no unwanted lumps or bumps (refer to Figure 6-5).

When notching an edge, don't cut through the stitching at the seamline.

My favorite way to notch an edge on light- to mid-weight woven fabric is by using my pinking shears. I trim or grade the seam with the pinking shears, cutting to within ⅛ inch of the stitching line. Pinking automatically notches the edge, so I'm on to the next step in no time.

Don't be confused between notches that are match points marked on the pattern paper (see Chapter 4) and notches that you cut out of the seam allowance at an outside curve. Even though the word is the same, they are two different sewing terms.

Trimming seams eliminates bulk from the seam allowances that are stitched and then turned right side out so that the seamline is on the edge. Trim as close to the stitching line as possible, leaving enough seam allowance so that the stitches don't pull off the fabric (see Figure 6-5).

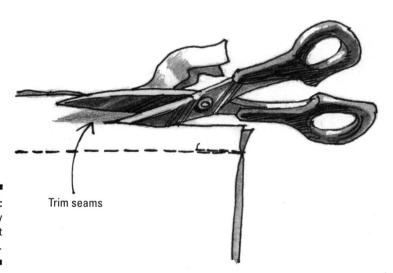

Figure 6-5:
Trim away
the bulk at
the seams.

Trim seams

Chapter 7
Hems and A-Ha's

*H*ave you ever bought a pair of pants and left them hanging in the closet until the dust settled on the hanger before shortening them? Have your kids outgrown their clothes before you could get to the hemming? If this sounds familiar, this chapter's for you. These tips, tricks, and techniques are my favorites for hemming and may keep you from procrastinating the next time a new outfit needs hemming.

But, first, what are hems and why do you need them? A hem is a turned-up edge that's stitched in place at the bottom of skirts, pants, shorts, sleeves, and drapery panels. Besides making the edges neat, hems add weight to an edge, so the garment or drapery hangs better with a hem than without one.

Marking a Hem

Before you can sew the hem, you need to mark it. To get a hem an even distance from the floor, you also need a helper. (My husband, while reluctant, became really good at this once he understood what he had to do.) You have two roles to fill when marking hems: the hem-ee and the hemmer.

If you're the hem-ee

As the hem-ee, you wear the garment, so the hem is marked to fit you. Here's what you do:

1. **Try on the garment, wearing the same underwear and shoes that you'll be wearing when you wear the garment out of the house.**

   Because most people are lopsided, put the garment on with the right side out — or the hem is measured to fit the wrong side of your body.

2. **Stand on a hard floor, table, or stool.**

   Carpet can distort the measurements.

3. **Stand up straight with your hands down at your sides and don't lock your knees.**

   I locked my knees once and passed out!

If you're the hemmer

As the hemmer, your job is to measure and mark the hem of the garment worn by the hem-ee. This is what you do:

1. **Find a pleasing hem length by temporarily pinning up the hemline.**

   When hemming a skirt or dress, temporarily pin up the hem to a pleasing length — not all the way around, just about 12 inches or so in the front.

   For slacks, temporarily pin up the hemlines so the creases break slightly at the top of the shoe. This is personal preference, so, if you have a favorite pair of pants, notice how they're hemmed and compare. Pin both hems so that they are even at the heel and creases. Now, skip ahead to the section "Finishing the Raw Edges of the Hem," later in this chapter.

   By temporarily pinning up a section of the garment at the proper length, you create a *hem fold*. This fold allows you to measure the hem for the rest of the garment more accurately.

2. **Using a yardstick, measure the distance from the floor to the hem fold and tightly wrap a thin rubber band around the yardstick the proper distance from the floor.**

3. **Pin through a single thickness at the hem fold by using two pins and pinning parallel to the floor. Remove the rest of the pins so that the hemline hangs free.**

4. **Using the rubber band on the yardstick as a guide, pin-mark the hemline even with the rubber band, pinning all the way around the garment.**

   Place pins about every 2 to 3 inches, pinning parallel to the floor. Pin-mark a few inches, move, and then measure and pin-mark again until the entire hemline is marked.

   Move around the hem-ee rather than the other way around. This way, the hem-ee doesn't shift weight and distort the hemline.

Deciding on the Hem Allowance

After you measure and mark the hemline, decide how deep you want the hem allowance — that's the distance from the folded hemline to the finished edge of the hem. Hem allowances range from ¼ to 3 inches depending on the type of garment and the fabric.

When you're sewing a project, the hem allowance is marked on the pattern. If you're altering a ready-made garment and are clueless about the best hem allowance for your project, refer to Table 7-1 for some general guidelines.

Table 7-1	Recommended Hem Depths
Garment	**Recommended Hem Allowances**
T-shirts, sleeves	⅝ to 1¼ inches
Shorts, slacks	1¼ to 1½ inches
Jackets	1½ to 2 inches
Straight skirts and coats	2 to 3 inches

Finishing the Raw Edges of the Hem

After you measure and mark the hemline and determine the proper hem allowance, even up the hem allowance and finish the hem edge.

Even up the hem allowance by measuring from the hemline to the raw edge. Say that you need the hem allowance to be 2½ inches. On your project, the hem depth varies from 2½ inches to 3 inches, so measure down from the hemline 2½ inches and mark around the hem edge by using a fabric marker. Then trim off the excess fabric so that the hem allowance is an even 2½ inches all the way around.

You may be working on a knit or a woven fabric. The hem edge of each fabric type is finished differently:

- ✔ Knits that don't run don't need to have the hem edges finished, although they may look better. If you choose not to finish the hem edge, skip ahead to the section "Hemming Things Up."

- ✔ Knits that curl, such as T-shirt knits and fleeces, are hemmed with twin needles, so skip ahead to the section "Hemming Knits."

- ✔ Finish the raw hem edges on woven fabrics so that they don't ravel. (Chapter 6 tells you how to finish raw edges.)

Quick-fix hemming with Res-Q-Tape

You're getting ready for work and reach in the closet for the only suit that isn't at the cleaners. With one leg in the trousers, you slip and catch your big toe in the hem and rip it out. You really don't know one end of the needle from the other, so you grab the Res-Q-Tape. The hem is fixed, and you're out the door in five minutes.

Res-Q-Tape is a very sticky, double-faced tape that won't harm fabric. Find it on the notion wall of your local fabric store or through your favorite sewing mail-order source.

If you have a sewing machine that has only a straight and zigzag stitch, finish the hem edge by sewing on hem tape or hem lace, as follows:

1. **Pin the hem tape to the hem edge.**

   Place the hem tape or lace on the right side of the fabric, overlapping the raw hem edge about ¼ inch. Then pin-baste the tape to the hem edge. (Once you are proficient, you can sew on the tape or lace without basting.)

2. **Set your machine like this:**

   - **Stitch:** Straight
   - **Length:** Appropriate for the fabric
   - **Width:** 0 mm
   - **Foot:** All-purpose

3. **Sewing with the right side of the fabric up, stitch the hem tape or lace in place without stretching it.**

Hemming Things Up

You've marked the hem, evened up the hem allowance, finished the raw edge, and now you're ready to pin up the hem and sew.

Pin up a hem the same way for both hand and machine blind hemming. Pin through both fabric layers, pinning ¼ to ⅜ inch from and perpendicular to the finished edge, as shown in Figure 7-1.

Figure 7-1:
Pin the hem
the same
way
whether
blind
hemming by
hand or
machine.

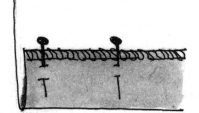

Hand blind hemming

If you don't have a blind hem stitch on your machine, or until you have mastered blind hemming by machine, stitch your hems this way by hand:

1. **Thread the needle with one 15- to 18-inch length of thread, one shade darker than the fabric.**

   If the thread is much longer, it tangles and wears out before you use all of it.

2. **Lay the hem across your lap so that the inside of the garment is up and the hem is perpendicular to your body. Fold the hem allowance up to where the pins enter the fabric.**

   Approximately ¼ to ⅜ inch of the hem allowance is showing.

3. **Take the first stitch on the single layer of the hem allowance, poking the point of the needle down into the fabric and then bringing it up no farther than ⅛ inch from where it entered.**

4. **Stitching from left to right (if you're right-handed) or right to left (if you're left-handed), take another stitch, picking up one fine thread (at the edge of the fold and where the pins enter the fabric) from the garment side of the project.**

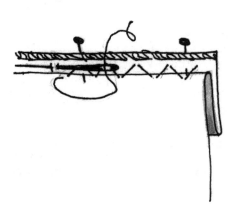

The goal here is for the stitches to be as invisible as possible on the right side of the project, so take the finest stitch possible on the garment side of the project. Continue stitching, taking one stitch on the hem allowance and then taking the next stitch on the garment where the hem is folded back to the pins. Continue until the hem is stitched.

Machine blind hemming

Once you use your sewing machine to blind hem, I bet you won't go back to doing it by hand. This is what you do:

1. **Set your machine like this:**
    - **Stitch:** Blind hem
    - **Length:** 2 to 2.5 mm/10 to 12 spi
    - **Width:** 2 to 2.5 mm
    - **Foot:** Blind hem

2. **Fold the hem allowance back to where the pins enter the fabric and place it under the blind hem foot.**

    The right side of the project is against the feed dogs, the wrong side is up, and the hem fold is snuggled up against the guide in the foot.

3. **Make the first few stitches on the hem allowance; then the zigzag bites into the fold.**

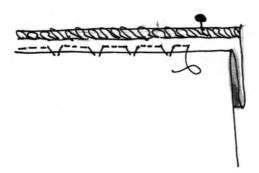

Like hand blind hemming, the goal here is for invisible stitches, so, if the stitch is grabbing too much of the hem fold, it's too wide. Use a narrower stitch width.

4. **Remove the work, pull the threads to one side of the fabric, and tie them off. Gently press the hem allowance from the wrong side of the project, applying more iron pressure on the hem fold than on the top of the hem allowance.**

Hemming Pegged or Straight Hems

Whether making pants or rehemming ready-made pants, the hem allowance is tapered to conform to the shape of the pant leg. If you don't taper the hem allowance, the hem edge is shorter than the leg circumference. What happens? The hemming stitches pull at the fabric, so the pant leg puckers at the top of the hem allowance. Yuck. This is how you taper a hem allowance:

1. **Measure, mark, and finish the hem edge, leaving about a 1½- to 2-inch hem allowance.**

2. **Rip out each inseam (the one on the inside of the legs) and each outseam (the one on the outside of the legs)** *only* **up to the hem fold.**

3. **Restitch the inseam and the outseam, sewing from the new hemline fold-out to the finished edge.**

   By tapering these seams from the hemline fold-out to the finished edge, they fit comfortably into the circumference of the opening.

Hemming Knits

Knits stretch. Because of this, traditional hand and machine blind hemming techniques don't hold up to a lot of wear. Duplicate commercial hemming techniques for your handmade projects and when rehemming ready-mades by hemming with your twin needles.

Twin needles are sized in two ways: by the distance the needles are from one another and by the needle size and point type. For example, a 4.0 - #80/12 Universal twin needle means

- ✔ You have two needles that are 4 mm apart.

- ✔ Each needle is a size 80 (European) or 12 (American sizing).

- ✔ Each has a Universal point.

Only sewing machines with top- or front-loading bobbins (a category that includes most machines) can use twin needles. If your bobbin goes in the side, the needles sit in the machine sideways and won't work. If you can't use twin needles in your machine, fuse the hem by using fusible web (see the manufacturer's instructions on the package on how to use it).

Follow these steps to hem knits:

1. **Mark, press, and pin up the hem as previously described.**

2. **Set your machine like this:**
   - **Stitch:** Straight
   - **Length:** 3 to 4 mm/6 to 9 spi
   - **Width:** 0 mm
   - **Foot:** Embroidery
   - **Needle:** 4.0 mm 80/12 Universal twin

3. **Thread your twin needle by following the instructions in your Operating Manual.**

4. **With the right side of the project up, place the hem so that the presser foot rests on a double layer of fabric (the hem allowance and the garment) and sew.**

   It's easier to sew straight and even when the foot rests completely on a double layer of fabric.

5. **After sewing around the hem, pull the threads to the wrong side and tie them off securely (see Chapter 6).**

6. **Carefully trim away the excess hem allowance above the stitch.**

Part III

Fashion Fundamentals

The 5th Wave
By Rich Tennant

"The intruder was no match for the old woman. She took him down and hand stitched him to the carpet before he knew what was happening. Someone unzip his mouth so we can hear what he has to say."

In this part . . .

When the pattern guide sheet of your fashion project tells you to "Sew in the zipper," you may be left scratching your head. How in the world are you supposed to do that? Your first step should be to turn to Chapter 9 of this chapter. There you find step-by-step instructions on how to sew in a zipper. I also give you the skinny on sewing hooks and eyes, darts, tucks, pleats, sleeves, pockets, and other sewing delights! Sprinkled throughout this part you also find projects that help you firm up your fashion fundamentals.

Chapter 8

Shaping Things Up

In This Chapter
▶ Seeing the art of darts
▶ Gathering the easy way
▶ Tuck, tuck, tuck . . . pleat
▶ Stretching your skills with elastic

*D*arts, gathering, pleats, tucks, and elastic enable you to give form to otherwise lifeless pieces of fabric. You can use these structural elements separately or together to turn a potato sack into a creation that conforms to all sorts of contours not only in clothing but in almost anything made of fabric.

Darting Around

Darts are little wedges of fabric, pinched out and stitched to shape pattern pieces at the waistline, back waist, shoulder, bustline, and hips, as shown in Figure 8-1.

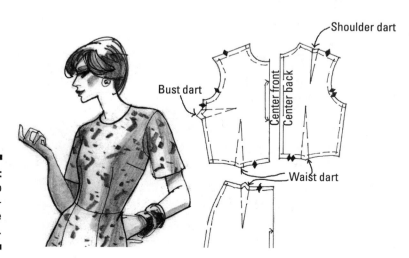

Figure 8-1:
Darts help your projects take shape.

Shoulder dart

Bust dart

Center front

Center back

Waist dart

Darts are marked on paper patterns with stitching lines and sometimes a foldline that converges to the point of the dart. (See Chapter 4 for more information on how to decipher the markings on patterns.)

Making the dart

To construct perfect darts every time, just follow these steps:

1. **Mark the dart with pins or a fabric marker. (See Chapter 4 for more about marking elements from a pattern.)**

2. **Fold the dart, right sides together, matching at the foldline and pinning perpendicular to the stitching line, at the dots marked on the pattern piece.**

3. **Place a strip of invisible tape, the length of the dart, next to the stitching line.**

   The tape forms a stitching template that helps to keep your sewing straight.

4. **Starting at the wide end of the dart, lower the presser foot and sew next to the tape for a perfectly straight dart.**

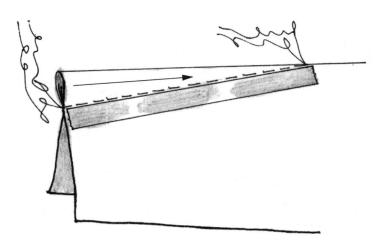

Pull out the pins before sewing.

Finishing the dart

After sewing your dart, you need to press it so that the dart forms a clean, smooth line in the fabric. Just follow these easy steps:

1. **Remove the tape and press the dart flat and together.**

   Place the dart on the ironing board with the wrong side of the fabric up. Place one edge of the iron over the stitching line with the rest of the iron over the fold of the dart; then press the dart flat from the stitching line out to the fold. This procedure is referred to as *pressing the dart flat and together.* By pressing over the seamline, you are setting the stitches so that they blend well into the fabric.

2. **Tie off the thread tails at the point of the dart (see Chapter 6 for the how-to's on tying off threads).**

3. **Press the dart to one side.**

   Press horizontal darts so that the bulk of the dart is down. Press vertical darts so that the bulk of the dart is toward the center.

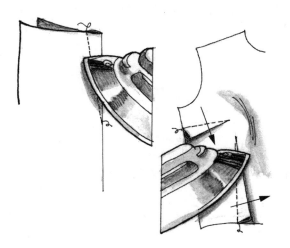

Gathering No Moss

You can gather fabric by using three methods. The method you use depends on the type of fabric you're working with.

Gathering with two threads

The two-thread method works best for creating fine, controlled gathers on light-weight fabrics such as batiste, challis, charmeuse, gauze, gingham, georgette, lace, silk broadcloth, and voile. (See Chapter 2 for more information on fabrics.) Just follow these steps:

1. **Set your machine like this:**
   - **Stitch:** Straight
   - **Length:** 2.5 to 3 mm/9 to 13 spi
   - **Width:** 0 mm
   - **Foot:** All-purpose or embroidery
   - **Upper tension:** Loosen slightly

2. **Thread your bobbin with a thread that contrasts with the thread going through the needle.**

3. **Sew a row of gathering stitches ½ inch from the raw edge, leaving at least a 2-inch thread tail.**

   Do not backstitch at the beginning or end.

   When sewing the seam together at the 5/8-inch seamline, the gathering stitches will be just inside the seam allowance.

4. **Sew a second row of gathering stitches ⅜ inch from the raw edge, leaving at least a 2-inch thread tail. Be careful not to cross stitching lines.**

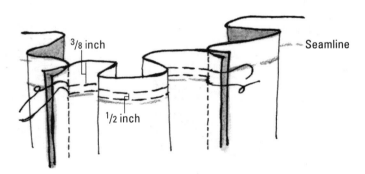

5. **Pull up the gathers by pulling on the contrasting bobbin threads.**

   Working from the ends toward the center, hold the bobbin threads taut in one hand while sliding the fabric along the stitches with the other. Adjust the gathers as needed for the desired fullness. Then remember to put your upper tension back to the normal setting for regular sewing.

   Not only are the gathers even, but by using two threads, you also have a back-up thread if the first thread breaks.

Gathering over a cord

Gathering over a cord is a terrific way for gathering mid- to heavy-weight fabrics such as chambray, chintz, corduroy, light-weight denim, linen and wool suiting, oxford, pique, poplin, and seersucker. The cord technique also works well when you gather yards of fabric all at once when sewing ruffles. Just follow these steps:

1. **Set your machine like this:**
   - **Stitch:** Straight
   - **Length:** 2.5 to 3 mm/9 to 13 spi
   - **Width:** 3 to 4 mm
   - **Foot:** Embroidery

2. **Cut a long strand of pearl cotton (a twisted embroidery floss available through your local fabric or craft store) or dental floss or reel off multiple strands of any thread long enough to accommodate the area to be gathered. For example, if you're gathering 10 inches, the cord should be 12 to 14 inches long.**

   If you're using thread, slightly twist the strands together — making a sort of cord — before sewing over it.

3. **Place the fabric under the needle with the wrong side up. Leaving the foot up, pierce the fabric with the needle ½ inch from the raw edge.**

4. **Center the "cord" under the foot, and lower the presser foot.**

5. **Zigzag over the cord.**

   The zigzag stitches create a channel for the cord to slide through.

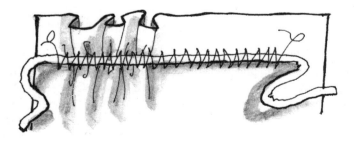

6. **Pull up the gathers by sliding the fabric down the cord.**

   You can easily adjust the gathers, and the cord doesn't break when working the stitches up and down for dense gathering.

Gathering with a gathering foot

A *gathering foot* is not standard issue with most sewing machines, but the time this foot can save you may make it worth the expense. This foot not only gathers light- to mid-weight fabrics automatically but, because of the way it's made, can also gather and attach a ruffle simultaneously.

Follow these steps to gather using a gathering foot:

1. **Set your machine like this:**

   - **Stitch:** Straight
   - **Length:** 3 to 4 mm/6 to 9 spi
   - **Width:** 0 mm
   - **Upper tension:** Tighten slightly
   - **Needle position:** Left (optional)

2. **Run a test strip on a scrap of fabric.**

   The amount the fabric gathered depends on the fabric weight, the upper thread tension, and the stitch length. Adjust and test for the desired gathering in the following ways:

   - **For more gathers:** Use a lighter-weight fabric, tighten the upper tension more, and lengthen the stitch.
   - **For fewer gathers:** Use a mid-weight fabric, a normal upper tension, and shorten the stitch length.

3. **After you have the test gather just right, sew the real gather, guiding the needle ½ inch from the raw edge.**

   Then this is what I do: Gather another long strip of the fabric you're using in your project, making sure that you gather enough. Cut off as much gathering as you need and sew it as directed in your pattern guide sheet.

   If you are gathering the ruffle and attaching it to the flat piece, lower the foot onto the ruffle fabric so that the right side of the ruffle fabric is up. Then slip the flat piece of fabric in the slot of the foot with the right side of the fabric down and sew.

   Remember to put your upper tension back to the normal setting for regular sewing.

Tackling Tucks

Tucks are stitched folds that run the full length of the garment. You usually use tucks to decorate or embellish a project, but occasionally you use tucks for fitting detail.

Knowing how to sew three types of tucks should take care of most of your tucking needs. Figure 8-2 shows you examples of the three most common tucks: plain, pin, and shell.

Figure 8-2:
Three types
of tucks
tackle
today's tuck
tasks.

You often find plain tucks on either side of a blouse or shirt (on the front of a tuxedo shirt, for example). Pin tucks pop up most often on heirloom christening gowns and fine blouses. Shell tucks commonly are sewn on the edge of T-shirt neckbands and on lingerie hems and edges.

Plain tucks

Plain tucks are anything but plain! They come in two tasty varieties:

- ✔ **Blind tucks:** The stitching line is right next to the fold of the next tuck, which hides the tuck's stitching.
- ✔ **Spaced tucks:** Space between the fold of the tuck and the stitching line highlights the stitching.

You make both types of tucks in the same way. Just follow these steps:

1. **Using a fabric marker, mark the tuck stitching lines at the dots on the paper pattern, transferring them to the fabric. (Chapter 4 tells you all about working with patterns.)**

2. **Fold the tuck, wrong sides together, matching and pinning the fabric together at the dots on the stitching lines.**

3. **Sew the tuck by lowering the presser foot and sewing on the stitching line.**

To help you keep the width of your tucks even, guide the edge of the fold along the lines marked on the needle plate of your sewing machine. For example, to sew a ½-inch-wide tuck, guide the tuck fold along the ½-inch line on the needle plate.

Pin tucks

Very narrow tucks are called *pin tucks* (because they are as narrow as a pin). The easiest way to make these delicate tucks is with your sewing machine and a twin needle.

A *twin needle* is one needle base that fits up in the needle bar and a crossbar with two needles mounted in it. Twin needles work only on sewing machines with top- or front-loading bobbins (most models have one of these bobbin types), so check to see what type of machine you're working with. If your bobbin goes in the side of the machine, the twin needle sits in the machine sideways and doesn't work.

To sew pin tucks using a twin needle, follow these steps:

1. **Set your machine like this:**

   - **Stitch:** Straight
   - **Length:** 2.5 to 3 mm/9 to 13 spi
   - **Width:** 0 mm
   - **Foot:** Embroidery
   - **Upper tension:** Tighten slightly

2. **Thread your machine for a twin needle, as shown in your machine's Operating Manual.**

3. **Mark the center of the tuck grouping by gently pressing a crease on the right side of the fabric (like you press a crease in a pair of pants).**

   For example, if you're making nine pin tucks across the front of a shirt, press the fold where you want the middle of the fifth tuck to be.

4. **Open the fabric flat and stitch the first tuck, centering the crease under the foot.**

5. **Pull out a generous thread tail and, without cutting the thread, turn the fabric 180 degrees.**

6. **Lower the foot a presser foot width away from the first tuck and sew the second tuck.**

To prevent the fabric from distorting, I like working out from the center of the tuck grouping. Stitch one tuck by sewing north to south and the next tuck by sewing south to north, working from the center tuck evenly out to the side tucks.

If you're sewing a lot of tucks and want them very close together, invest in a *pin tucking foot*. The underside has from three to five narrow channels, depending on the brand. After you make the first tuck, the other tucks simply ride under one of the channels in the foot for the straightest tucks ever.

Shell tucks

Shell tucks look like a row of little scalloped shells on a neck edge (refer to Figure 8-2). Sometimes shell tucks are used on the neck edge of delicate tank top in lieu of a facing (another piece of fabric that finishes an edge).

Follow these steps to make shell tucks by using a blind hem stitch:

1. **Set your machine like this:**
   - **Stitch:** Blind hem
   - **Length:** 2.5 to 3 mm/9 to 13 spi
   - **Width:** 5 to 6 mm
   - **Foot:** Embroidery

2. **Fold down and press the edge you're tucking about ⅝ inch.**

3. **Place the folded edge so that the fabric is halfway under the foot and the bulk of the fabric is to the *right* of the needle.**

4. **Lower the presser foot and sew.**

   The needle takes a few stitches on the right and then zigzags off the edge at the left, pulling up a little shell in the fabric.

You can also stitch a shell tuck with the reverse blind hem stitch. The reverse blind hem stitch looks like the blind hem stitch (three to four straight stitches and then a zigzag). But rather than the zigzag kicking to the left, it kicks to the right. Why is this difference important? Instead of putting the bulk of the fabric to the right, the reverse blind hem stitch enables you to sew with the bulk of the fabric to the left, which makes sewing the stitch much easier.

To sew a shell stitch with the reverse blind hem stitch, follow Steps 1 and 2 in the preceding list of steps. Then place the folded edge halfway under the foot so that the bulk of the fabric is to the *left* of the needle. When you lower the foot and sew, the needle takes a few stitches on the left and then zigzags off the edge at the right, pulling up a little shell in the fabric.

You Can't Beat Pleats

Pleats are folds in the fabric that control fullness. You find pleats in all sorts of places, including the following:

- Around a whole garment, such as on a pleated skirt
- In sections, such as at the waistline of a pair of trousers
- As a single pleat, like a kick pleat in the back of a skirt

You make most pleats by folding a continuous piece of fabric and then stitching the folds to hold them in place. The pattern guide sheet explains how to fold and construct pleats for a particular project; refer to the pattern often as you sew your pleats.

To make a pleat, mark it as you would a dart or other symbol found on the pattern tissue (see marking instructions Chapter 4). Then you fold the pleat on the foldline and stitch the pleat on the stitching line.

Types of pleats

When you look through pattern catalogs and fashion magazines (and probably your own closet), you see a variety of types of pleats. Become familiar with the different types of pleats and where you find them on clothing (see Figure 8-3):

The types of pleats include the following:

- **Knife pleats:** Have one foldline and one placement line and are pleated in one direction. You often find several knife pleats clustered together on one side of a garment, where a cluster faces one direction and another cluster faces the opposite direction — like at the top of a pair of trousers.

- **Box pleats:** Have two foldlines and two placement lines. The folds of each pleat face away from each other, and the back side of the folds may or may not meet. You most commonly see box pleats down the center front of a dress or skirt.

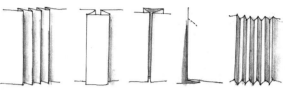

Figure 8-3:
Look for knife pleats, box pleats, inverted pleats, kick pleats, and accordion pleats in garments in your closet, in stores, and in catalogs.

- **Inverted pleats:** Have two foldlines, but they come together at a common placement line.

- **Kick pleats:** Have one foldline and one placement line and are usually found at the hem edge at center back of a slim skirt. Besides adding a style, kick pleats give the skirt enough room for comfortable walking.

- **Accordion pleats:** Sorry — you can't make these pleats at home. Accordion pleats look like the bellows of an accordion, providing a kicky, flared effect. These pleats are permanently set into the fabric by a commercial pleater. Purchase accordion pleated fabric by the yard.

Making a pleat

Regardless of the type pleat you're making, with the exception of the accordion pleat, pleats are all made just about the same. Once you know how to make a kick pleat, you have the basic skills needed to make the others.

You often find simple knife pleats in trousers. To create a knife pleat, follow these steps:

1. **Mark the pleats at the dots as directed on your project's pattern guide sheet.**

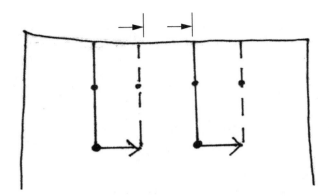

2. **Fold and pin the pleat, bringing the foldline over to meet the place-ment line.**

3. **Stitch the pleat on the stitching line.**

Getting Elastic

Besides adding shape and form to a project, elastic usually adds comfort in terms of wearing the garment.

Elastic comes in a variety of configurations depending on its intended use. Refer to Chapter 2 for more information on the different types of elastic and which type may be appropriate for your project.

In this section, I tell you how to use elastic thread to create a gentle control called *shirring*. You also discover the easy way to put elastic through a casing. And, if you want to know how to sew elastic to an edge, I show you two techniques — one using a sewing machine and one using a serger.

For shirr

Shirring sort of resembles scrunched gathering. (See "Gathering No Moss," earlier in this chapter, for more information on gathering.) However, although gathering and shirring are both means for controlling fullness, gathering is usually done and then set in a seam — as in a gathered ruffle or a gathered skirt — that goes on a waistband. Shirring involves several equidistant rows of gathering.

The best fabrics for shirring are soft, light-weight wovens that have been preshrunk, such as batiste, charmeuse, and calico. The best knit fabrics for shirring are tricot, cotton T-shirt knits, and interlocks.

Shirring can be done by using regular thread on the top and bobbin. However, my favorite way (and the easiest to fit) is to shirr by using elastic thread in the bobbin.

You need the following magic ingredients for shirring success:

- **Quality elastic thread:** You can get elastic thread at your local sewing machine dealer. It has a stretchy core wrapped in cotton and is a little beefier than what you typically find on the notion wall at the fabric store.

- **Paper adding-machine tape:** Your local office supply store should stock this tape. I have a roll that I keep with my sewing stuff because it comes in handy for other sewing jobs.

Armed with the proper tools, follow these steps to shirr:

1. **Set your machine like this:**
   - **Stitch:** Straight stitch
   - **Length:** 3 to 4 mm/6 to 9 spi
   - **Width:** 0 mm
   - **Foot:** Embroidery
   - **Upper tension:** Tighten slightly

2. **Wind the bobbin with elastic thread.**

3. **Place the bobbin on the bobbin winder and place the tube of elastic thread on your lap. Loosely tie the elastic thread onto the bobbin and then wind the bobbin slowly, guiding the elastic thread onto the bobbin evenly.**

   If your machine has a self-winding bobbin, wind the bobbin by hand.

   Don't stretch the elastic thread while winding. If you do, the elastic thread stretches out while it's on the bobbin, and all the zip is zapped.

4. **Thread the bobbin case as though it were a normal sewing thread, pulling it through and snapping it into the bobbin tension.**

The weight of the fabric determines how much the fabric shirrs, so you need to perform a test to see how your fabric behaves. Cut a strip of fabric 10 inches long and about 6 inches wide and then do the following steps on your test strip before shirring the real deal.

5. **Place a strip of adding machine tape under the fabric; then place the fabric and tape under the presser foot with the right side of the fabric up.**

   The tape prevents the fabric from shirring before you want it to. After you remove the tape, the fabric shirrs beautifully.

6. **With the right side of the fabric up and the adding machine tape under the fabric, sew the first row of shirring across the top of the strip.**

7. **When you reach the end of the fabric, pull out enough thread so that at least 1 inch of elastic thread is left out at the end of the first row of stitching.**

   Doing so ensures that the elastic thread doesn't pull out of the stitching when it's caught in a seam.

8. **Sew a second row next to the first, sewing a presser foot distance away.**

9. **Repeat Steps 4, 5, and 6 until you shirr the desired amount of fabric.**

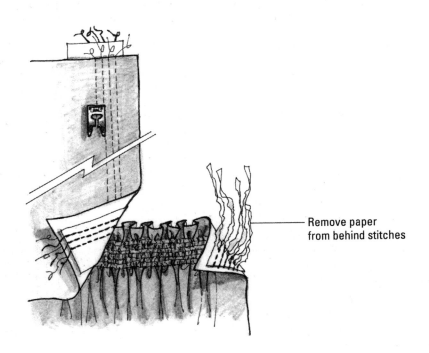

Remove paper from behind stitches

10. **Tear off the adding machine tape from behind the stitches.**

The fabric shirrs as the elastic thread relaxes. If the 10-inch test fabric strip shirrs to 5 inches, you know to use a 2:1 ratio when shirring a dress bodice, a cuff on a sleeve, or a waistline.

When you shirr at the wrist of a sleeve or waistline, remember to catch each row of shirring in the seams at both ends. This way, the elastic threads are secured in the seam and don't pull out.

Elastic in a casing

A *casing* is a fabric tunnel that holds a drawstring or elastic at waistlines, wrists, and ankles to shape a garment. Traditionally, you create a casing in one of the two following ways:

- ✔ By folding down and stitching a casing, using fabric at the top of a waistline. You often see and use this method for the waistband on a pair of pull-on shorts.

- ✔ By sewing another strip of fabric to the wrong side of the fabric. This method is popular at the waistlines of dresses and at the back of jackets.

In this section, you make a casing by using the fold-down method. Pattern instructions often tell you to create the casing, and then thread the elastic through the casing with a large safety pin or *bodkin* (a little tool that pinches together over the end of the elastic like a pair of tweezers with teeth).

I've made hundreds of casings. I can't tell you how many times I've gotten to within 2 inches of the end and given the elastic one last tug, just to have the safety pin or bodkin pull off the end before the elastic was all the way through the casing. If that didn't happen, then the safety pin or bodkin caught in the seam allowances. By the time the elastic was through the casing, I felt like I had acute arthritis in both hands. Painful and frustrating!

So, with help from my friend Karyl Garbow, we devised the following technique for creating elastic casings. Our technique takes about as long as the conventional method, but you don't lose the elastic, and your hands aren't stressed. The trick is to start with a length of elastic that is longer than the circumference it's going in. Elastic is often packaged in several-yard lengths so there's enough elastic for several treatments.

Try this fold-down method at the wrist or ankle of a pair of pants or a top. You can also use this method for the waistline of pull-on shorts, pants, and skirts:

1. **Set your machine like this:**
   - **Stitch:** Three-step zigzag
   - **Length:** 1 to 1.5 mm/25 spi or fine
   - **Width:** 4 to 5 mm
   - **Foot:** All-purpose

   If you're using a serger, use the following settings:
   - **Stitch:** Three-thread overlock
   - **Length:** 3 mm
   - **Width:** 5 mm
   - **Foot:** Standard

2. **Overcast the raw edge of the casing so that the fabric does not ravel.**

   To *overcast,* guide the fabric so that the stitches catch the fabric on the left and sew just off the edge at the right.

3. **Fold down the casing toward the inside of the project the width of the elastic plus ⅝ inch. Press the casing into place.**

4. **Set your machine with the following settings:**
   - **Stitch:** Straight
   - **Length:** 2.5 to 3 mm/10 to 12 spi
   - **Width:** 0 mm
   - **Foot:** All-purpose or edgestitch
   - **Needle position:** Left (optional)

5. **Edgestitch around the top of the casing, sewing ⅛ inch from the folded edge. (See Chapter 6 for more on edgestitching.)**

   The edgestitch foot has a guide in it that keeps your sewing straight. It's not a standard foot, so ask your dealer whether they make one for your machine.

6. **Leaving the elastic in one long strip, place and pin the elastic into the casing, snuggling it up against the edgestitched fold.**

   Pin parallel to and just under the elastic. Lots of elastic will be hanging off either end of the casing, which you cut to fit later.

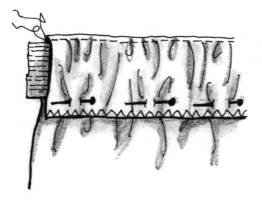

7. **Anchor one loose end of the elastic with a pin. Using your all-purpose foot, stitch under (but not through!) the elastic.**

   Rather than stitching the casing down all the way around, leave a 2-inch opening in the casing for the elastic ends to pull through.

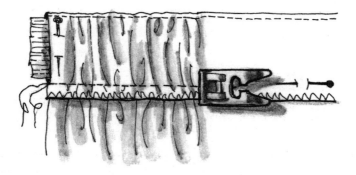

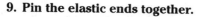

8. **Pull the elastic taut through the opening in the casing until it fits comfortably around your waist.**

9. **Pin the elastic ends together.**

   Don't cut off the elastic until you check that it stretches enough to fit over your hips. Nothing is worse than sewing in the elastic and then discovering that you can't pull up your pants.

10. **Cut the elastic to fit, adding a 1-inch overlap at both ends.**

11. **Overlap one end of the elastic over the other 1 inch and sew a square to really secure the ends.**

    Join the elastic at the overlap by straight stitching across the top, down the side, across the bottom, and then up.

When you have a shorter piece of elastic to work with or are replacing elastic that's shot, thread the elastic through the casing. Instead of using a safety pin or bodkin that can sometimes pull off the end or get hung up on the seam allowances, cut a small slit in the elastic and thread a bobby pin through it. The bobby pin has smooth ends and is narrow enough to easily slide through almost any casing, as shown in Figure 8-4.

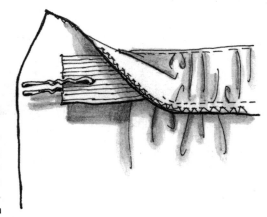

Figure 8-4:
Use a bobby pin to pull elastic through a casing.

Elastic on an edge

Elastic sewn into ready-made clothing is stitched on an edge of an opening and then flipped over and topstitched. This factory technique is very easy to duplicate with your sewing machine or serger.

You can use the following technique to apply elastic to just about anywhere you need elastic on an edge, including waistbands, sleeves, and pant legs:

1. **Set your machine like this:**

   - **Stitch:** Overlock
   - **Length:** Longest (as described in your Operating Manual)
   - **Width:** 5 mm
   - **Foot:** All-purpose

   If you're using a serger, use these settings:

   - **Stitch:** 3-thread overlock
   - **Length:** 3 to 3.5 mm
   - **Width:** 5 mm
   - **Foot:** Standard

2. **Using your fabric marker, mark off the *edge of the fabric* at the garment opening in eight equal parts.**

   Chapter 1 tells you more about markers. Eighths, rather than quarters, are easier to work with.

3. **Stretch the elastic around your waist (wherever the elastic is being sewn) until it is comfortable.**

   Remember that you need about a 1-inch extra length to overlap each end of the elastic.

4. **Using your fabric marker, mark off the *elastic* into eighths.**

5. **Pin the elastic into the opening, matching the marks on the elastic with the marks on the garment opening.**

   When putting elastic into a waistband or leg opening, leave one of the side seams open. It's easier to sew in the elastic and adjust the fit at a seam.

6. **Sew the first couple of stitches to anchor the elastic to the casing.**

7. **Stop and reposition your hands, grabbing the fabric and elastic in front of and behind the presser foot.**

   Stretch the elastic to fit the fabric, sewing from pin to pin so that the fabric and the elastic edges match up. Stitches will catch with the fabric and elastic on the left side of the stitch and then swing just off the edges on the right side of the stitch.

   Remove the pins as you get to them so that you don't sew over them and break a needle.

   When serging, serge from pin to pin, removing pins before getting to them and guiding the elastic so the knife slightly trims away the excess fabric.

8. **Change the settings on your machine as follows:**
   - **Stitch:** Straight
   - **Length:** 3 to 3.5 mm/8 to 9 spi
   - **Width:** 0 mm
   - **Foot:** Embroidery
   - **Bobbin:** Thread with elastic thread (see "For shirr," earlier in this chapter)

9. **Flip the elastic over so that the overcasting stitches (those that were used to sew the elastic to the edge) are to the wrong side of the project and then topstitch the elastic.**

   With the right side up, guide the edge of the casing, following a line on your needle plate and so the topstitching just catches the bottom edge of the elastic.

10. **Now that the elastic is stitched in place, sew up the side seam, catching the elastic ends in the seamline.**

The serger combined with the elastic applicator foot makes quick work of elastic application. Adjust the tautness by tightening or loosening the adjustment screw on the foot.

Chapter 9

Zippers and Company

- -

In This Chapter

▶ The four-minute zipper — really!

▶ Buttonhole basics

▶ Hooks, eyes, and snaps made simple

- -

*E*arly in my sewing career, I remember searching through the catalogs for patterns without zippers or buttonholes. After a while though, I didn't have many choices, and the styles were so boring that I had to overcome my fear if I wanted to make anything with pizzazz. I took a deep breath, chose patterns with zippers and buttonholes, and in the process picked up some cool shortcuts.

After you read this chapter, you will no longer be zapped by zippers or baffled by buttonholes!

Yes, Virginia, There Are Easy Ways to Put in Zippers

Pattern guide sheet instructions often assume some knowledge of sewing and have been recommending the same zipper application techniques for decades. In my search for an easier way, I ran across some great factory methods, which I share with you in this section.

At first glance, these techniques may look complicated, but they overcome the typical roadblocks most folks have when sewing in zippers. So follow along with me step-by-step, and you'll have a really professional-looking project with a zipper you'll love to use.

You can use several methods to sew zippers in. The two most common methods are sewn in one of two ways:

✔ **A centered application:** The zipper teeth are centered at the seamline, such as down the center back of a dress.

✔ **A lapped application:** A flap of fabric that overlaps the zipper teeth. You find lapped zipper applications on the sideseams of skirts, pants, and pillows.

Breaking a few rules

Regardless of whether you're sewing a centered or a lapped zipper, follow these tips. Some of them are a bit hard to believe, but these tips will save you a lot of frustration — take my word for it:

✔ **Use a zipper that's longer than necessary:** How much longer doesn't really matter — just go longer. This way, the *zipper pull* (the part you tug on to open and close the zipper) is out of the presser foot's way when you sew the top of the zipper. The results? Nice, even stitching at the top of the zipper. After you sew the zipper in and the zipper pull is at the bottom of the zipper, you cut the zipper to fit the opening when you finish sewing on the waistband or facing.

✔ **Use ½-inch tape — like Scotch Magic Mending Tape — and baste in the zipper across the back without using pins:** The tape holds everything flat and in place, and sewing through it doesn't damage the needle or the fabric.

✔ **Use ½-inch tape on the right side of the project as a topstitching guide when sewing in the zipper:** This way, the stitching lines are parallel, and the zipper application looks as good as in ready-made clothing. (Who cares whether the zipper looks good from the wrong side, anyway?)

Putting in centered zippers

Sewing in a centered zipper is as easy as following these steps (see Figure 9-1):

1. **Before taking the paper pattern off the fabric, use the points of your scissors to clip into both layers of the seam allowance ¼ inch to mark the bottom of the zipper placement.**

2. **Remove the pattern paper from the fabric and then place and pin the seam, right sides together.**

   Put two pins parallel and close together in the seamline and at the zipper placement clips you marked in Step 1 as a reminder to stop sewing when you get to them.

3. **Starting from the bottom of the seamline and using a 2.5 to 3 mm (10 to 12 spi) stitch length, sew the ⅝-inch seam.**

   Stop and securely backstitch at the bottom of the zipper placement clip and double pins.

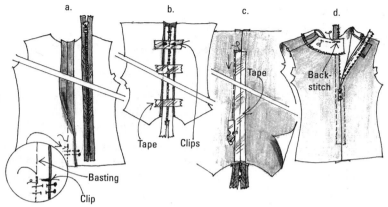

Figure 9-1:
Heres' a
great way
to put in a
centered
zipper.

4. **Remove the work, cutting the threads off at the fabric.**

5. **Set your machine like this:**
   - **Stitch:** Straight
   - **Length:** 4 to 6 mm/4 spi
   - **Width:** 0 mm
   - **Foot:** All-purpose

6. **Starting at the backstitching, baste the remainder of the seam together at the ⅝-inch seamline, leaving generous thread tails (refer to Figure 9-1a).**

7. **Remove the pins, press the seam flat and together, and then press the seam open (see Chapter 5).**

8. **Match the bottom of the zipper with the clips in the seam allowance, centering the zipper teeth over the seamline.**

9. **Using the ½-inch Scotch Magic Mending Tape, tape across the zipper every inch or so.**

   The zipper pull is up on the zipper tape, out of the way (refer to Figure 9-1b).

10. **On the right side of the fabric, place a strip of ½-inch tape over the basted seamline, centering the seamline under the tape.**

   This is your stitching guide or template.

11. **Set your machine like this:**
   - **Stitch:** Straight
   - **Length:** Appropriate for the fabric

- **Width:** 0 mm
- **Foot:** Zipper

12. **Move your zipper foot so that the toe of the foot is to one side of the needle.**

    A zipper foot has one toe (rather than two toes like the all-purpose foot) so that you can move it from one side of the needle to the other for easy zipper application. Moving the toe in this step prevents the foot from riding over the zipper teeth (see your Operating Manual and Figure 9-1c).

13. **Starting from the bottom of the zipper, stitch next to the tape, sewing across the bottom and then up one side of the zipper on the right side of the fabric.**

    Don't backstitch; you pull the threads through to the wrong side and tie them off later.

14. **Sew in the other side of the zipper, guiding next to the tape template.**

    Move the toe of the foot to the other side of the needle. Sew next to the tape, starting back at the bottom and sewing up the other side of the zipper.

15. **Pull off the tape from both sides of the project.**

    Remove the basting stitches by pulling on the bobbin thread.

    Before cutting off the zipper, try on the project. Does everything fit like you want it to? If it does, then pull the zipper pull to the bottom of the zipper before cutting off the excess zipper.

16. **Pull the zipper pull to the bottom of the zipper and securely back-stitch over the zipper coil at the ⅝-inch seamline (refer to Figure 9-1d).**

    Backstitching prevents the zipper from coming off the track so that you can safely cut off the zipper. Then, when you're sewing the rest of the project together, a seam (usually from a waistband or facing) intersects at the top of the zipper tape over the teeth or coil, preventing the pull from coming off the track.

Putting in lapped zippers

Sewing in a lapped zipper is as easy as following these steps:

1. **Follow Steps 1 through 6 for a centered zipper application (see the previous section).**

2. **Set your machine like this:**
   - **Stitch:** Straight
   - **Length:** Appropriate for the fabric
   - **Width:** 0 mm
   - **Foot:** Zipper

3. **Position the zipper in the seam.**

   Match the bottom of the zipper with the clips in the seam allowance. Position the zipper face down so that the right-hand edge of the zipper tape is on the right-hand side of the seam allowance. Center the zipper teeth over the seamline. You sew this side of the zipper only to the seam allowance, and remember that the zipper pull is up on the zipper tape, out of the way.

4. **Move your zipper foot so that the toe is to the right-hand side of the needle, and sew the zipper to the seam allowance.**

   (Moving the toe prevents the foot from riding over the zipper teeth — see your Operating Manual.)

5. **Move the zipper foot so that the toe is to the left-hand side of the needle; then form a fold in the seam allowance by turning the zipper face up so that the edge of the fold is close to the zipper teeth or coil.**

6. **Stitch over the fold, sewing through all thicknesses.**

7. **Tape-baste across the back of the zipper.**

   From the wrong side of the project, spread the zippered seam as flat as possible and gently press. Tape-baste across the seam allowance and zipper, placing the tape every inch or so. Flip the project over.

8. **Tape the stitching template on the right side of the project.**

   Place a strip of ½-inch tape so that the edge of the tape is even with the seamline.

9. **Sew in the zipper from the right side of the project, guiding next to the tape template.**

   Move the toe of the foot to the right-hand side of the needle. Sew next to the tape, sewing across the bottom, pivoting at the corner, and then sewing up the right-hand side of the zipper.

10. **Finish the lapped zipper application by following Steps 15 and 16 in the previous section.**

Buttonhole Basics

What comes first, the button or buttonhole? Both — and neither. To make the buttonholes, you need to know the size of the buttons, so you have to have the buttons before you can make the buttonholes.

I buy buttons in the size that the back of the pattern envelope recommends and sew the buttonholes in the same direction the pattern recommends — if the buttonholes on the pattern are horizontal, I make them that way. Then I know that the buttons are in the best proportion to the garment and give me the best fit and look.

Sizing buttonholes

Even though the buttons may measure ½ inch, they may vary in thickness. Thicker buttons need longer buttonholes than flatter ones. For example, a ½-inch, half-round, ball button needs a longer buttonhole than a ½-inch, flat, four-hole button. The fastest and easiest way to determine how long to make the buttonholes is to do the following:

1. **Cut a strip of paper about 5 to 8 inches.**

   Cut a longer strip when working with larger buttons.

2. **Wrap the paper strip around the button and across the widest diameter, finger-pressing a crease at the edge of the button.**

3. **Pull the button out of the paper strip and measure the length of the paper strip from the fold to the finger-pressed crease.**

   The buttonhole must be this length for the button to easily slip through it.

Double-check that the buttonhole is just the right length for your button by test-stitching it on an interfaced fabric scrap. This way, you can adjust the buttonhole length longer or shorter so that it's just the right size before putting it in your project for good.

Marking buttonholes

Buttonholes are positioned ½ inch from the finished edge. To prevent sewing the buttonhole too close to the edge, stick a strip of ½-inch-wide Scotch Magic Mending Tape the length of the opening, placing one straight edge even with the finished edge.

Using your seam gauge, stick another strip of tape parallel to and a button-hole-length away from the first. Place a third strip of tape perpendicular to the long tapes and ¼ inch from the marked buttonhole. All this taping gives you a guide that keeps buttonholes straight and even.

Sewing buttonholes

You can probably make buttonholes by hand, but unless you have the practiced hand of a master tailor, your buttonholes just won't look right unless you stitch them with a sewing machine. The sewing machine companies have done a wonderful job of making buttonholes easier to create, and each brand and model has its own special way of making them.

Buttonholes consist of two long sides made with short, narrow zigzag stitches called _satin stitches_, and with wider zigzag stitches, called _bartacks_, on the ends.

Some machines make buttonholes in one step, and others make them in two, three, or four steps. Most machine brands have a patented method of button-hole making that's pretty darn good, so read your Operating Manual to determine how the process works with your make and model.

I show you how to make a buttonhole in 11 easy steps, which works even on the most basic zigzag machine and looks great every time.

Make a test buttonhole. Using the same fabric, thread, interfacing, and presser foot that you're using in the project, mark and stitch a test buttonhole. This way, you know that buttonholes are long enough for the button and that the stitch length of the buttonhole stitches is adjusted properly for the fabric.

You can follow these steps to make buttonholes on most machines (consult your Operating Manual for instructions specific to your sewing machine):

1. **Set your machine like this:**
   - **Stitch:** Zigzag or buttonhole
   - **Length:** 0.5 to 0.8 mm/60 spi or fine setting
   - **Width:** 2 to 2.5 mm
   - **Foot:** Buttonhole
   - **Needle position:** Left (read your Operating Manual)

2. **Place the fabric under the foot so that the finished edge of the project is even with the back edge of the presser foot, and the needle starts sewing at the edge of the tape.**

   The short length of tape must be at the side edge of the foot so that the needle doesn't stitch through it.

3. **Sew down the left side of the buttonhole, stopping at the tape and with the needle in the right side of the stitch.**

4. **Lift the presser foot, pivot the fabric 180 degrees, and lower the foot.**

5. **Lift the needle all the way out of the fabric.**

6. **Move the stitch width to 4.5 or 5 mm.**

7. **Holding back on the fabric slightly so that it won't move, take four or five stitches, creating the bartack.**

   Stop with the needle out of the fabric.

8. **Set the stitch width back to where you had it in Step 1 and then sew the other side of the buttonhole.**

   Stop — with the needle out of the fabric — when the needle reaches the edge of the tape.

9. **Move the width to where it was for the first bartack (4.5 to 5 mm).**

   Holding back on the fabric slightly so that it won't move, take four or five stitches, creating the bartack. Stop with the needle out of the fabric.

10. **Set the width to 0 mm and stitch up and down a few stitches, holding back on the fabric and stitching in place.**

    Doing so creates a machine-made knot.

11. **Pull threads to the back of the fabric, tie them off, and then cut off the threads.**

Cutting open buttonholes

I open buttonholes two ways: by using the seam ripper or by using a buttonhole cutter and block. If you plan on making a large number of buttonholes, buy a cutter and block. This tool saves you time and cuts open buttonholes very accurately.

 Prevent your buttonholes from coming undone before their time. Put a drop of FrayCheck on the knot on the back side of the buttonhole by dipping the point of the pin in the liquid and dotting it on the thread. Then, before cutting the buttonhole open, dribble a thin bead of FrayCheck on the cutting space, between the two sides of the buttonhole. Let the FrayCheck dry and then cut open the buttonholes.

Using a ripper

Carefully cut open your buttonholes with a ripper by following these steps:

1. **Score the cutting space between the two rows of stitching by running the back side of the ripper blade between the two rows of buttonhole stitches.**

   Doing so separates the threads, allowing you to more easily cut the buttonhole open, without cutting the buttonhole stitches.

2. **Place a pin at one of the bartacks.**

   The pin acts like a brake and prevents you from cutting open the buttonhole past the bartack.

3. **Starting at the opposite bartack end, push the point of the ripper through the fabric, cutting the fabric between the sides of the buttonhole.**

   Before getting to the end of the buttonhole, use the same motion as you do when pinning and bring the point of the ripper up and in front of the pin. This way, you can push hard through the fabric without cutting too far.

Using a cutter and block

These little tools are really great. Find them through your local sewing machine dealer or mail-order source.

Follow these steps to cut open your buttonholes by using a cutter and block:

1. **Center the buttonhole over the little wood block.**

2. **Center the cutter blade over the cutting space in the buttonhole.**

3. **Push down firmly on the cutter, cutting through the fabric to the wood block.**

   Tada! You're done.

Marking the button placement

You can mark the button placement before removing the paper pattern piece, but I like marking the button placement after I've made and cut open the buttonholes because it's more accurate.

Follow these steps to mark the button placement:

1. **Hold the project so that the buttonholes and button opening are wrong sides together.**

   If the project has an overlapping front placket (like the front of a T-shirt), then hold it as though the front placket is buttoned.

Sport snaps (the buttonhole alternative)

Sport snaps, which hold up to a good deal of wear and tear, were available only for clothing manufacturers — until now. Several companies make and sell commercial-grade sport snaps to the sewing market. These snaps are quite tailored and often make a wonderful alternative to buttons and buttonholes.

Snaps from the very simple sew-on type to the heavy-duty sport snap have two sides — a ball and a socket. Instead of sewing them onto a project as you do with traditional snaps, sport snaps attach to the fabric in two ways:

- By poking a hole, as with the post-style snaps

- By pushing prongs through the fabric, as with the prong-style snaps

Sport snaps range from the smallest size, 12 (about ¼ inch), to the largest size, 27 (about ¾ inch). When shopping for snaps, consider the project and where you are placing the snaps before buying the first thing you see. For instance, you probably don't want a size 27 snap at the crotch of a pair of toddler's overalls. The snap is just too big and bulky.

Don't mix snap parts from one brand to another. Manufacturers make snap parts to function in harmony and won't guarantee their product if you use a wrong part or tool.

Each brand of sport snap has its own method of application, so make sure that you have the proper snap-setter tool(s) for the brand. Read the instructions for application thoroughly before putting them on your project. This way, you're assured of a snapping success. As with buttonholes, apply a test snap, using the same fabric, number of layers, and interfacing, before putting them on your finished project.

2. **Mark the end of the cutting space at the bartack.**

   From the button side of the opening, push a pin straight through the project so that it goes in at the buttonhole opening, right next to the bartack. Using a fabric marker, mark the button placement at the pin.

   - For horizontal buttonholes, mark button placement nearest the finished edge.

   - For vertical buttonholes, mark button placement so that all the buttons are placed either at the top or at the bottom of the bartack.

3. **Before sewing on the button by hand or machine (see Chapter 5), double-check that the button is placed three-fourths to a full button-diameter's distance from the finished edge and then adjust the placement as needed.**

Remove buttons from the card the easy way: On the back side of the card, slide a pin under the fine wire that holds the buttons on the card. Pull the button off the front of the card. The pin prevents the wire from pulling through the card. The pin often ends up bent — if it is, throw it away.

Yer Hooks, Eyes, and Sew-On Snaps

You've probably seen hooks and eyes sewn at the top of a zipper placket and at a waistband. Like other fasteners, hooks and eyes come in different sizes designed for different uses. The fine (size 0) hooks and eyes work well on babies' and children's clothing. Heavier, size 3 hooks and eyes work better on adults' clothing.

General-purpose sew-on snaps range from a small, fine-sized snap used on children's clothing, to larger, heavier sizes for adults' clothing. Snaps, hooks, and eyes come in a black finish to use on dark fabrics and a nickel finish to use on light-colored fabrics. Snaps are also made out of a clear nylon that blends with any color.

Hooks and eyes come together on a card or in a little box and usually have two types of eyes available:

- **Straight eye:** This eye works best on lapped edges where one side of the garment overlaps the other, like at a waistband.
- **Round or loop eye:** This eye works best on abutted edges where one side meets the other, like at the top of a centered zipper placket.

To close an opening, you sew hooks and snaps in similar locations. The choice between the two is one of personal preference. When closing two sides of a project, decide whether you would rather hook them together or snap them together. Then stitch them in place by using a hand whipstitch (see Chapter 5).

Sewing on the hook, round eye, and ball side of the snap

Follow these steps to sew on a hook, round eye, or ball side of a snap:

1. **Thread a hand needle with a doubled thread and knot the end (see Chapter 5).**

2. **Sew on the hook side or ball side of the snap first.**

   You don't want the stitches showing through the facing or waistband to the right side the project. So carefully work the hand needle down and then up through the inside of the waistband or facing, sewing through only one layer of the fabric.

3. **Lightly dab the back of the hook (or socket side of the snap) with a glue stick.**

Some snaps have holes in the center of both the ball and socket. To position them correctly, simply push a pin straight through the center of the ball, and then through the fabric; push another pin straight through the socket of the snap and then through the fabric. Snap. Are both sides of the snap in the right spot to close properly? If not, make the minor adjustments and sew them on.

 4. **Thread the hook or snap onto the needle, pushing it down to the surface of the fabric.**

    Sew on the hook or snap, taking three or four small whipstitches through the same hole. Sew the stitches carefully so that the stitches don't show through to the right side of the project.

 5. **Sew a knot.**

    When you take the last stitch, leave some slack so that you have a loop. Thread the needle through the loop and then pull the stitch tight to the fabric. Repeat to knot another stitch. Clip the thread off at the fabric.

 6. **Repeat Steps 1 through 5 for each hole.**

 7. **Before "knotting off" the second hole, pass the needle and thread through the fabric to the end of the hook, without stitching through to the right side of the waistband or facing.**

    Stitch around the end of the hook a couple times so that the stitches hold the hook flat and against the project.

 8. **Sew on the round eye by following Steps 1 through 6 above.**

    Because the hook and round eye are sewn on abutted edges, you don't want the stitches showing from the right side of the project.

Sewing on the straight eye and socket side of the snap

Because the eye and socket side of the snap gets a great deal of rough wear, you sew them on the *underlap,* the part of the project that's under the closure, like the button side of a project.

Whipstitch through the holes as I describe in Steps 1 through 6 in the preceding section, sewing straight down through the hole and completely through all the layers of the fabric. Bring the needle back up through the back of the fabric and through the hole in the eye or snap. Whipstitch through all the holes, knotting the thread as I describe in Step 5 in the preceding section.

Chapter 10

Sleeves: The Long and the Short of It

- -

- -

Sleeves are easy to put in when you know how. In this chapter, I show you the easiest methods, first by not putting in a sleeve at all, but by facing or binding off a sleeveless armhole. Facing the armhole gives you practice staystitching, seaming, trimming, notching, pressing, and understitching. (If these terms are new to you, read Chapter 6.) The wonderful technique I show you for binding off an edge is a factory method not usually found in traditional pattern guide sheet instructions. You'll love it.

Next, I tackle sleeves, starting with the raglan sleeve. Raglan is not the best style for sloping shoulders, but it's easy to sew and looks good when you use the right shoulder pad underneath. I save set-in sleeves for last. These sleeves are actually sewn into an armhole. The easiest set-in sleeves I cover are either gathered or set in flat, before you sew up the side seam.

Sleeveless Armhole Facings and Bindings

Have you ever cut off the sleeves of a T-shirt or sweatshirt to make it sleeveless? Cutting off the sleeves does give you extra room and ventilation, but after a while, the armhole stretches out, never to be the same size again. Because it's only a T-shirt or a sweatshirt, it's no big deal. But for your other clothes, the armholes are finished with either a facing or binding that keeps those armholes in shape and looking good for the life of the garment. By the way, if you want to bind off the armholes in that T-shirt or sweatshirt, use the following techniques to give your old favorites staying power.

Facing sleeveless armholes

A facing is a piece of fabric that has been reinforced with a piece of interfacing (see Chapter 2 for more on interfacings and how to use them) that is then stitched to an opening and turned back toward the inside of the project to finish off the opening. Facings are attached not only to armholes but also to other areas such as necklines and hem edges.

Follow these easy steps for the best finished armholes in town:

1. **Cut out and interface the armhole facing by using fusible interfacing as shown on your pattern guide sheet instructions.**

2. **Placing the right sides together and matching the notches, pin and sew the facing together, backstitching at the top and bottom of the seam.**

3. **Place the facing in the armhole, right sides together and matching the notches.**

   Double notches are at the back of the armhole, single notches are at the front of the armhole. If you mistakenly place the left facing into the right armhole, the seam allowances have different curves and won't match.

4. **Starting at the underarm seam, sew the facing on the armhole at the ⅝-inch seamline.**

   Backstitch at the end of the seam.

5. **Clip the seam allowance at the inside curves to within ⅛-inch of the seamline.**

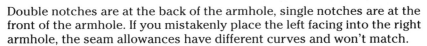

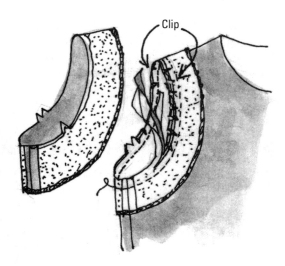

Clip

Armholes and armhole facings are inside curves, so clip into the seam allowance by using your scissor tips, clipping almost to the stitching line at the front and back of the armhole (see your pattern guide sheet and Chapter 6 for info on clipping seams). Clipping releases the seam allowance so that it won't bunch up when you turn and press the facing to the inside of the garment.

6. **Trim the facing seam allowance to ½ inch.**

   Trimming one seam allowance narrower than another is called *grading the seam*. When you do this, the facing falls automatically toward the narrower seam allowance, making it easier to turn and press the facing.

7. **From the wrong side of the fabric, press the seam allowance toward the facing.**

8. **Understitch the facing seam by sewing ¹⁄₁₆ inch away from the seam-line on the facing side of the seam allowance (see Chapter 6 for more information on understitching).**

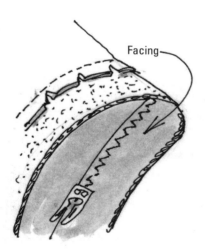

Facing

Understitching helps the facing turn toward the inside of the garment and stay there.

9. **Press the facing toward the inside of the garment and tack down the facing by stitching-in-the-ditch.**

   Sewing from the right side of the garment, center the crack of the seam under the needle. Sew, guiding the stitches so that they bury themselves in the crack of the seam. Don't backstitch; simply pull the threads to the facing side and tie them off.

Binding sleeveless armholes

Using binding is a particularly clean way to finish an edge on an armhole, neckline, or other hem edge. You sew a doubled band to the wrong side of the garment and then bring the folded edge of the binding over the seam allowance toward the right side of the garment and edgestitch it in place. This commercial binding method ensures a sensational ready-to-wear look on any bound edge.

Remember, this technique works best on light- to mid-weight fabrics.

Cutting the binding

When cutting your own binding, cut it four times the finished width and then add another ½ inch for the seam allowances (two, ¼-inch seam allowances = ½ inch).

So, for a ½-inch finished binding width, you start with a strip that's 2½ inches wide. I always cut a little longer binding than I need so that I don't run out.

Sewing the binding

Follow these steps to construct the binding that goes around the edge of the armhole:

1. **Trim the garment armhole seam allowance to ¼ inch.**

   If you have pinking shears, use them for trimming because pinkers automatically notch the seam allowance for you, making the seam allowance easier to work with (see Chapter 6 for more information on notching seams).

2. **Staystitch around the trimmed armhole under the arm from notch to notch. (Chapter 6 tells you more about staystitching.)**

3. **Fold and press the binding in half the long way so that the *wrong* sides of the fabric are together.**

4. **Open the binding strip, then fold down the short end ½ inch and press.**

   This is the end that overlaps the binding at the other end, giving the opening a nice, finished look.

   After pressing this short end, fold and press the binding strip back to its original position.

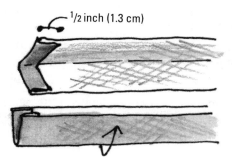

½ inch (1.3 cm)

5. **Starting slightly to the back side of the underarm seam (and with the short hemmed end first), pin the binding to the *wrong side* of the garment so that all of the raw edges are even.**

6. **When you get back to where you started pinning on the binding, overlap the binding at the opening by about ½ inch, then cut off the binding strip.**

   This way, the binding ends up long enough.

7. **Set your machine like this:**

   - **Stitch:** Straight
   - **Length:** 2.5 to 3.5mm/10 to 12 spi
   - **Width:** 0 mm
   - **Foot:** All-purpose

8. **Sew the binding to the armhole using a ¼-inch seam allowance, back-stitching at the end of the seam.**

9. **With the wrong side of the garment up, press the seam allowance toward the binding side.**

10. **Fold, pin, and press the band in shape around the opening.**

    Fold the edge of the band over the opening, toward the right side of the project, so that the edge of the band covers the seam allowance and the previous stitching line.

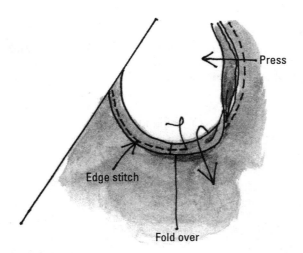

11. **Edgestitch the band to the opening, guiding ⅛ inch from the folded edge of the band. (See Chapter 6 for more on edgestitching.)**

Raglan Sleeves

You find raglan sleeves on garment tops — from sweatshirts to cashmere sweater sets. What makes them different from traditional set-in sleeves is that the seams on the front run from the neck edge diagonally across to the underarm, then up the back to the neckline in the back.

Because the raglan sleeve covers the shoulder, either a seam or dart shapes the top of the sleeve so that it fits smoothly at the shoulder line. The most common way to shape a raglan sleeve is with a dart. Just follow these steps:

1. **Sew and then press the shoulder dart.**

   Placing the right sides together, pin the shoulder dart as shown in your pattern guide sheet. Sew the dart starting from the wide end, stitching to the point (see Chapter 8 for more information on sewing darts).

2. **Pin the sleeve to the garment, with the right sides together and matching the notches, and then sew at the ⅝-inch seamline.**

3. **Sew the garment side seams, right sides together at the ⅝-inch seamline, backstitching on both ends of the seam.**

4. **Trim the seam allowance to ⅜ inch from notch to notch _at the underarm seams only._**

   This keeps the underarm seam from bunching up (and cutting off the circulation under your arm).

5. **Press the front and back shoulder seams open, from the notches up to the neckline. (See Chapter 5 for more tips and tricks of perfect pressing.)**

Big News about Set-In Sleeves and Armholes

Set-in sleeves have a seam that goes all the way around your arm where your arm connects to your torso. Instead of going diagonally across your body from the neckline as with raglan sleeves, a set-in sleeve starts at the underarm (or armpit), travels up, runs over your shoulder, and then goes straight back down again to the underarm.

So here's the big news: Set-in sleeves are bigger than the armholes they go into. They're bigger so you can comfortably move your arms around. This extra fabric in the sleeves causes a lot of sewers major sleeve-setting difficulties. So how do you get the sleeve in there — shrink it? Yes, and no. In this section, I share some tricks with you to help make set-in sleeves less mysterious.

Sewing sleeves in flat

Setting sleeves in flat means that the side seams of the shirt or bodice are open (not sewn yet), and the sleeves are not sewn into a tube. Even if the pattern says to sew the underarm sleeve seam first, try this flat method, which is a lot easier. By sewing with the sleeve against the feed dogs (rather than the other way around), the excess sleeve fabric works itself into the armhole seam almost automatically. Follow these steps to relieve your sleeve-sewing worries:

1. Sew and press the shoulder seam of the shirt (as per the pattern instructions) and then open the shirt flat so that the right side of the fabric is up.

2. Pin the sleeve to the shirt, right sides together, matching the front and back notches, and centering the sleeve cap at the shoulder seam.

3. Sewing with the sleeve side down against the feed dogs, stitch the sleeve into the shirt at the ⅝-inch seamline.

   The feed dogs on your sewing machine feed the underlayer of fabric a little faster than the top layer of fabric, which is directly under the presser foot. Use this to your advantage when sewing in a sleeve. Sewing with the sleeve side down allows the feed dogs to ease in just enough fullness of the sleeve so that it fits perfectly into the armhole.

4. Trim the seam allowance to ⅜ inch under the arm from notch to notch only. Then overcast the edges of both seam allowances together by using the three-step zigzag on your sewing machine or serge them together (see Chapter 6 for the details of overcasting).

5. Pin and sew the garment side seam and underarm at the ⅝-inch seamline, sewing the entire side seam and underarm sleeve seam in one step.

   Start sewing the seam from the hem edge, then up through the underarm seam.

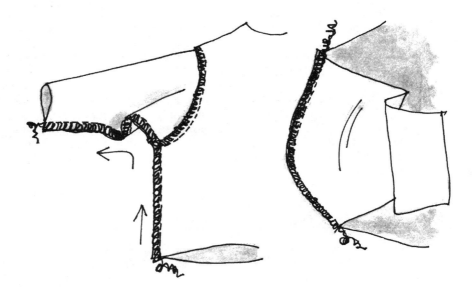

Sewing sleeves in the round

Setting sleeves in the round means that you sew together the side seams of the shirt or bodice and then stitch together the sleeves at the underarm seams. This technique gives you a better fit and is recommended for gathered, fitted, or tailored sleeves.

The easiest set-in sleeve to sew is the gathered sleeve. Because the gathering stitches are sewn at the sleeve cap from dot to dot or from notch to notch, the fullness at the sleeve is cinched in enough to comfortably fit the armhole (review the tricks of two-thread gathering in Chapter 8).

The information in this section may look more involved than what you see in the pattern guide sheet instructions, but by following these easy steps, you're assured of success:

1. **Using a fabric marker, transfer the dots on the armhole and sleeve seamlines from the paper pattern pieces to the fabric. Also mark the top of the sleeve cap.**

    These dots are additional match points and also tell you where the gathering stitches are sewn on the sleeve cap (for example, pattern guide sheet instructions may direct you to gather "from dot to dot").

    If you don't find a dot at the top of the sleeve cap pattern, just mark one there or make a tiny clip into the seam allowance yourself. This way, when putting in the sleeve, the mark at the top of the sleeve cap matches up with the shoulder seam.

2. **Place, pin, and sew the garment, right sides together, at the side seams; place pin and sew the sleeve, right sides together, at the underarm seam, following your pattern guide sheet instructions. Press the seam open or to one side (see Chapter 5 for more on pressing seams).**

3. **Sewing with the right side of the sleeve up, stitch two rows of gathering stitches on the sleeve cap, sewing from notch to notch (or dot to dot).**

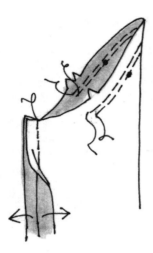

Sew the gathering stitches so that the row of stitching closest to the seamline is ½ inch from the raw edge, and the second row is sewn ¼ inch from the raw edge.

4. **Pin the sleeve into the armhole, right sides together, pinning at the notches, dots, and underarm seams. Pull on the bobbin threads, working the gathers down the stitches until the fullness of the gathered sleeve fits the armhole.**

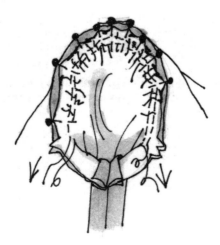

Gather half the sleeve at a time. Gather the back half of the sleeve from the back notches to the dots, then from the dots to the top of the sleeve cap. For the front half of the sleeve, gather from the front notches to the dots, then from the dots up to the top of the sleeve.

By gathering the sleeve section by section, you're able to distribute the fullness evenly, working from one small area to the next.

Double notches are at the back of the armhole and sleeve; single notches are at the front of the armhole and sleeve. If you get the left sleeve into the right armhole, the seam allowances have different curves, won't match, and the garment really feels funny when it's on (ask me how I know this).

5. **Stitch the sleeve to the armhole at the ⅝-inch seamline, backstitching at the end of the seam.**

   Sewing with the sleeve side up, start sewing at the underarm seam, guiding your needle just to the left of the first row of gathering stitches.

6. **Starting at the notches, clip into the seam allowance, clipping to within ⅛ inch of the seamline at the inside curves.**

7. **Trim the seam allowance to ⅜ inch from notch to notch, cutting away the excess seam allowance from both the garment and the sleeve at the _underarm seam only_.**

   This way, the sleeve is comfortable, and your circulation isn't cut off under your arms.

8. **Overcast the trimmed underarm seams together from notch to notch.**

   Overcast the raw edges together by using a three-step zigzag stitch with your sewing machine or 3-thread overlock with your serger (see Chapter 6 for more on overcasting). Tie off threads at either end of the overcast edges.

9. **Press the armhole seam flat and together all the way around, pressing from the seamline out to the raw edge. Then gently press the seam back together.**

Chapter 11

A Pocket Full of Ideas

In This Chapter

▶ The ins and outs of inseam pockets

▶ Patch pockets for every size and shape

▶ Pocket patterns for everybody

▶ Making a pocket collage shirt

▶ Moving a pocket from one place to another

▶ Covering stains with a cool appliqué

*I*n this chapter, I tell you how to sew pockets by using the shortcuts that professionals use. I also include a really great project that lets you use the power of pockets to conceal even the worst of shirt disasters!

A Little Pocket Primer

Pockets are little pouches sewn on or into pants, shirts, and other garments (even decorative home interior items such as pillows — see Chapter 15), all for the express purpose of holding pennies and other portable paraphernalia (or, just to look clever, as in the case of accessories for your living areas).

✔ *Inseam* or *set-in pockets* are stitched in a seam, as shown in Figure 11-1.

✔ *Patch pockets* are those that attach like a patch to the surface of the fabric, as you can see in Figure 11-1.

Figure 11-1:
Pocket
types:
inseam
pockets and
patch
pockets.

Patch pockets

Inseam
pockets

Stitching All-in-One Inseam Pockets

The easiest inseam pocket to make is one in which you cut out a pattern that includes the pocket, pocket lining, and the garment itself all in one piece. Even though your pattern may call for pocket lining pieces to be cut and sewn to the garment separately, the construction steps are the same.

1. **Mark the pocket opening on your fabric.**

   The pocket openings are usually marked with dots on the seamline on the pattern paper. So, using your fabric marker, mark the pocket placement by transferring those dots onto your fabric (see Chapter 4 for information on marking your fabric).

2. Stay the pocket opening.

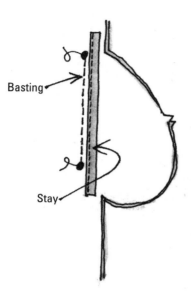

Basting

Stay

Staying an area means to stabilize it so that it doesn't stretch out. For example, staystitching prevents a curved edge from stretching out of shape while you're working on the project (see Chapter 6 for more on staystitching). To stay the pocket, you use a strip of twill tape.

Cut a piece of twill tape 2 inches longer than the length of the pocket opening. Place the tape on the wrong side of the front pocket seamline, centering it next to the marks for the pocket opening. Stitch it to the front pocket fabric only. This is a pocket stay and makes the pocket opening "stay" in shape, even when you hang your hands in your pockets for hours at a time.

3. Set your machine like this:

- **Stitch:** Straight
- **Length:** 3.5 to 5 mm/5 to 9 spi
- **Width:** 0 mm
- **Foot:** All-purpose
- **Upper tension:** Loosened
- **Bobbin thread:** Contrasting color to needle thread

4. Pin and baste the pocket opening shut (see Chapter 5 for more information on basting).

Pin the garment and front and back pocket pieces, right sides together. Baste the pocket closed, basting the pocket opening from dot to dot. This way, after you stitch and press the pocket, you can pull out the basting stitches and expect a perfectly formed pocket opening!

5. **Set your machine like this:**

   - **Stitch:** Straight
   - **Length:** 2.5to 3 mm/10 to 12 spi
   - **Width:** 0 mm
   - **Foot:** All-purpose
   - **Upper tension:** Normal
   - **Bobbin thread:** Matching color to the needle thread

6. **Pin the garment, right sides together, and then sew up the side seam, starting from the bottom of the project, pivoting at the pocket opening dots.**

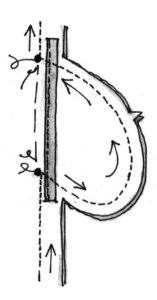

7. **Clip from the raw edge to the dots at the top and bottom of the *back* pocket seam allowance only.**

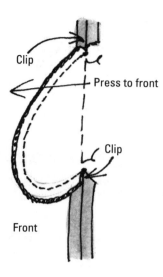

When you press open the clipped seam allowance, the pocket falls toward the front of the garment. Why is this a good thing? When the garment is worn, the pocket is pushed toward the front of the garment. By clipping the seam allowance, the side seam isn't pulled out of whack.

8. **Press the pocket seams flat and together, from the wrong side of the garment.**

Then, again from the wrong side, press the side seams open by pressing the pocket toward the front of the garment.

9. **Remove the basting stitches by simply pulling out the contrasting bobbin thread.**

Cool, huh?

Putting Together Patch Pockets

In this section, you cut, shape, and stitch an unlined patch pocket with square corners and an unlined patch pocket with curved corners. You also unravel the mysteries of creating patch pockets with self-lining and with a separate lining. Finally, you discover the most professional pocket-application technique ever.

But how do you know what pocket style is best to make? Here's my formula: For body types that are round, select a pocket and garment style that has square and rectangular lines. For figures that are thin and angular, choose pocket and garment styles that are curved and rounded. By using an opposite-shaped pocket, you de-emphasize figure flaws.

Pocket placement is also an important consideration. If you're very busty, a curved pocket placed over the bust is a bad choice — you may want to omit the pocket altogether. For those of us with generous back sides, don't even think about sewing curved patch pockets in that area of the physique . . . they just emphasize the obvious.

Unlined patch pockets with square corners

I like sewing this pocket on shirts, even when the pattern doesn't call for one. This cornering technique works really well, so you can have the squarest corners going. Just follow these steps.

1. **Cut out the square-corner pocket by following the pattern guide sheet instructions or by using one of the pocket patterns found in this chapter (see "Using the Pocket Patterns," later in this chapter).**

2. **Using your sewing machine, overcast the top edge of the pocket facing (see Chapter 6 for more information on finishing raw edges).**

3. **Press the pocket side seams toward the wrong side of the pocket.**

4. **Fold and press up a triangle the width of the seam allowance at both pocket corners.**

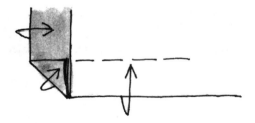

5. **Fold up and press the bottom of the pocket on the seamline, enclosing the triangle in the seam allowance.**

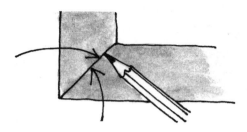

6. **Using your fabric marker, mark the angle of the miter so that the ink of the marker touches both fabric edges on the angle.**

7. **Unfold one pocket corner.**

   When connected, the marked lines make a large triangle in the corner, which becomes the *stitching line* of the miter.

8. **Fold the triangle in half so that the side and bottom pocket seams are right sides together; stitch the miter on the marked line.**

   Before trimming out the excess fabric, turn the corner right side out and check that the miter is at a right angle.

9. **Turn the pocket corner wrong side out again, trimming the seam allowance to ¼ inch and tapering it at the corner (see Chapter 6 coverage of trimming away fabric at a point or corner).**

   Repeat for the other corner of the pocket. Press the corner seams open.

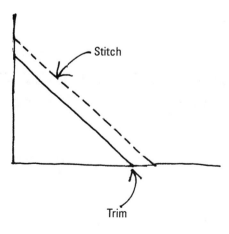

10. **Fold the pocket facing on the foldline toward the right side of the pocket. Sew the seams at both sides of the pocket.**

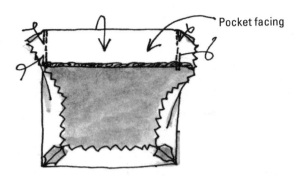

Pocket facing

Backstitch at the top and bottom of both seams.

11. **Trim away the excess seam allowance at the corners.**

12. **Turn the pocket right side out and press.**

Now your pocket is ready to attach to your project.

Unlined patch pockets with curved corners

The biggest challenge with a curved corner pocket is getting both curves the same shape.

Follow these steps and see how easy it is when you're using the right tools:

1. **Cut out the curved-corner pocket by following the pattern guide sheet instructions or by using one of the pocket patterns found in this chapter (see Figure 11-2).**

2. **Using your sewing machine or serger, overcast the top edge of the pocket facing (see Chapter 6 for more information on finishing raw edges).**

3. **Set your machine like this:**

   - **Stitch:** Straight
   - **Length:** 3.5 to 4 mm/6 to 7 spi
   - **Width:** 0 mm
   - **Foot:** All-purpose

4. **Easestitch-plus to shape the curved corners.**

   Sewing upward on the wrong side of the fabric, easestitch-plus from about 1½ inches above the curve to 1½ inches to the other side of the curve, sewing ¼ inch from the raw edge. Repeat for the other corner.

   Using your sewing machine, easestitch-plus by guiding the fabric so that the needle sews ¼ inch from the raw edge. While you're sewing, hold the fabric very firmly behind the foot so that it bunches and piles up.

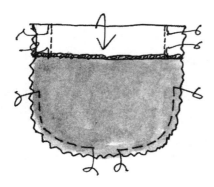

5. **Press and shape the corners of the pocket around a pocket former.**

   Making sure that both pocket corners come out in exactly the same shape is a challenge — to say the least. So try a pocket former and shape the corner around this template. You can find pocket formers at your local fabric store or sewing supply mail-order company.

   If you can't locate a pocket former, make one out of a piece of cardboard. Cut a 4-inch-by-4-inch square of cardboard. (Cardboard found on the back of writing tablets works well for this.) Set a small salt shaker or bottle of paper correction fluid in the corner, then trace around the bottom curve of the container with a pencil, creating a smooth curve at the corner. Trim the corner by following your pencil line. This is your pocket former.

With the wrong side of the pocket up, snug the gentlest curve of the pocket former into one of the corners and gently steam-press the seam allowance up to the seamline, shaping the curve of the pocket corner around the curve of the pocket former.

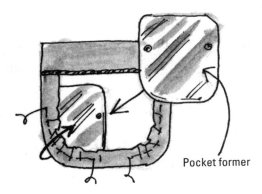

Pocket former

6. **Fold down, pin, and stitch the pocket facing.**

   Fold the pocket facing on the foldline, putting the right sides together. Sew the seams at both sides of the pocket. Backstitch at the top and bottom of both seams. Trim away the excess seam allowance at the corners (read more about trimming corners in Chapter 6).

7. **Turn the pocket right side out and press.**

   Now your pocket is ready to attach to a project.

Lined patch pockets

Sometimes you want more oomph to the pocket so that it can hold more of whatever you're putting in it or to give the pocket a smoother-looking finish. You can do this by lining it. The decision is usually a function of the fabric, the style of the pocket, and the type of project.

If you're making a self-lined pocket, make sure that your fabric is lightweight like cotton oxford — wool coating is way too heavy for a self-lining.

1. **Prepare the pocket pattern by folding down the pocket facing and folding the paper pattern on the foldline at the top of the pocket.**

2. **Prepare the fabric for layout and cutting in one of two ways:**

   • **For self-lined pockets:** Fold the fabric into a double layer, so that the right sides are together and the fold is perpendicular to the lengthwise grain (see Chapter 4 for more about grainlines). Lay out the pocket pattern on the fabric and cut out the pocket so that the top of the pattern is on the fold.

- **For pockets with a separate lining:** Following the pattern guide sheet instructions, cut two separate pocket pieces — one out of the project fabric and one out of the lining fabric.

3. **Pin the pocket and lining together, with right sides together.**

4. **Set your machine like this:**

   - **Stitch:** Straight

   - **Length:** 2.5 to 3 mm/10 to 12 spi

   - **Width:** 0 mm

   - **Foot:** All-purpose

5. **Stitch around the sides of the pocket, sewing ⅝ inch from the raw edge and backstitching at the end(s) of the seamline.**

   If you have a pocket former, use your fabric marker and trace the curve of the pocket former onto the fabric at the seamline of both corners. Stitch over the traced lines, and the corners turn out to be the same shape.

6. **Trim away the excess seam allowance at the corners.**

   If the pocket has curved corners, notch the curves with your pinking shears or scissors (read up on notching outside curves in Chapter 6).

7. **Slash the center back of the lining, cutting the slit on the bias.**

Slashing means to cut into a piece of fabric either in the center of it or from an edge to the center of it. You cut a slash on the bias so that the fabric won't ravel when you pull the pocket right side out through the slash.

8. **Turn the pocket right side out through the slash.**

   In this commercial patch pocket technique, instead of turning the pocket through a seamline, you turn the pocket right-side out through the slash.

9. **Using the point of your blunt-end scissors, push out the corners and curves of the pocket.**

   Because the slash is in the center of the lining, a point turner tool works more easily into the curves and corners, helping to create a really good-looking pocket.

10. **Press the pocket so that the seamline is on the outside edge of the pocket.**

    If leaving the slash open bothers you, slip a strip of fusible web under the slit and fuse it shut by following the manufacturer's instructions (see Chapter 2 for more information on fusible web).

    Your well-made pocket is ready to attach to a project.

Attaching patch pockets

Attach your pocket the easy way by edgestitching it in place by following these steps:

1. **Pin your already-made pocket to the project by following your pattern guide instructions.**

   Patch pockets are usually intended to hold something, so instead of placing them so that they're stitched flat as a pancake to the project, position them so that there is a little slack at the top.

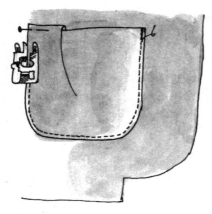

Need an easy-to-sew gift? Make this simple hair barrette and gift box. Add a low-sew greeting card, and you'll dazzle the lucky recipient with your creative talents. (See Chapter 3.)

Bring your holidays home by sewing and dressing Father Time. Everything you need to create this classic heirloom comes in a kit, and sewing the project is very easy (see Chapter 19). Set the scene for a

Dress your window treatment (see Chapter 16) to match your table with these napkins (see Chapter 13). Make rich tapestry place mats your guests are sure to admire (see Chapter 13). Then change the seasons indoors by making different place mats and a matching "flag" for your quick-change cornice.

Spruce up any room with a trim and border pillow (see Chapter 12) or an easy envelope pillow (see Chapter 15). Make one, the other, or both out of coordinating fabric.

Making Bravo Bear gives you practice sewing curves and corners and stuffing soft, 3-D projects. Bravo Bear's face and paws are appliqued with trim and felt. The tie dresses Bravo up to coordinate with the rest of the room decoration. (See Chapter 19.)

You start creating this casual, elegant look by turning a square of home-decor fabric into a table-cloth to dress your table (see Chapter 13). Make complementary napkins (see Chapter 13) and finish by fashioning a French Country cornice out of the same fabrics (see Chapter 16).

Redo a room in a weekend by making a duvet cover and dust ruffle (see Chapter 14) and matching pillow shams (see Chapter 15). Top off the window with some shirred and flipped panels on a continental rod (see Chapter 16). Tie in all the fabric coordinates by making a flanged trim and border pillow (see Chapter 15).

Having trouble finding a
shower curtain you like at
the store? Then make a curtain and a topper to match.
Use a coordinating fabric
and shirr a double panel topper onto spring rods. This
splash of color adds pizzazz
to an otherwise ho-hum
room. (See Chapter 16.)

Wrap yourself or someone you love in the warmth and softness of this hat, scarf, and jacket. It requires no pressing, doesn't ravel, and is very easy to sew. Kids of all ages enjoy this ensemble.
(See Chapter 19.)

Don't be a stuffed shirt — sew one! You can easily turn a shirt into a pillow, complete with secret hiding places for the remote control or a favorite toy. You can also make a flanged pillow to match (see Chapter 15). Top your window with a cornice that's perfect for the den or a child's room (see Chapter 16).

Place mats aren't just for the table anymore. You need only four mats to make this great vest. Use six mats to put together this handmade jacket, and then add hand-running stitches for hand-stitched elegance. (See Chapter 19.)

Make this reversible cape, and your little ones become Dracula, Little Red Riding Hood, or a favorite super hero. Just add a ready-made sweat suit or shirt and pants underneath to complete the outfit. (See Chapter 19.)

Watch out! You may have a tough time getting this cape off your gremlin to wash it. Remember to make this project out of washable fabrics and durable grosgrain ribbon. (See Chapter 19.)

This tulle skirt, cape and overskirt combination, and veil can create the look of a bride or princess. Tie the lace overskirt around her waist over a white leotard and tights. Add the crowning touch with a lovely lace veil for hours of fun and fantasy. (See Chapter 19.)

The overskirt converts to a cape when worn over her shoulders and a pink leotard and tights. This fun ensemble is easy to sew and makes a wonderful addition to any dress-up box. (See Chapter 19.)

When you spill ink or tea down the front of a favorite shirt, don't throw it out! Cover up the stains by placing a pocket collage or a giant applique over the mess. Make the pocket collage to coordinate with a pair of favorite pants. (See Chapter 11.)

When your child's favorite jumper or dress gets too short, add a ruffle and some colorful rickrack to the hem. You can also add rickrack at the edge of the pocket and applique a strip of matching ribbon. You'll end up with a jumper that looks better than it did when it was shorter! (See Chapter 17.)

Test drive your decorative stitches by sewing this belt sampler of many colors; you can also stitch it tone-on-tone for a subtle, textured look. Next, make an easy fitting belt using woven Guatemalan belting (see Chapter 17). Stack leftover belting, rickrack, and buttons over handmade paper; then stitch everything together to create a one-of-a-kind greeting card (see Chapter 5).

2. **Set your machine like this:**

   • **Stitch:** Straight

   • **Length:** Appropriate for the fabric

   • **Width:** 0 mm

   • **Foot:** Edgestitch or blind hem

   • **Needle position:** (Optional) Adjust the needle position so that you're sewing ⅛ inch from the edge of the pocket

3. **Edgestitch around the pocket (read more about edgestitching in Chapter 6).**

   Guide the edge of the pocket along the blade in the foot, backstitching at the top of the pocket as shown. If this is a topstitched pocket that's not likely to get a lot of tough wear and tear, don't backstitch. Instead, pull the threads to the back and tie them off (see Chapter 6 for more information on backstitching and tying off threads).

Using the Pocket Patterns

Sometimes, I just want to put a pocket on a project, and the pocket's not part of the original pattern. Instead of rifling through other patterns or buying another pattern to find just the right pocket, I dig into my reserve of pocket patterns when the inspiration strikes.

The shirt pocket pattern in Figure 11-2 has three different styles:

- Rectangular pocket
- Rounded pocket
- Chevron pocket

1. **Fold pattern tracing material or leftover pattern paper the length of the pocket in half the long way.**

2. **Place the pocket pattern under the pattern paper, lining up the pattern on the fold of the pattern paper.**

3. **Trace off the desired pocket by following the key in Figure 11-2.**

   While you're at it, why not trace off all three styles? Then you can have a ready pocket pattern resource when you need it!

After you trace off these pocket patterns, safely store them between the pages of this chapter!

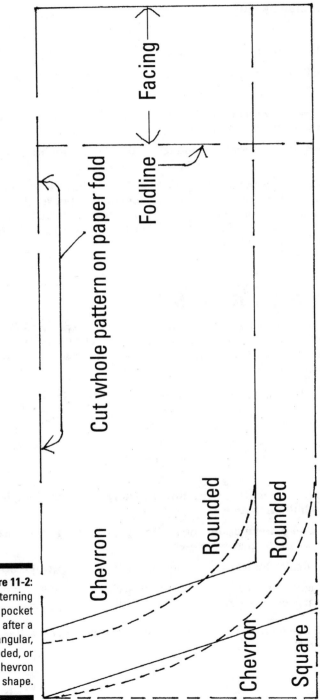

Figure 11-2:
Patterning
your pocket
after a
rectangular,
rounded, or
chevron
shape.

Making a Cool Pocket Collage Shirt

My husband ruined three shirts in one week with the same leaky pen. Go figure. So instead of throwing them away (the shirts, not my husband and his leaky pen), I artfully stitched a pocket collage, covering the ink stains on the front of his, and now my, favorite shirt. You can see the end result in the color section of this book. This is how it works:

1. **Dig through your fabric stash for fabric that matches the color and/or design of your injured garment.**

   My favorite stained shirt is the white one with the blue and black stripes. So I located fabrics with black, white, and blue in them.

2. **Trace off the pocket patterns and cut out the pockets.**

   Using the pocket patterns in Figure 11-2, cut out three different pocket styles from three coordinating fabrics.

3. **Make the unlined pockets by following the steps in the section "Putting Together Patch Pockets," earlier in this chapter. Pin the pockets to the front of the shirt, creatively arranging them so that they cover the stains.**

4. **Edgestitch the pocket to the front of the shirt. (Read more about edgestitching in Chapter 6.)**

Moving a Pocket and Making a Stain-Covering Appliqué

I stained a brand-new, day-old shirt with iced tea and couldn't get out the stain. Instead of throwing away my new shirt, I stitched new life into it, as shown in the color section of this book, by following these easy steps:

1. **Using your seam ripper, remove the existing breast pocket by cutting through the stitches with a seam ripper (see Chapter 6 for ripping instructions). Set the pocket aside.**

   You will sew it on in another place later.

2. **Cut out an 18-inch square of contrasting fabric (I used a patchwork fabric of red, white, and blue). Cut that square into two triangles, cutting the square apart from the upper-left corner to the lower-right corner.**

3. **Turn under and press the outside edges of each triangle ⅝ inch, following the instructions in the section "Unlined patch pockets with square corners," earlier in this chapter, for making a square pocket.**

4. **Place and pin a triangle on the right side of the shirt front so that the longest side of the triangle is positioned ¾ inch from the finished edge. Repeat for the left side of the shirt front.**

   If your shirt has a strip of fabric where the buttonholes and the buttons are stitched (this is called a *placket*), snug the long edge of the triangle up to the long edge of the placket.

5. **Edgestitch around the three edges of the triangle, sewing on the right side of the shirt front (see Chapter 6 for more details on edgestitching). Rather than backstitch, pull the threads to the wrong side of the project and tie them off. Repeat for the left side of the shirt front.**

6. **Place, pin, and sew the pocket you ripped off the shirt in Step 1, wherever you want it, edgestitching it in place.**

   I put mine near the lower edge of the shirt, halfway between the shirt opening and the side seam. This way, the pocket is in the perfect position for keys.

Part IV
Sewing for the Home

The 5th Wave   By Rich Tennant

"Maybe a shower curtain wasn't the best thing to try and make into an evening dress."

In this part . . .

I know it's wrong to play favorites, but I just can't help it — this part of the book is probably the coolest set of chapters you'll ever read. In this part, I show you how you can create new looks for just about any room in your house. After you read the chapters in this part, you'll no longer have to settle for store-bought napkins, place mats, duvet covers, pillows, or curtains. You will be able to make your own — in hours! — in exactly the colors and fabrics that you like best.

Chapter 12

Assembling and Working with Home Decor Materials

· ·

In This Chapter

▶ Home decor trims, cord, braids, and fringes — what they look like and how to use them
▶ Making and sewing on piping like a pro
▶ Creating a trim and border pillow
▶ Sewing tassels with no hassles
▶ Sewing a reversible table runner

· ·

*H*ere are the top three reasons I love home decor projects (and think you will too):

   ✔ I don't have to alter the fit of a home decor project if I've overeaten during the holidays.

   ✔ I have the personal satisfaction of knowing I beautified the room myself and saved a fortune.

   ✔ Home decor projects are fast and easy to sew.

I tell you all about the special materials involved in home decor projects in this chapter.

A Few Words about Home Decor Fabric

All fabrics are not created equal. Although you can use some home decor fabrics to make clothing and use some fabrics for clothing in your home decor projects, you have better results using the right fabric for the job.

Home decor fabrics differ from other fabrics in several ways:

   ✔ Many home decor fabrics are heavier in weight (and therefore less drapable, but generally more durable).

✔ Home decor fabrics are usually at least 54 to 60 inches wide, rather than 45 inches wide.

✔ Home decor fabrics have a strip of color bars that are match points, printed on the selvages (see Chapter 4 for more on selvages) so, when you sew one panel to the next, the design matches perfectly at the seamline.

A whole world of home decor fabrics awaits you at the fabric store. Go in and explore — just remember to ask for the home decor section!

Always check the bolt end of your home decor fabrics for proper cleaning and care instructions. They differ widely.

Braving Braid Basics

Braid is a flat home decor trim with two finished edges. The two most common types of braid are:

✔ **Gimp:** A flat braid usually glued to furniture to conceal upholstery tacks. You can also stitch gimp to the edge of decorator cord-edge trim (see the following section for the details on cord).

✔ **Mandarin:** A dressier, ½-inch dimensional gimp (meaning that it has a texture), great for outlining pillows, place mats, and other home decor projects. You can also use mandarin braid in crafting by gluing it to handmade boxes and decorating lamp shades.

Conquering Cord

Cord is a round, twisted strand of fibers that look like rope. Cord can be anywhere from ⅛ inch to ½ inch around and is made out of cotton, shiny rayon, spun satiny rayon, or a combination of fibers, each with its own texture.

The most common kinds of cord include the following:

✔ **Cable cord:** A twisted cotton or cotton/polyester cord used as a filling for fabric-covered piping (see the following section for more information on piping). Preshrink the cable cord before using it in a project. *Piping* (or welting) is made by covering the cable cord with a strip of fabric called a casing. The casing has a ¼-inch to ½-inch seam allowance so that it can be sewn into the seam at the edge of a pillow, slipcover, or sofa cushion cover. Piping gives a crisp, tailored finish to the edge.

✔ **Cord-edge trim:** A twisted cord with a lip edge of flat gimp sewn to it. The twisted cord is pretty by itself and is not covered with a casing like cable cord. The lip edge makes it easy to insert the trim at a seam in a pillow or at the edge of a window cornice, swag, or jabot (see Chapter 16 for more information on window treatments).

Cord-edge trim is a "dry-clean only" trim. So, remember that the fabric you use in your projects must be compatible with the trim.

✔ **Filler cord:** A web-covered cotton cord used inside piping. It's softer and fatter than cable cord and is manufactured at diameters up to 1¾ inches thick.

Because of its loose construction, don't preshrink filler cord before covering it, and dry-clean the projects instead of washing them.

✔ **Chair tie:** A twisted decorator cord 27 to 30 inches long with tassels on both ends. Traditionally used to attach cushions to chairs, chair ties also make nice drapery tie-backs.

✔ **Tie-back:** A twisted decorator cord that's shaped into a three-sectioned loop. A color-coordinating ring cinches the loop so that the tassel hangs in the center loop. The side loops encircle a drapery and hold it back by looping over the hardware attached to the wall.

For information on attaching cord to your projects, see the next section in this chapter.

Attaching Decorator Trims: A Primer

Here are some sewing guidelines to keep in mind as you sew home decor trims onto your projects:

✔ Use a size 14/90 to 16/100 Universal point or sharp needle in your sewing machine. Home decor fabrics can get very thick under the presser foot and need a sharp, heavy needle.

✔ Use a little longer stitch length (6 to 8 spi) than for garment sewing. Again, the longer stitch length makes sewing the extra thicknesses created by the fabric and trim a lot easier.

✔ In certain cases when the fabric moves sluggishly under the presser foot, lighten up the foot pressure (see your Operating Manual for instructions on how to do this). A *wedge* is also helpful when sewing up and over uneven thicknesses.

When sewing uneven thicknesses (such as when hemming jeans by sewing up and over the thick jean seams and then back down to the level hem allowance), use a wedge under the heel to level the presser foot when approaching and coming off the heavy seams. Wedges are available through your local sewing machine dealer, fabric store, or sewing mail-order source. Look for them by the brand names of Jean-A-Ma-Jig or Hump-Jumper.

If you don't want to buy a wedge, make one by cutting out a 6-inch square of denim. Fold it in half and then in half again until you have four layers of fabric. Continue folding this denim square until the wedge is as thick as needed, so when the foot rests on the wedge and the thick seam, the foot is level.

- Prevent unnecessary needle breakage by sewing slowly over thick areas.

- Start sewing a trim at the center of any side of a pillow or cushion unless the project instructions say explicitly to do otherwise.

- Fabric and trim must be equal lengths; don't pull or stretch the trim to fit an edge.

- When making pillows and slipcovers or covering cushions, sew the trim to the top pillow piece first. Then sew the back pillow piece to the trimmed front fabric piece. This way, if you get any stitch distortion, it shows on the back rather than the front of the project.

Making and Attaching Piping

Call me crazy, but I love sewing piping in a seam. I like seeing it in seams to set off style lines in a garment. I love seeing it at the edge of a pillow or cushion because it says "quality." You can purchase piping by the yard or make it to match a specific project. It's made by cutting and seaming long strips of fabric and encasing the cable or filler cord in the fabric strip (see preceding section for more information on cable and filler cord). Piping is very easy to make and insert when you know how. Want some practice? Then make the pillow I tell you about in the section "Making a Trim and Border Pillow," later in this chapter.

Making your own piping

If you're lucky enough to find piping to match your project, buy it. If not, this section tells you how to make your own piping to match your project.

You make piping, which is also sometimes called *welting,* by covering a cable cord with a strip of fabric called a *casing* ("Conquering Cord," earlier in this chapter, tells you more about cable cord). The casing has a ¼-inch to ½-inch seam allowance so that the casing can be sewn into the seam at the edge of a pillow, slipcover, or sofa cushion cover. Piping gives a crisp, tailored finish to the edge.

To make your own piping, just follow these steps:

1. **Measure the perimeter of the area you want to pipe and add 2 inches or so for overlap and seaming for each length of piping you want to insert.**

   For example, if you want to pipe the edge of a pillow and the pillow has a perimeter of 30 inches, you need 32 inches of piping. If a seat cushion has two seams you want to pipe and each seam measures 40 inches around the perimeter, you need to make 84 inches of piping.

2. **Preshrink and cut a length of cable cord the same length of the area you want to pipe. (See Chapter 2 for more information on preshrinking.)**

   Prevent the cable or filler cord from uncontrolled fraying by taping around the end of the cord before cutting through it and leave the tape on for the duration of the project.

3. **Determine how wide to cut the fabric casing that covers the cording.**

   Wrap your tape measure around the cording so that it's snug. This is the circumference of the cord. Now take the circumference measurement and add an inch for seam allowances.

4. **Cut enough fabric strips so that, when they're seamed together in one long length, you have enough fabric to cover the length of the cable or filler cord.**

   Cable or filler cord is covered with either a straight- or bias-cut fabric casing, depending on the shape of the seam it's going in. If you want to sew the piping to straight seams (such as the edges of a rectangular slip-cover or square pillow), cut the fabric into strips either across the grain or on the lengthwise grain (see Chapter 4 for more information on grainlines). If you want to sew the piping to a curved edge, like a round pillow, cut the fabric strips on the bias (see Chapter 4 for more information on the bias).

   If you can't cut one strip of fabric that's long enough to cover the entire length of the cord, cut as many small strips as you need and sew them together with a ½-inch seam.

5. **Prepare your machine with the following settings:**

   - **Stitch:** Straight
   - **Length:** 3 mm/9 spi
   - **Width:** 0 mm
   - **Foot:** Zipper or piping

   Most sewing machines come with a zipper foot as standard equipment. If you sew on a lot of piping, buy a piping foot. The underside of the foot has a deep groove that automatically guides over the cording for straight sewing and even piping application. A foot I like and use a lot is called a "Pearls and Piping Foot." It's manufactured by Creative Feet and designed to fit any brand or sewing machine model by Creative Feet. Call 800-776-6938 for more information (or see the appendix).

6. **With the right side of the fabric out and starting at one end, sandwich the cord in the casing — like you would put a hot dog in a bun.**

   Don't pin the casing around the length of the cable cord before sewing. If you do, it takes forever, and you'll never want to look at another piece of piping as long as you live. Instead, start sewing and slow down the machine; use your hands to guide the fabric and cording together as you sew.

You can use the following technique to attach piping to the edge of pillow, a seat cushion slipcover, or anywhere two seams come together.

Attaching piping

When attaching piping to a pillow, attach the piping to the front pillow piece first and then sew the back to the front.

1. **Starting anywhere but at a corner, pin the piping to the right side of the fabric so that the raw edges of the piping and the fabric are even.**

   Keep the piping in one long length until you are absolutely sure that you have enough to go around the project. Don't stretch the piping to fit the edge or the seamline ends up puckered.

2. **Set your sewing machine like this:**
   - **Stitch:** Straight
   - **Length:** 3 mm/9 spi
   - **Width:** 0 mm
   - **Foot:** Zipper or piping

3. **Sew on the piping at the ½-inch seamline, pulling out the pins as you get to them. Stop sewing about 2 inches before the end of the piping.**

   If you're sewing trim to a straight edge, skip to Step 5.

   If you're pinning and sewing around a corner, clip the seam allowance of the piping up to, but not through, the stitching line. With the needle in the fabric, raise the foot and pivot slightly, nudging your index finger into the corner of the piping so that it bends around your finger, away from the needle. Lower the presser foot and continue stitching. You may have to stitch a gentle curve rather than a sharp corner to accommodate the bulk of the piping.

4. **Rip out the stitching that holds the fabric casing around the filler cord, opening the casing about 1 inch on both ends. Tape the ends of the cable cord together.**

5. Turn one edge of the casing under, overlapping the fabric and pinning it to the other end. Then stitch on the rest of the casing at the seam allowance to join them together.

6. Place and pin the piped seam allowance to the nonpiped seam allowance with the right sides together.

7. Place the project under the presser foot so that the stitching from Steps 2 through 5 is where you can see it.

Place the project under the foot so that, when sewing, the needle falls between the stitching line and the bump of the piping.

By guiding your work this way, you're sewing close enough to the piping that the previous row of stitching won't show when the project is turned right side out.

Attaching cord-edge trim

You attach cord-edge trim the same way you attach cording and piping (see the preceding set of steps). Then, when you reach the starting point, overlap the two ends of the cord. Cut the cords so they each have at least a 3-inch tail. Overlap, pin the ends, and sew.

Making a Trim and Border Pillow

You can get some experience sewing in piping and cord-edge trim by making this fun trim and border pillow (see the color section of this book). This small pillow coordinates with the Bravo Bear that I show you how to make in Chapter 19.

To make a trim and border pillow, you need the following supplies (in addition to the Sewing Survival Kit I tell you about in Chapter 1):

✔ 1 14-inch pillow form

✔ ½ yard of 48-inch-wide to 54-inch-wide upholstery velvet

✔ 1 10-inch square of home decor fabric that coordinates with the velvet

✔ Thread that matches the fabric

✔ 1½ yards of cord-edge trim that matches the fabric

✔ (Optional) 4 decorator tassels to coordinate with the fabric (see "Attaching Tassels," later in this chapter, for more information on tassels)

Just follow these steps to create the pillow:

1. **Cut a 14-inch square from the upholstery velvet and set it aside.**

2. **From the remaining velvet, cut four 2¾-by-14-inch strips.**

3. **Set your sewing machine like this:**

   - **Stitch:** Straight
   - **Length:** 3 mm/9 spi
   - **Width:** 0 mm
   - **Foot:** Zipper or piping

4. **Sew the cord-edge trim to two opposite sides of the 10-inch fabric square, using a seam allowance the width of the lip of the cord. (See "Attaching piping" and "Attaching cord-edge trim," both earlier in this chapter, if you need more information on attaching the trim.)**

   "Decenter" your needle position so that it sews next to the piping on the lip edge of the trim. (Turn to Chapter 1 for information on needle position.)

5. **Sew the fabric strips onto the two opposite ends of the 10-inch pillow square.**

   You sandwich the cord-edge trim between the velvet strip and coordinate fabric, and the velvet strip is longer than the edge of the square. That's okay. After sewing, trim the longer edge of the strip so that it's even with the edge of the square.

6. **Repeat Steps 3 through 5 for other two sides of the pillow square.**

7. **Press the cord-edge-trimmed pillow square from the wrong side, pressing the seam allowances to one side.**

8. **Using your dressmaker's chalk and trimming scissors, trim each corner on both pillow squares into a gentle curve.**

   Doing so makes it easier to sew the tassels and prevents the "bunny ear" effect in each corner of your pillow when it's finished.

9. **If you are using tassels, pin one in each corner of the cord-edge-trimmed square, pinning them so that the loops are caught in the seam allowance.**

10. **With the right sides together, pin and stitch the pillow together, using a ½-inch seam allowance and leaving a 5-inch opening on one side to turn the pillow through.**

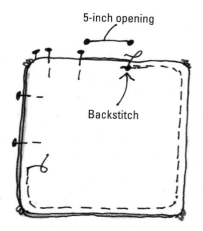

11. **Press the seams flat and together (see Chapter 5 for more information on pressing seams flat and together).**

12. **On either side of the opening, clip into the seam allowance just shy of the seamline. Press the seam allowance toward the center of the pillow cover.**

13. **Trim the seam allowance to about ¼ inch, trimming out the fabric bulk at the corners. Then turn the pillow cover right side out.**

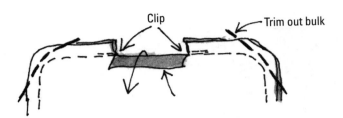

Clip

Trim out bulk

14. **Stuff the pillow form into the pillow cover and hand slipstitch the opening to close it (see Chapter 5 for more information on hand slipstitching).**

Jazzing Things Up with Fringe

Fringe is a decorative edging made of packed, hanging yarns. Decorator fringes are a lot of fun to work with and add richness and value to your home decor projects.

The following list tells you about the most common types of fringe that you may run across:

- **Ball fringe:** A decorative fringe constructed with a gimp edge and cotton pompons. Use it to trim whimsical home decor projects, children's rooms, and costumes.

- **Boucle fringe:** A fringe constructed with permanently kinked, nubby yarns called *boucle yarns*. Boucle fringe can be short, long, looped, or bullion.

- **Bullion fringe:** A long fringe with twisted, looped ends. It's used a lot on pillows, upholstery, and slipcovers. It even makes nice doll hair.

- **Butterfly fringe:** A fringe with cut edges on two sides that are connected by an open threaded area. When you fold butterfly fringe in half the long way and stitch it to a project, you create a double-thick row of fringe.

- **Chainette fringe:** A fringe constructed of many short or long chainette ends. Use it for garment sewing, window treatments, and table toppers (see Chapter 13 for the instructions for making a table topper).

- **Moss fringe:** A short, cut fringe that looks like a brush after the fringe has been sewn in a pillow or slipcover and the chainstitch is removed from the edges.

- **Tassel fringe:** A fringe with many tiny tassels attached to a length of gimp.

The lip edge of the fringe makes it easy to sew to the edge or in a seam of a pillow or cushion. Follow the instructions in Steps 1 through 3 and Steps 5 through 7 in the sections "Attaching piping" and "Attaching cord-edge trim," both earlier in this chapter. Then, when you reach the starting point, overlap the two ends of the fringe. If you're using moss or brush fringe, just butt the fringe ends together at the join so that it's not so thick.

Attaching Tassels

Tassels are made of thread strands tied and banded at the top. You have a top loop on each tassel that can be as short as ½ to 1 inch or up to 3 inches long. This loop is what you find sandwiched in the seam of a table topper or a pillow and used on window treatments.

The method you use to attach tassels depends on the length of the tassels. You attach short-looped tassels (½ to 1 inch) by hand and long-looped tassels (over 1 inch) by machine.

Attaching short-looped tassels

Follow these steps to attach short-looped tassels:

1. **Thread and knot a hand needle with a doubled thread. Place a drop of seam sealant on the knot and then pull the needle and thread up through the center so that the knot snugs up inside the tassel.**

2. **Pass the needle and thread around and through the short loop several times.**

3. **Finish sewing on the tassel by sewing a knot (see Chapter 5 for the details on making knots).**

Attaching long-looped tassels

Follow these steps to attach long-looped tassels:

1. **Place the tassel on the right side of the fabric so that the head of the tassel is ½ inch outside the seamline and the tassel loop is inside the seam allowance.**

   The tassel itself is positioned toward the center of the project.

2. **Machine stitch, catching the long loop in the stitching at the seamline.**

Making a Reversible Table Runner

Try your hand at sewing tassels by making this easy table runner (as shown under Father Time in the color section). You can create this pretty runner to "run" either the width or the length of a table — use it rather than place mats or a tablecloth and impress even your fussiest dinner guest!

To make the runner, you need the following supplies (in addition to the tools in the Sewing Survival Kit that I tell you about in Chapter 1):

- ✔ ½ yard of 60-inch-wide tapestry fabric (tapestry fabric is a special kind of home decor fabric)
- ✔ ½ yard of 60-inch wide lighter-weight home decor fabric that complements the tapestry fabric
- ✔ Thread that matches the fabric
- ✔ 2 decorator tassels
- ✔ 1 yardstick

1. **Take one piece of the 18-by-60-inch fabric and, using your dressmaker's chalk, mark the mid-point of the short ends.**

2. **At the marks, fold the fabric toward the center, as though you were making a paper airplane. Press the edge of each fold.**

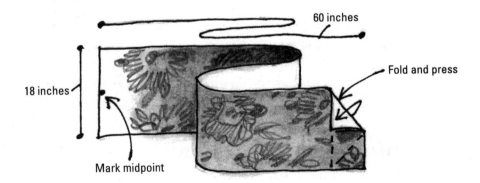

60 inches

18 inches

Fold and press

Mark midpoint

3. **Cut your table runner along each of the foldlines on both ends of the fabric. Each end should form a point.**

4. **Repeat Steps 1 through 3 for the other piece of fabric to create the reversible side of the runner.**

5. Pin the tassels to the right side of the tapestry fabric so that the loop is in the seam allowance and the top of the tassel is as close to the seamline as possible.

You need enough room for the presser foot to ride next to the tassel to sew the seam, so adjust the tassel placement as needed.

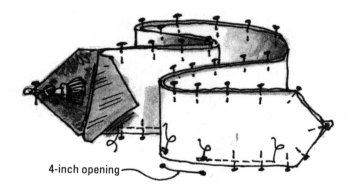

4-inch opening

6. Pin the contrasting fabric to the right side of the tapestry fabric.

7. Starting on one long side, sew all the way around the table runner, using a ½-inch seam allowance. Leave approximately a 4-inch opening. Backstitch at each end of the stitching line.

Instead of stitching to a very sharp point at the ends, sew a gentle curve around the points, catching the tassel cord in the seamline.

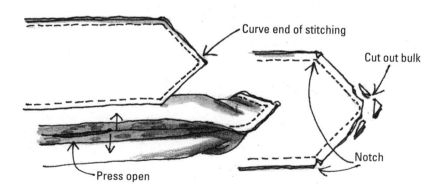

Curve end of stitching

Cut out bulk

Press open

Notch

8. Trim excess fabric and tassel cord from around the points of the runner.

9. **Press the seam flat and together (see Chapter 5 for more information on how to press things flat and together). At the opening, press the seam back toward the center of the runner on both edges (as if it were turned right side out).**

   This makes the opening almost invisible and easier to close by hand.

10. **From the wrong side, press the seam allowance open over a seam roll or seam stick (if you have one), pressing as close to the points as possible.**

    If you don't have a seam roll, press the seam open as well as possible by using your iron and ironing board.

11. **Turn the runner right side out and press the edges.**

12. **Close the opening with hand slipstitches (see Chapter 5 for more information on hand slipstitching).**

Chapter 13

Quick-Change Table Toppers

I know what you're thinking — napkins, place mats, and tablecloths — they're squares and rectangles. What's to know? Believe it or not, you can finish an edge several ways, and I cover my favorite fast and easy techniques in this chapter.

Selecting Your Fabric for Table Toppers

Whether you're making place mats, napkins, or tablecloths, here are a few things to keep in mind when selecting fabric.

✔ Before buying a fabric simply because you like the color or design, consider the fiber content, the fabric finish, and what you want to make. Fabrics such as all-cotton or all-linen are absorbent but very wrinkle-prone, so you may want to choose fabrics blended with a little polyester. A fabric finish such as Scotchgard also repels stains and spills, so the fabric may not have the absorbency needed for napkins but works great as a tablecloth.

✔ Don't use fabrics that consist of more than 50-percent synthetic or man-made fiber. They're just not absorbent, and the stains and odors remain in the fabric even after repeated washings.

✔ Using fabrics with preprinted stripes, plaids, or checks helps you cut straight, and hemming is as easy as following the lines in the fabric.

✔ Don't use knits. Tightly woven fabrics work better and last longer as napkins and tablecloths.

✔ Look at the wrong side of the print. Will it limit your napkin-folding possibilities because it's not pretty enough on the wrong side? If so, choose another fabric or use it for something other than a napkin, where the wrong side won't matter.

✔ If you want a light- to medium-weight fabric, look for bandannas, broadcloth, calico prints, chambray, chintz, duck, gingham, kettle or weaver's cloth, light- to mid-weight linen and denim, muslin, percale, poplin, and seersucker.

✔ For heavier-weight fabrics, look for damask, double-sided fabrics, linen, sailcloth, and terry cloth.

Making Napkins

Friends and family members usually expect handmade gifts from me — and I've made some really gorgeous things through the years. But the most appreciated gifts were the 160 napkins (20 sets of eight) I made for everyone one holiday season. Napkins are fast and easy to make and are good for our environment.

First, I used up fabric that coordinated with my friends' color schemes and lifestyles — Sally works with chimpanzees, so she got a jungle print; my classically-tailored pal, Carol, got the black and white stripes. I used a cheerful juvenile print for our son's day-care provider.

Besides making the napkins that season, I went to garage sales and flea markets and bought wonderful baskets for pennies. When December arrived, I baked up loaves of my favorite pumpkin bread and included the recipe along with the napkins in the basket. What a hit!

Napkin sizes

Tables 13-1 and 13-2 tell you how much fabric you need to make napkins of various sizes. The size of each unfinished napkin is shown in inches; the amount of fabric for each set of napkins is shown in yards.

Table 13-1 Yardage for 45-Inch Fabric

Unfinished Napkin Size	*Six Napkins*	*Eight Napkins*	*Ten Napkins*	*Twelve Napkins*
15 inches	⅔	1	1⅓	1⅓
18 inches	1½	2	2½	3
20 inches	1⅔	2¼	2⅞	3½
22½ inches	1⅞	2½	3⅛	3¾

Table 13-2 Yardage for 54- to 55-Inch Fabric

Unfinished Napkin Size	*Six Napkins*	*Eight Napkins*	*Ten Napkins*	*Twelve Napkins*
15 inches	⅞	1¼	1⅔	1⅔
18 inches	1	1½	2	2 inches
20 inches	1⅔	2¼	2⅞	3⅓
24 inches	2	2⅔	3⅓	4

Sewing basic table napkins

After making 160 napkins, I discovered a fast, efficient way to make them. These little beauties come together so quickly that you may be tempted to create a set for special dinner parties, family celebrations, or holidays. To make these napkins, you need the following materials in addition to your Sewing Survival Kit (see Chapter 1):

- Napkin fabric (see Tables 13-1 and 13-2 for yardage)
- Thread that matches the napkin fabric

Just follow these steps to have napkins in no time:

1. **Cut the napkin squares (see Tables 13-1 and 13-2 for suggested sizes).**
2. **Set your sewing machine like this:**
    - **Stitch:** Three-step zigzag
    - **Length:** 1 to 1.5 mm/24 to 30 spi
    - **Width:** 5 mm
    - **Foot:** All-purpose

If you're using a serger, set your serger like this:

- **Stitch:** Balanced three-thread overlock;
- **Length:** 2 mm
- **Width:** 3 to 5
- **Foot:** All-purpose

3. **Overcast the opposite edges of the fabric squares with your sewing machine or serger.**

   Place the raw edge under the foot so that the needle catches the fabric on the left and swings off the raw edge at the right. (See Chapter 6 for more information on overcasting raw fabric edges.)

4. **Overcast the other two opposite edges of each napkin.**

5. **Pin and press a ¼-inch hem on two opposite edges of the fabric square.**

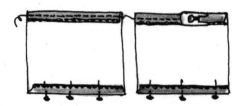

By pinning the hems this way, the corners turn out sharp and square.

6. **Set your machine like this:**

   - **Stitch:** Straight
   - **Length:** 3.5 mm/9 spi
   - **Width:** 0 mm
   - **Foot:** All-purpose

7. **With the right side of the fabric up, topstitch around the hem edge, guiding the right edge of the presser foot even with the folded edge of the hem. Backstitch at the end of the topstitching.**

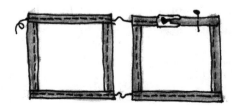

See Chapter 5 for more information on topstitching.

Making fringed and stitched napkins

Impress even the pickiest eater with these napkins (see the beautiful setting shown in the color section). No extra trim to buy — simply pull out threads from the fabric edges, thereby creating fringe to match. (By the way, this fringing technique works on the edges of place mats, too.)

To make these napkins, you need the following materials in addition to your Sewing Survival Kit (see Chapter 1):

- Napkin fabric (see Tables 13-1 and 13-2 for yardage)
- Thread that matches the napkin fabric
- ½-inch transparent tape
- 1 large hand tapestry needle

Follow these steps to make the fanciest napkins on your side of the street:

1. **Cut a strip of fabric across the grain, perpendicular to the selvages, in the desired length.**

   For example, to make several 15-inch napkins, cut a 15-inch-wide strip of the fabric across the grain. After this longer strip is fringed, it's cut into squares.

2. **Cut off the finished selvage edges on both sides of the fabric strip.**

3. **Using the tape, mark the fringe depth (¾ to 1 inch) at the top and bottom of the fabric strip.**

   Doing so marks where the fringe stops.

4. **Using the hand tapestry needle, remove the crossgrain threads up to the edge of the tape.**

Do this by starting at the top edge of the strip and working the point of the needle under one of the long threads in the strip. When you have pulled up on this one thread enough to create a loop, pull the thread out all the way across the fabric. You'll see a short length of fringe appearing on the long edge of the strip. Continue pulling out threads until you have fringe along both long edges of the strip. Stop when the fringe is at the edge of the tape.

5. **Cut the long fabric strip into napkin squares.**

   For example, if your fabric strip is 15 inches wide, cut the strip into 15-inch squares. After cutting each square, two edges of the squares are fringed, and two edges of the squares are not.

6. **Tape-mark the fringe depth on the nonfringed edges. Using the hand tapestry needle, remove the lengthwise threads up to the edge of the tape as you did in Step 4.**

7. **Set your machine like this:**

   - **Stitch:** Zigzag
   - **Length:** 2.5 to 3 mm/10 to 12 spi
   - **Width:** 3 mm
   - **Foot:** Embroidery

8. **Place the fabric under the needle so that the edge of the fringe is halfway under the foot.**

   When the fabric moves under the foot, the needle catches halfway into the fringe and halfway into the fabric at the edge of the fringe.

9. **Lower the foot and sew around all the edges so that the stitches catch in the fabric on the left and zigzag into the fringe on the right.**

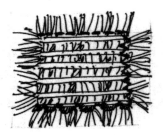

This stitching groups the fringe into neat tufts on the edge and prevents the fabric from fraying when you wash the napkins. When pivoting at each corner, stop with the needle in the left side of the stitch, lift the foot, adjust the fabric, lower the foot, and proceed. By doing this, you have an extra stitch at each corner for more security.

Instead of backstitching to secure the ends when you finish sewing, pull the threads to one side of the fabric and tie them off (see instructions in Chapter 6 for tying off threads).

Perfecting Place Mats with Fringed Edges

Add pizzazz to pizza night, dazzle to dinner, sizzle to your steak with these fringed-edge place mats. You need the following materials, plus your Sewing Survival Kit:

- ✔ Yardage of 54- to 60-inch tapestry fabric: ⅝ yard makes four place mats; 1¼ yards make eight place mats
- ✔ Thread to match the tapestry fabric

Preshrink the tapestry fabric in cold water and line dry. You care for the finished place mats this way, too. If you don't, you'll end up with place mats much smaller than you originally made them.

To make the place mats, just follow these steps:

1. **Square up the fabric.**

   For the place mats to end up exact rectangles, the larger piece of fabric they're made from must start off as an exact rectangle. If it's not squared up, your next dinner party may feature place mats that are new trapezoid shapes.

   Start by pulling out a thread from selvage to selvage, across the grain, on both the top and bottom edges.

   Then trim the short excess fringe up to and even with both pulled-thread edges. Doing so ensures that the fringe is even on both ends of the finished mats. The tapestry fabric strip should measure approximately 54 to 60 inches by 18 inches.

2. **Measure down from the top edge 1 inch and pull out a thread straight across the width of the tapestry fabric. Repeat for the bottom edge of the tapestry strip.**

   This "pulled thread line" marks the edge of the fringe.

3. **Starting from the pulled thread line, pull out crosswise threads creating a 1-inch fringe at both the top and bottom of the tapestry strip.**

4. **Set your machine like this:**

   • **Stitch:** Zigzag

   • **Length:** 2.5 mm/10 spi

   • **Width:** 3 mm

   • **Foot:** Embroidery

5. **Place the fabric under the needle so that the edge of the fringe is halfway under the foot. Lower the presser foot.**

   When the fabric moves under the foot, the needle catches halfway into the fringe and halfway into the fabric at the edge of the fringe.

6. **Overcast the two long edges, guiding the fabric so that the needle zigs into the fabric on the left side of the stitch and then zags into the fringe on the right side of the stitch.**

7. **Cut the fringed strip into four equal widths.**

   Each mat measures approximately 18 by 14 inches.

8. **Set your machine like this:**

   • **Stitch:** Overcast

   • **Length:** 4 to 6 mm/5 to 6 spi

   • **Width:** 4 to 5 mm

   • **Foot:** All-purpose

   If you're using a serger, set your serger like this:

   • **Stitch:** Three-thread overlock

   • **Length:** 3 mm

   • **Width:** 4 to 5 mm

   • **Foot:** All-purpose

9. **Finish the long edges of the place mat (see Chapter 6 for more information on finishing edges).**

10. **Set your sewing machine like this:**

    • **Stitch:** Straight

    • **Length:** 3 mm/9 spi

    • **Width:** 0 mm

    • **Foot:** All-purpose

11. **Fold and press ½-inch hems on the long edges of each mat. Topstitch, guiding the hem edge along the ¼-inch line in the needle plate. Remember to backstitch at the beginning and end of each fringed edge.**

Turning Out a Tablecloth

After you sew this square tablecloth, simply place it on your table so that the points are centered on the sides and ends of the table — that's called *setting the square on point.* You can also use this tablecloth over another tablecloth to add color accents and dimension to your eating space. To make the tablecloth, you need the following materials in addition to your Sewing Survival Kit:

✔ Tablecloth fabric (see "Selecting Your Fabric for Table Toppers," earlier in this chapter, for some suggestions): You need 1¼ yard of 45-inch-wide fabric for a 43-inch table square or 1½ yards of 54- to 55-inch-wide fabric for a 52-inch table square.

✔ Thread that matches the fabric.

✔ 4 tassels (optional).

These few simple steps create a tablecloth you'll be proud to eat on:

1. **Cut the tablecloth fabric square.**

   For example, if you're working with 45-inch-wide fabric, cut a square 45 by 45 inches; if you're working with 54-inch fabric, cut a 54-inch square.

2. **Set your sewing machine like this:**

   - **Stitch:** Three-step zigzag
   - **Length:** 1.5 to 2 mm/13 to 15 spi
   - **Width:** 5 mm
   - **Foot:** All-purpose

   If you're using a serger, set your serger like this:

   - **Stitch:** Balanced three-thread overlock
   - **Length:** 2 mm
   - **Width:** 3 to 5 mm
   - **Foot:** All-purpose

3. **Finish the opposite edges of the square.**

   Place the raw edge under the foot so the needle catches the fabric on the left and swings off the raw edge at the right. Repeat by finishing the edges of the two opposite edges.

4. **Pin and press a ½-inch hem on two opposite edges of the fabric square. Repeat for the other two sides.**

   Doing so ensures that the corners fold in correctly for secure hemming.

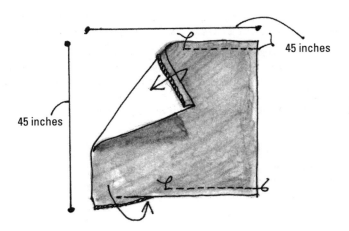

45 inches

45 inches

5. (Optional) Slip in and pin four tassels — one at each corner.

6. Set your machine like this:

- **Stitch:** Straight
- **Length:** 3.5 mm/7 spi
- **Width:** 0 mm
- **Foot:** All-purpose

7. **With the right side of the fabric up, topstitch around the hem edge, guiding an even distance from the edge. Backstitch at the end of the topstitching.**

   If you would rather fringe the edges, refer to the fringing and stitching instructions in the section "Making fringed and stitched napkins."

Chapter 14

Clever Cover-Ups for the Bedroom

. . . .

In This Chapter

▶ Speed gathering a dust ruffle

▶ Making a duvet cover

. . . .

*W*ant to change your bedroom decor as easily as you change your clothes? You can refresh the look of your sleeping chambers by making the easy dust ruffle and duvet cover that I describe in this chapter. Create matching window treatments from Chapter 16 and pillow shams and throw pillows from Chapter 15, all by using your beautiful fabric and the know-how you develop from reading this book.

The biggest challenge with most home decor projects is handling the length, bulk, and weight of the larger pieces of fabric. Clear away some space on the floor, move the stuff off the dining room table, and get sewing!

Making a Dust Ruffle

A bed skirt, often called a dust ruffle, fits between the mattress and box springs. A ruffled or pleated skirt drops to the floor, covering up the unsightly bed frame or side rails.

I like making my own bed skirts, even if I buy a ready-made comforter, because I use better fabric and sew in more gathers for a really rich look to the bedroom. Like other home decorating projects, the most challenging part is handling the volume of fabric.

When working with a great volume of fabric, hold the fabric taut in front of and behind the presser foot as you sew. Sew a few inches, then reposition your hands, keeping even tautness in front of and behind the foot as you proceed along the length of the seam. Doing so keeps the machine from getting clogged by a backup of fabric.

The dust ruffle that I present in this section is three-sided — the headboard side doesn't have a ruffle on it.

This dust ruffle is for a bed without posts or a foot board. For beds of special design, buy a bed skirt pattern specifically suited for these variations.

To make this dust ruffle, you need not only your Sewing Survival Kit (see Chapter 1) but also enough base fabric to cover your box springs and enough ruffle fabric to fall, or "drop", the distance from the top of the springs to the floor. One flat sheet does the trick for the base fabric that goes between the mattress and the box springs; select a size as close to the dimensions of your box springs as possible (this sheet doesn't show so it doesn't matter what color it is).

You make the ruffle itself by sewing strips of fabric together. The number of strips you need (and consequently, the amount of fabric) depends on the size of your bed and the width of your fabric. Consult Table 14-1 to determine the correct yardage.

I recommend that you stick to polyester-cotton blends (for easy care) in solid colors (things get more complicated when you have to match patterns). Also pick up thread that matches the fabric, masking tape, and pearl cotton.

Table 14-1		Yardage for Bed Skirt	
Bed Size	*Fabric Width*	*Yardage*	*Number of 20-inch Strips to Cut*
Twin	45-inch	4½	8
	54-inch	4	6
	60-inch	3½	7
Double	45-inch	5	9
	54-inch	4	8
	60-inch	4	8
Queen	45-inch	5	9
	54-inch	4½	8
	60-inch	4	7
King	45-inch	5½	10
	54-inch	4½	8
	60-inch	4½	8

Measuring the box springs

In order to make the ruffle the right size to cover the box springs entirely, you need to measure your box springs. Take the mattress off your bed and follow these steps:

1. **Measure the top width, the top length, and the drop.**

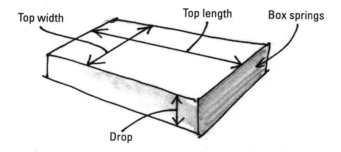

2. **Add the following to the measurements you took in Step 1 to account for the seam allowances and hems:**

    • **Top width:** Add 1½ inches.

    • **Top length:** Add ½ inch.

These measurements help you determine you how much fabric to cut out for the base of the dust ruffle (for more information, see the next section).

Measuring and cutting the fabric and sheet

Have the measurements you took in the previous section handy as you follow these steps:

1. **With the hem edge of the sheet at the top, cut the flat sheet the width and length that you calculated in Step 2 of the previous section.**

    The hem edge of the sheet ends up on the end of the dust ruffle where your head goes.

2. **Cut the appropriate number of fabric strips for your bed's size (refer to Table 14-1).**

    The strips should be 20 inches long by the width of the fabric; cut the strips perpendicular to the selvage.

Sewing the ruffle strips together

As you follow these steps, you create a very long strip of fabric. As the long strip takes shape, fold it up and let it rest in your lap for easy handling.

1. **Finish and hem one short side of one of the fabric strips with a ¾-inch hem (see Chapter 6 for more information on finishing seams and Chapter 7 for details on hems). Repeat for a second fabric strip.**

   The hemmed edges of these two strips are the ends of the bed skirt that are at the head of the bed.

2. **Set your machine like this:**
   - **Stitch:** Straight
   - **Length:** 3 mm/9 spi
   - **Width:** 0 mm
   - **Foot:** All-purpose

3. **Pin and sew the fabric strips together, creating one long ruffle strip.**

   Place the short raw edge of the hemmed strip to the short raw edge of one of the unhemmed strips, with right sides together. Sew a ½-inch seam, backstitching at both ends. Place, pin, and stitch another unhemmed strip to the longer strip, sewing the short raw edges, right sides together.

   Continue adding shorter strips to the longer one so that the last strip added is the other hemmed strip.

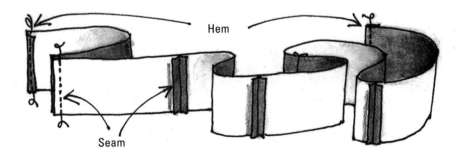

Hem

Seam

Double hemming the ruffle strip

Home decorating projects are made with double hems. This gives the fabric extra weight at the hem edges and a professional, finished look.

Before you double hem your dust ruffle, try it on the bed for size. Pin up the raw edge 4 inches to simulate a 2-inch double hem. Then hold the test double hem even with the top edge of the box springs, letting the ruffle drop down to the floor. If the length isn't right, lengthen or shorten your hem allowance according to the following steps.

Because the hem is turned up twice, you don't need to finish the edge before hemming. Just follow these steps:

1. **Double hem one long edge of the ruffle strip.**

   Place the fabric on the ironing board, wrong side up, so that the hem edge is on the board the long way. Press up a 1¾-inch hem the length of the long strip. Turn up, press, and pin up the hem again, so that the hem is doubled and 2 inches wide.

2. **Set your machine like this:**
   - **Stitch:** Straight
   - **Length:** 3 mm/9 spi
   - **Width:** 0 mm
   - **Foot:** All-purpose

3. **From the right side, sew a 2-inch hem, guiding an even distance from the edge.**

   Stick a strip of masking tape across the bed of the machine, so that the left edge of the tape is 2 inches to the right of the needle and parallel to the lines marked in the needle plate. Use the edge of the tape as your stitching guide.

4. **Press the hem again.**

Speed gathering the ruffle strip

As you follow these steps, you see your dust ruffle coming together in front of your eyes:

1. **Find a ball or skein of pearl cotton (a twisted embroidery floss available through your local fabric or craft store) or any fine string.**

   You use the pearl cotton or fine string as a cord to help you evenly gather the fabric. This cord must be long enough to fit the length of the ruffle strip. To prevent it from tangling, leave the cord in the ball, skein, or package until you're ready to use it.

2. **Set your machine like this:**
   - **Stitch:** Zigzag
   - **Length:** 2.5 to 3 mm/9 to 13 spi
   - **Width:** 3 to 4 mm
   - **Foot:** Embroidery

3. **Place the fabric under the needle, ½ inch from the raw edge and with the *wrong side of the fabric up*. Leaving the foot up, pierce the fabric with the needle.**

   The long strip is in your lap and on the floor.

4. **Center the end of the cord under the foot and on top of the fabric. Anchor the beginning end of the cord by wrapping it around a pin in figure-8 style.**

   This way, the cord won't slide out of the stitching as you sew. It doesn't matter which side of the needle the cord is on.

5. **Zigzag over the cord.**

   The stitches create a channel for the cord to slide through — gathers are easily adjusted, and the cord won't break as you work with the fabric.

6. **Mark the edge of the ruffle and the edge of the bed skirt base into eight equal sections.**

   Fold the ruffle strip in half the short way, then in half again, and in half again until you have folded it into eighths. At the edge where the gathering stitches are, press a short crease at the folds, pressing from the gathering stitches to the raw edge. These are your eight match points.

   Using your tape measure and fabric marker, measure around the three sides of the base fabric and divide that measurement into eighths. Using a fabric marker or pencil, mark the bed skirt base fabric into eighths along the three raw edges.

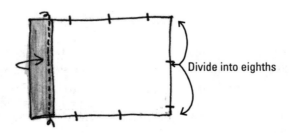

Divide into eighths

7. **Pin the ruffle to the sheet, right sides together, matching the marks around the three sides of the base sheet.**

8. **Pull up and adjust the gathers from pin to pin.**

   Starting at the head end of the bed skirt, pull on the gathering cord, adjusting the ruffled fullness to fit from the end to the first mark. Pin the ruffle to the base fabric, pinning every 2 to 3 inches. Gather, adjust, and pin the next section as before. Repeat until you have pinned all the sections to the base fabric. When you're finished pulling up the gathers, the gathered piece fits the flat piece, and the gathers are even.

Attaching the ruffle to the sheet

Follow these steps to complete the dust ruffle:

1. **Set your machine like this:**

   - **Stitch:** Straight
   - **Length:** 3.5 to 4 mm/6 to 8 spi
   - **Width:** 0 mm
   - **Foot:** All-purpose

2. **With the ruffle side up, sew the ruffle to the base fabric using a ⅝-inch seam allowance, backstitching at the beginning and ends of the seam.**

   Your gathering stitches are ½ inch from the raw edge. When sewing the seam, the ⅝-inch seamline is just to the left of the gathering stitches.

 Hold the fabric taut in front of and behind the presser foot as you sew. Sew a few inches and then reposition your hands, keeping even tautness in front of and behind the foot and along the length of the seam. This keeps the seam smooth and pucker-free.

Creating a Quick Duvet Cover

A duvet is a fluffy comforter that's slipped into a duvet cover. You make the duvet cover in this section out of bedsheets, so your duvet is as easy to care for as the sheets on your bed.

Because duvet covers are much cheaper than the duvet itself, you can afford to have several color-coordinating covers — a wardrobe of room accessories to match your moods or the changing seasons.

To make this duvet cover, you need the duvet you intend to cover at hand so that you can measure it. You also need the following materials, in addition to your Sewing Survival Kit (see Chapter 1):

- ✓ Flat sheets to cover the front and the back of the duvet. Lay the duvet on a large table or the floor and measure its width and length. Take your duvet measurements to the store and buy two flat sheets slightly larger than the width and length measurements of the duvet. Duvets and flat sheets vary in size by manufacturer, so double-check that the sheets you buy are large enough to cover your duvet.

- ✓ Thread that matches the sheets.

- ✓ One standard-weight zipper that's half the width of the finished duvet cover.

To cut and make the duvet cover, follow this short list of steps.

1. **Lay one sheet on the table or floor, wrong side up. Center your duvet on the sheet so that the edges of the duvet are inside the hemmed edges of the sheet.**

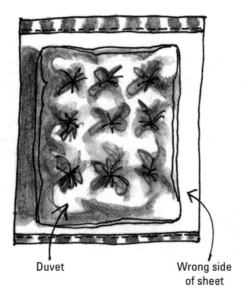

Duvet   Wrong side
                of sheet

2. **Cut out the sheet the same size as the duvet, cutting off the excess fabric from the bottom, sides, and top.**

    This piece is the duvet top.

If you need a little more length, rip out the hems at the top and bottom of each sheet and then press the hems flat before cutting.

3. **Using the first cut sheet as a pattern, cut the second sheet the same size as the first sheet.**

   This piece is the duvet back.

4. **Insert the zipper on one short end of the duvet cover by using a centered zipper application (read more about zipper application in Chapter 9).**

   After you stitch in the zipper, remove the basting stitches and unzip it. (You need the zipper unzipped to turn the duvet cover right side out.)

5. **Set your machine like this:**

   • **Stitch:** Straight

   • **Length:** 3 to 3.5 mm/8 to 9 spi

   • **Width:** 0 mm

   • **Foot:** All-purpose

6. **Starting and stopping at the ends of the zipper, pin the top and lining right sides together. Then sew the rest of the duvet together by using a ⅝-inch allowance.**

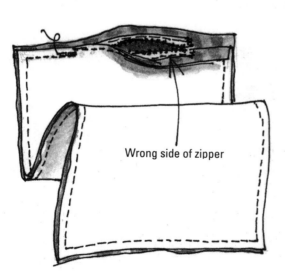

Wrong side of zipper

7. **Turn the duvet cover right side out through the zipper opening and then slide in your duvet.**

Chapter 15

Praiseworthy Pillows

. . . .

In This Chapter

▶ Starting with the right materials

▶ Covering a pillow form

▶ Sewing a flanged pillow sham

▶ Sprucing up a room with a fringed pillow

▶ Turning a favorite shirt into an unusual pillow

. . . .

*P*illows have the power to add life to any room of your house. You can choose fabric for pillows that coordinates with your curtains, wallpaper, or sofa, creating a unified look for a room. Find out how in this chapter.

Selecting Materials for Pillows

Pillow perfection starts with the right materials. Keep these tips in mind as you shop for materials for your pillows:

✔ **Fabrics:** Buy home decor fabrics that have a cotton fiber content of 50 percent or more. Also look for cotton/polyester blends because they are durable and easy to care for.

If you use a cotton novelty print, corduroy, denim, duck, chintz, twill, or poplin to make your pillow, preshrink the fabric before making the pillow cover.

The amount of fabric you need depends on the size of the pillow you want to cover and the kind of pillow cover you want to make. To decide how much fabric you need, see the yardage instructions I give in the various sections in this chapter.

✔ **Thread:** Of course, you need thread to match your pillow fabric. Any all-purpose thread will do the job!

✔ **Trims:** The trims you use must also be compatible with your fabric from a fiber and washability standpoint. When in doubt, show your fabric and trim choices to a sales associate at your local fabric store to confirm the care and use compatibility between your trims and fabrics.

✔ Many of the home decor fabrics recommend "Dry Clean Only" care. If you choose such a fabric, make the pillow covers removable and have them dry cleaned to preserve their "brand-new" appearance.

✔ **Stuffing:** The easiest stuffing to work with is premade pillow forms. These timesaving fabric-covered pillows are a given size, shape, and density and just pop into a decorative pillow cover. They're available in many sizes and a variety of price ranges.

Making a Pillow by Using a Pillow Form

In this section you see how easy it is to make a pillow cover from start to finish. This pillow cover features an "envelope" closure in the back that makes it very easy to sew and very easy to take care of — when you want to wash the pillow cover, you just "unseal" the envelope and remove the pillow.

Although styles and shapes may change, the basic construction steps are about the same from one pillow cover to the next. At the end of the chapter, you also get some practice by making three quick pillows to keep for yourself or give away.

The amount of fabric you need for this project depends on the size of the pillow you want to cover. Measure your pillow form (or take it with you to the store) and ask the sales associate in the fabric store to cut enough yardage so that you can create three fabric squares exactly the size of your pillow form. You may have a little bit of fabric left over.

Measuring your pillow form and cutting the pillow front

Measure your premade pillow form, from seam to seam across the middle, before cutting the fabric for the pillow cover. Even though the package may say the pillow form is a 16-inch square, dimensions do vary, even within the same manufacturer.

After you measure your pillow form, cut one square the same size as the pillow form. This piece becomes the front of your pillow. For example, if you have a 16-inch pillow form, you cut one square of fabric 16 by 16 inches.

Making an envelope closure on the pillow back

The easiest way to close a pillow is by slipping the pillow form in the pillow cover through an envelope opening in the back. Here's how to do it:

1. **Measure and cut the back pillow cover pieces.**

   You use two pieces of fabric to create this envelope closure. Cut two pieces of the pillow fabric that measure the width of the pillow by half the length of the pillow, plus 4 inches.

   For example, for a 16-inch square pillow, cut two pieces of fabric 16 by 12 inches.

2. **Finish one long edge of each back pillow piece.**

   (See Chapter 6 for more about finishing edges.)

3. **Fold, press, and topstitch a 2-inch hem on the long finished edge of each back pillow piece.**

   (See Chapter 5 for more information on topstitched hems.)

4. **Overlap the back pillow pieces 2 inches at the hemmed edges, so the back envelope piece measures the same as the front pillow piece. Pin the back pillow pieces together at the top and bottom of the hemmed opening.**

   For example, for a 16-inch pillow, when you overlap the back pillow pieces, the finished size of the back is 16 inches square.

Preparing the corners

Square pillows often end up with "bunny ears" or unintentionally exaggerated corners. Prevent this by following these steps:

1. **Pin the back and front pillow pieces together with the right sides together.**

2. **Using a fabric marker and ruler, draw a line across the corner at the intersection of the ½-inch seam allowance.**

Taper the lines out to the edge of the fabric to a point one-fourth the length of the side of the pillow. Do this for each corner.

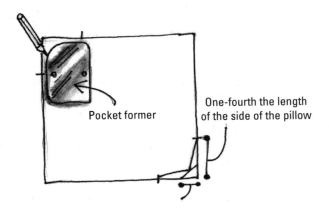

Pocket former

One-fourth the length
of the side of the pillow

Take your fabric marker or dressmaker's chalk and use the pocket former as your template. Simply trace around one of the sharper curved edges of the tool to taper and smooth out all eight pillow cover corners. Remember to trace the same curve on the pocket former for each pillow corner so that all the corners match.

Sewing the pillow cover together

Follow these steps to put the pillow cover together:

1. **If you want cord edge, fringe, a ruffle, or piping sewn on the edge of the pillow, sew it on the front pillow piece.**

   (Read more about cutting, sewing, and joining these trims in Chapter 12.)

2. **Place and pin the pillow top and envelope back, right sides together, so that the envelope hems overlap each other by about 2 inches.**

   Make sure that the raw edges of the front and back pillow pieces are even around the perimeter of the pillow cover.

3. **Set your sewing machine like this:**

   - **Stitch:** Straight
   - **Length:** 2.5 to 3 mm/10 to 12 spi
   - **Width:** 0 mm
   - **Foot:** All-purpose

4. **Using a ½-inch seam allowance, sew the top and back pillow pieces together around all four edges, backstitching at the ends of the seam. Press the seams flat and together before turning the pillow cover.**

5. **Turn the pillow cover right side out and pop in the pillow form.**

Now lay your head on your sensational new pillow and take a nap.

Creating a Flanged Pillow Sham

Your first question about this project may be "What's a flange?" It's a flat border around the perimeter of the pillow cover. What's a sham? It's a removable pillow cover. (See the bedroom setting in the color pages of this book; the flanged pillow shams are on the bed right up against the brass bed frame.)

Make shams not only for rectangular sleeping pillows but also for large, square European-style bed pillows and floor pillows. (In Chapter 14, you find out how to make a bed skirt and duvet cover. You can put the finishing touches on that bedroom by making matching flanged pillow shams.)

The amount of fabric you need for this project depends on the size of the pillow you want to cover. Measure your pillow form (or take it with you to the store) and ask the sales associate in the fabric store to cut enough yardage so that you can create three pieces of fabric exactly the size of your pillow form plus 18 inches. You may have a little bit of fabric left over.

To make a beautiful pillow sham with a 3-inch flange, follow these steps:

1. **Measure your pillow and add 6 inches to the length and the width measurements.**

   These measurements help you cut a piece of fabric the right size in the next step. For example, if you start with a pillow that's 26 by 20 inches, then your measurements are 32 by 26 inches.

2. **Cut one piece of fabric the length and width that you calculate in Step 1.**

3. **Measure half the pillow length and add 4 inches.**

   These are the measurements for the sham's back pieces. The back pieces form an envelope that lets you take the pillow out and put it back in again.

4. **Cut two back "envelope" pieces of the length that you calculate in Step 3 and the width that you calculate in Step 1.**

5. **Finish one short edge of each back envelope piece.**

   (See Chapter 6 to read more about finishing raw edges.)

6. **Fold, press, and topstitch a 2-inch hem on the finished edge of each back envelope piece.**

   (See Chapter 5 for more information on topstitched hems.)

7. **Overlap the back envelope pieces 2 inches at the hemmed edges, pinning the back envelope pieces together at the top and bottom of the hemmed opening.**

8. **Place and pin the top sham and envelope back, right sides together, so that the raw edges of the front and back sham pieces are even around the perimeter.**

9. **Using a ½-inch seam allowance and a straight stitch, sew the top and back sham pieces together, backstitching at the ends of the seam. Trim away the excess fabric at the corners (see Chapter 6 and read up on trimming seam allowances at the corners). Press the seams flat and together.**

   I wish I could tell you what settings to use on your machine, but you could be using any one of 100 fabrics. I suggest sewing a test strip of stitches on your fabric and adjusting your stitch length if necessary.

10. **Put the sham on the ironing board and press as much of the seam open as possible, pressing around all four sides of the sham.**

11. **Turn the sham right side out and press the seam flat and together along the seam line.**

12. **Using your fabric marker or dressmaker's chalk, mark a border around the sham, marking 3 inches in from the seamed edge.**

    This marks the stitching line of the flange.

13. **Stitch around the sham, sewing on the markings made in Step 12, 3 inches in from the finished edge.**

Instead of machine-stitching the flange, thread a large tapestry needle with yarn and sew several rows of running stitches around the flange starting 3 inches from the finished edge (see Chapter 5 for the how-to's on working the hand running stitch).

Sewing a Fringed Envelope Pillow

Make this really easy pillow to match your Bravo Bear (one of the projects in Chapter 19). You can also make it to coordinate with your bedroom decor, using a companion fabric and a sensational decorator trim called bullion fringe that I discuss in Chapter 12. After making this easy pillow, you may amaze even yourself with your newfound creativity and sewing skills.

To make this project, you need the following materials in addition to your Sewing Survival Kit.

- ✔ 1 18-inch pillow form
- ✔ ½ yard of 48-or-54-inch-wide home decor fabric
- ✔ Thread that matches the fabric
- ✔ 1 yard bullion fringe to coordinate with the fabric

Follow these steps to create the pillow:

1. **Cut the fabric 18 by 46 inches.**

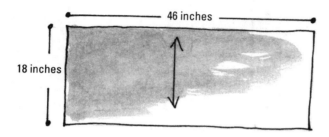

2. **Finish the short ends of the pillow cover.**

   (See Chapter 6 for more information on edge finishing.)

3. **Press and stitch a ½-inch hem on both short ends of the fabric.**

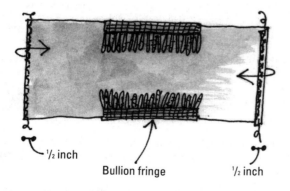

4. **Cut the bullion fringe in half and place it on the pillow cover.**

   (See information in Chapter 12 on how to safely cut the fringe so that it doesn't ravel unexpectedly.)

Place the trim on the right side of the fabric, centering it on the sides of the fabric strip so that the lip edge of the fringe is even with the raw edges.

5. **Fold the short ends toward the center, right sides together, so that the pillow cover measures 18 inches square.**

   The short ends overlap each other about 4 ½ inches and sandwich the bullion fringe in the seam line.

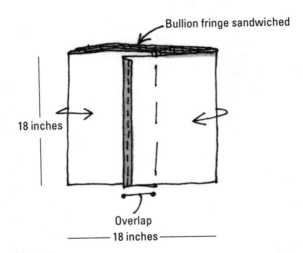

6. **Using a straight stitch and a 3 to 4 mm/6 to 9 spi stitch width, sew a ½-inch seam on both sides of the pillow cover, backstitching at both ends of each seam. Press the seams flat and together.**

7. **Turn the pillow right side out and pop the pillow form into the cover through the opening in the back.**

To make the pillow shown in the color pages, add the optional flap by following these instructions:

1. **Add a flap to your pillow by cutting out one triangle each from a coordinate fabric and lining so that one edge of the triangle is the width of the pillow.**

2. **Using a ½-inch seam allowance, sew cord-edge trim to the right side of two short sides of the coordinate triangle (see Chapter 12 for more on sewing on cord-edge trim).**

3. **Sew the lining to the triangle, right sides together, so that the trim is sandwiched between the coordinate fabric and lining.**

4. **Trim out the bulk from the point (see Chapter 6 for trimming out the bulk at the corners). Turn the flag right side out and press. Finish the raw edges (see Chapter 6 for more on finishing raw edges).**

5. **Hand-stitch the flap to the edge of the pillow by using a running stitch (see Chapter 5 for more on hand stitches), as shown in the color photo.**

Making a Pillow Out of Your Favorite Old Shirt

When my son grew out of his favorite flannel cowboy shirt, it was still good enough for someone to wear, but I couldn't bring myself to give it away. I was leafing through a mail-order catalog and saw clever pillow covers made from sweatshirts, sweaters, and blouses, so I thought, "Why not," and made a pillow like the one you see in the color pages of this book. This is a great way of preserving the little kid in all of us, or turning that "lucky shirt" into something really treasured by the recipient when you present it as a gift.

Although you can cut off the sleeves and shirttails to square up the shirt to fit the pillow cover, I keep them intact, turn them inside the shirt, and stuff them at the back of the pillow. The sleeves can make wonderful hiding places for action figures, toy cars, special rocks, and the remote control.

To make this project, you need the following materials in addition to your Sewing Survival Kit (see Chapter 1):

- 1 flannel shirt, cotton blouse, or team jersey
- 1 pillow form (fold the shirt into a square until it looks the way you want it to show in the final pillow, measure it, and then buy a pillow form that measures the closest to that size)
- Thread that matches the fabric

Follow these steps to make the pillow:

1. **Button up the front of the shirt.**

   If the shirt is not a button-up style, then skip to Step 4.

2. **Set your machine like this:**

   - **Stitch:** Straight
   - **Length:** 3 mm/9 spi
   - **Width:** 0 mm
   - **Foot:** All-purpose

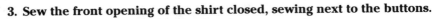

3. **Sew the front opening of the shirt closed, sewing next to the buttons.**

   If there's already a row of topstitching, just sew over it.

    If the foot keeps running into the buttons, if possible, de-center the needle to the far right or far left position. This way, just a skinny part of the foot rides next to and not over the buttons.

4. **Turn the sleeves inside out, pushing them back through the armholes, up to the shoulder seams. Pin them to the back of the shirt, out of the way.**

5. **Pop in the fabric-covered pillow through the open, shirttail end.**

   Snug the pillow up to the neck and into the shoulders.

6. **Pin the shirttail shut, pinning next to the bottom of the pillow from side seam to side seam.**

   This is the stitching line for the bottom of the pillow cover.

7. **Using a fabric marker or dressmaker's chalk, mark the stitching line on both the front and the back of the shirt. Remove the pins and the pillow form.**

8. **Turn the shirt inside out, placing right sides together and matching the marks made in Step 7. Pin the shirt together at the shirttail, pinning perpendicular to the marks and from side seam to side seam.**

9. **Sew the shirttail closed, pulling out the pins as you get to them. Backstitch at the beginning and end of the seam.**

    Depending on how much of a shirttail there is, you may want to trim it off, leaving about a ⅝-inch seam allowance.

10. **Turn the shirt right side out and pop in the pillow from the neckline end. Smooth the sleeves to the back of the pillow.**

    You're done!

Chapter 16

What to Do with Your Windows

"Save money. Make your own window treatments." This message might make a great bumper sticker for people who are transitioning to a new apartment or home or who are updating the abode they currently live in. This chapter tells you how to work with windows, and it tells you how to make some window treatments that are easy on the eyes — and the pocketbook!

The Wide World of Window Treatments

When it comes to dressing up your windows, you can choose from an almost countless number of treatments. The most common and easiest to make are the designs I cover in this book (some of which are shown in Figure 16-1 and in the color section of this book).

Use the following treatments, some of which are shown in the middle row of windows in Figure 16-1, for shorter, narrower windows:

✔ **Curtains:** A short treatment that stops at the window sill or just below.

✔ **Double cafe curtains:** Hang on rings that you string onto a rod.

✔ **Sheer panel curtains:** Have a stitched casing at the top and are slipped over a flat curtain rod.

Use the following treatments (see the two bottom windows in Figure 16-1) for longer, wider windows:

- **Drapes or draperies:** A long treatment that stops at the floor or "puddles" onto the floor.

- **Pinch-pleated draw draperies:** Hang on a traverse rod that draws over a flat rod.

- **Full-length triple pinch pleat draw draperies:** Hang on a two-way traverse rod.

- **Shirred draperies:** Shirred to a continental rod and are tied back to the window frame.

- **Sheer panel draperies:** Have a stitched casing at the top and are slipped over a flat curtain rod.

Use the following ideas alone or together with curtains or draperies for just about any window:

- **Cornice:** A rigid box covered with fabric and padded with a soft batting or contoured foam. (The top row of windows in Figure 16-1 shows various types of cornices.) Use a cornice alone over the top of a window or over draperies or vertical blinds mounted on a traverse rod (see the next section for information on the different rod types).

- **Poufs and rosettes:** Short lengths of fabric, pulled into a loop along the length of a drapery scarf, that fan out, creating soft, roselike poufs at the corners of the window.

- **Puddles:** Puddling means that the drapery fabric measures 12 to 20 inches longer than from the top of the rod to the floor. The hem edge is shirred in with a rubber band or cord then spreads out or "puddles" onto the floor.

- **Scarf or swag:** A soft, usually sheer fabric that drapes over the top of swag holders at each corner of the window (find several types of swag holders where drapery hardware is sold).

- **Tie-backs:** Made of fabric or drapery cord and tassels, tie-backs hold a drape open at the side of a window.

- **Window topper:** Any treatment mounted at the top of the window — from a cornice to a short skirt shirred onto a rod.

Figure 16-1:
Common
window
treatments.

The Rod's Connected to the Return: The Anatomy of a Window

Before making a window treatment, you need to know the basic language of windows and window treatments (shown in Figure 16-2):

- ✔ **The window width:** The distance measured across the window. Outside window width measures from one outside edge of the *trim mold* to the other outside edge of the trim mold. Inside window width measures from one side of the window to the other, inside the *window frame*.

✔ **The window length:** The distance measured from the top to the bottom of the window. Outside window length is measured from the outside edge of the *trim mold* to the bottom of the *apron*. Inside length is the distance from the top of the *window frame* to the *sill*.

✔ **Rod:** Holds the drapery or curtain in place over the window.

✔ **Overlap:** The amount the drapery overlaps in the center on a two-way draw traverse rod.

✔ **Return:** Where the rod or cornice turns the corner and "returns" to the wall. Depending on the depth of the return, you may have enough room for another rod to fit behind it, allowing you to layer your drapes.

✔ **Window sill:** This piece of trim extends from the window, usually at the bottom of the window.

✔ **Trim mold:** The wood that's nailed around the window to trim or finish the opening.

✔ **Apron:** A piece of wood that attaches under the sill. If a sill isn't present, the apron looks like a continuation of the trim mold.

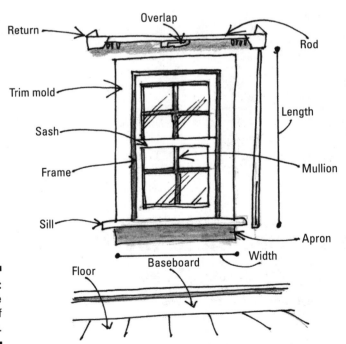

Figure 16-2:
The anatomy of a window.

Rods come in a variety of shapes and sizes (shown in Figure 16-3). The type of rod you use depends on what sort of window treatment you want to make:

✔ **Flat rods:** Used to hold shirred drapery panels by threading the rod through the casing at the top of the panels. A cornice, valance, or other window topper that goes over a curtain, shirred to a flat rod to finish the treatment.

✔ **Cafe rods:** Mounted either inside or outside the window frame; work well for straight, shirred, or pleated curtains.

✔ **Tension rods:** Best for lightweight curtains because they have a spring-type mechanism inside that tensions the rod between two walls or inside the window frame. (You use tension rods in the shirred and bloused shower topper that I show you how to make in the section of the same name, later in this chapter.)

✔ **Traverse rods:** Hold draperies that open and close either in a one-way direction (opening from one end) or in a two-way pattern (opening from the center) with the use of a drapery cord.

✔ **Continental rods:** Are available in wider 2-inch to 4-inch *drops* (the distance the rod drops down from the top of the window). You use continental rods for shirred panels like those described in "Simple Shirred Curtains and Draperies to Fit Any Window," later in this chapter.

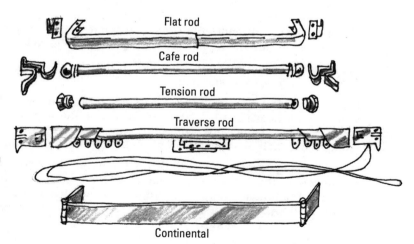

Figure 16-3:
Common drapery rods.

Flat rod

Cafe rod

Tension rod

Traverse rod

Continental

Measuring the Finished Width and Length

After you select the curtain or drapery style you want to use for your window and determine the sort of rod you need to use, measure your windows to determine the finished width and length of the treatment. Here's what you need to determine the finished length of specific treatments:

- **Curtains and drapes:** Measure from the top of the rod to the desired length — to the sill, apron, or floor.
- **Shower curtain:** Measure from the top of the rod to the floor.

And now for the finished width:

- **Curtains and drapes:** Measure the rod from end to end plus returns (the short ends of the rod that stick out from and "return" to wall).
- **Shower curtain:** Measure the rod width from end to end.

Keep these guidelines in mind for accurate measurements:

- **Install the curtain rod first.** When you take your measurements, you're able to measure accurately the finished width and length. Rods can attach to the window frame, the sides of the window frame (called an inside mount), at the sides of the window frame or trim mold (called an outside mount), on the wall above the frame, or at the ceiling.

- **Use a metal measuring tape.** Cloth measuring tapes may stretch or sag, causing inaccurate measurements.

- **If you're making window treatments for several windows, take measurements for each individual window.** Even in the same house where the windows look the same size, window measurements may vary enough that each treatment must be made to fit each individual window.

- **When making curtains for a window without an apron (see "The Rod's Connected to the Return: The Anatomy of a Window," earlier in this chapter), the finished length should be at least 4 inches below the window sill or below the bottom of the frame.** This way, your curtain is in proportion to the window.

Determining the Cut Fabric Length

After you know the finished length you need for your window treatment (see the previous section), you need to calculate the *cut length* of the fabric. You determine the cut length of the curtain or drape by taking the finished length and adding the following:

✔ The casing.

✔ The heading.

✔ The doubled lower-hem allowance. I tell you more about each of these measurements in the next few sections.

When you begin making window treatments, choose fabric that is either one color or a very small design. Treatments become much more difficult to work with when you have to contend with a large-pattern design.

The casing and heading

A casing and heading are at the top of a curtain or drape. A *casing* is a fabric tunnel that you thread onto a rod to hold up the curtain or drape. A *heading* is extra fabric above the casing that looks like a little ruffle after you thread the casing onto the rod. Although a casing is necessary for some curtains and drapes (that's how the curtain attaches to the rod), a heading can be decorative rather than functional.

Follow these easy steps to determine how much to add to the finished length of your curtain or drape to account for the casing and heading:

1. **Using your tape measure, measure the diameter of the curtain rod. Take that measurement and add another inch. Then add that number to the finished length of the curtain or drape.**

   This extra inch accounts for a ½-inch seam allowance, and you also have plenty of extra room for the rod to slide smoothly through the casing.

2. **Decide how long you want the heading and double that length. Then add that number to the finished length of the curtain or drape.**

   For example, if you want a 2-inch heading, add another 4 inches to the length of the fabric you need to cut.

Poufs, rosettes, puddles, and tie-backs

For each pouf, rosette, or puddle, remember to add an additional 20 inches to the cut length so that the fabric drapes properly. For example, if a drape has two poufs and two puddles, add an additional 80 inches to the cut length (20 inches × 4 = 80 inches).

Tie-backs don't require as much extra length as poufs and puddles. To figure out how much extra length you need for a tie-back, drape the tape measure on the rod and tie it back with as much slack as you like. Note the extra length and then add it to the cut length measurement of each drapery panel.

Doubled lower hems

Lower hems on curtains and drapes are doubled over and then stitched. These doubled lower hems add weight to the panels, which helps the fabric to hang straight and even.

The depth of the hem is determined by the fabric weight:

- **Sheer and lightweight fabrics:** Use a double-fold hem of 6 inches. Add 12 inches to the cut length.

- **Medium-weight fabric:** Use a 4-inch double fold hem by adding 8 inches to the cut length.

- **Heavy-weight fabric:** Use a 2-inch double fold hem by adding 4 inches to the cut length.

Determining the Cut Fabric Width

To determine the cut curtain or drapery width, you need to take the following into account:

- The fullness
- The width of the fabric
- The number of fabric panels needed for a particular treatment
- Seam allowances
- Double side hems

I tell you more about each of these factors in the next few sections.

Fabric fullness

When making your own window treatments, use these guidelines to determine how much fabric to buy:

- ✔ When using sheer and lightweight fabrics, use 2½ to 3 times the rod width (including the returns) for the finished width of the fabric panel.

- ✔ When using mid-weight fabrics, use 2 to 2½ times the rod width (including the returns) for the finished width of the fabric panel.

- ✔ When using heavy fabrics, use twice the rod width (including the returns) for the finished width of the fabric panel.

Panels and fabric width

When you're making curtains, drapes, slipcovers, dust ruffles, and other home decor projects that require a lot of fabric, pattern instructions tell you to cut so many *panels* for a particular project. Panels are nothing more than a length of fabric used at the widest width.

Home decor fabrics, which run from about 48 to 72 inches wide, are typically wider than fabrics used to make clothing. So they work better than the 36- to 45-inch fashion fabrics to cover large areas.

Most treatments use more than one fabric width, or panel, so that you have enough fabric spanning across the window for pulling up the gathers, pleats, and shirring. For example, in a set of sheer panel drapes, you may see three separate panels shirred onto a rod, and each finished panel may be made from two cut panels. (See the previous section to determine how much fullness you need for a particular window and fabric weight.)

Seam allowances

Seam allowances for home decor projects are usually ½ inch. For easy pattern matching, home decor fabrics have match points or color bars printed in the selvages, and if the fabric is printed, the print usually starts ½ inch in from the selvage. So, when you're deciding how wide to make each fabric panel, remember to add 1 inch *per panel* for the seam allowances (½ inch + ½ inch = 1 inch).

Double side hems

You sew side hems on both sides of a curtain or drape. Like lower hems, side hems are doubled so that the fabric hangs straight and even on the edges:

- ✔ For treatments using only one panel (like a shower curtain), add 4 inches for a 1-inch double hem on each side.

- ✔ For treatments using two or more panels, add 4 inches to the *finished width* of the treatment for a 1-inch double hem on each side.

Constructing a Window Cornice

Want to make quick and easy changes to your window treatments? The cleverest home decor product I've found, called the Quick-Change Window Cornice (by Bon Coeur Window Systems), gives you the tools to do just that. The best part is that the Quick Change Cornices look like expensive custom treatments for a fraction of the custom price. Just look at the color pages to find your favorite. So become a "quick-change artist" and give any room a new, custom look in an evening or less.

To make this window cornice, you need the following materials in addition to your Sewing Survival Kit (which I tell you about in Chapter 1):

- ✔ One Quick-Change Cornice Window Kit (see the appendix)
- ✔ 1½ yards of home decor fabric to cover two average-sized cornices that fit a 44-inch window

Covering your cornice

The body of the cornice is actually polyurethane foam, which you cut to fit your window according to the manufacturer's instructions. After preparing the body of the cornice, follow these steps to cover it with your fabric:

1. **Cut a piece of your fabric in the following dimensions:**

   - **Length:** 24 inches
   - **Width:** The width of the cornice (from the end of the left return to the end of the right return) plus 7 inches

2. **Lay the fabric wrong side up on a table or the floor and place the cornice on the fabric, foam side down. Position the cornice so that you have a 3¼-inch border at the top and both sides.**

3. **Using a credit card, tuck the fabric behind the top edge of the backing board, tucking from the center out.**

4. **Turn the cornice face up. Begin tucking the fabric into the top horizontal groove, smoothing the fabric from the center out.**

5. **Tuck the second, third, and fourth tuck grooves, keeping the fabric loose and straight ahead of the groove that you're tucking.**

   This way, the fabric tucks easily in the grooves as you're working toward the bottom edge

   You can tuck the fabric into one groove, all the grooves, some of the grooves, or none of them. This cornice offers options for almost any decorating taste.

6. **Tuck the fabric at the bottom edge behind the backing board (you may need to trim the excess fabric to 3¼ inches for a smooth finish).**

7. **Fold the fabric at the return ends as if you were wrapping a gift, tucking the fabric under the backing board.**

To finish, hang the cornice over the window by following the manufacturer's instructions.

Adding a "flag" to the cornice

I call this a flag because it reminds me of one (see the color photo). The flag hangs on the cornice after it's covered and is anchored only at the top so that you can easily change the flag and create a new look for your window treatment whenever the mood strikes you. To make the flag, you need your Sewing Survival Kit (which I tell you about in Chapter 1), plus the following:

✔ 1 yard of home decor fabric to make one flag that coordinates with the cornice fabric

✔ Thread that matches the fabric

✔ T-pins (look like a letter "T" and are available in the home decor department of fabric or craft stores)

✔ 1 tassel (see Chapter 12 for more information on tassels)

Here's how you create your flag:

1. **Cut two triangular-shaped pieces of fabrics in the following dimensions:**

   • **Base of the triangle:** The width of the cornice from return to return.

   • **Cut the yard of fabric in half from selvage to selvage:** Each panel measures approximately 54 to 60 inches wide by 18 inches deep. Fold one panel in half the short way to mark the center of the strip. Using dressmaker's chalk and a yardstick, draw a line from the center fold diagonally up to one corner to shape the short sides of the triangle. Cut out the triangle, cutting on the chalk mark and through both layers. Unfold the strip. Voilà, a triangle.

   For a different look, you can make the triangles less than the full cornice width, or you can make several smaller triangles to span the width of the cornice from return to return.

2. **Place and pin the triangle pieces so that the short edges are right sides together. Sandwich the tassel at the bottom point, pinning it in between the two triangle fabric pieces. Leave the long side (the base of the triangle) open.**

3. **Set your machine like this:**

   • **Stitch:** Straight

   • **Length:** 3 mm/9 spi

   • **Width:** 0 mm

   • **Foot:** All-purpose

4. **Using a ½-inch seam allowance, sew the two short sides together, catching both sides of the tassel cord in the seam by rounding the stitching line at the point of the triangle.**

5. **Trim away the excess seam allowance at the point and press the seam open (review the information in Chapter 6 on trimming away the fabric bulk at a corner).**

6. **Turn the flag right side out, pressing the edges flat and together.**

7. **Tuck the top of the flag under the cornice backing board, securing it between the backing board and the foam.**

   If the fabric is heavy, you may want to secure the flag with T-pins.

To achieve a different look, check out the cornice variations in the color pages. Tuck the flag or your favorite team pennant into one of the other tuck grooves on the face of the cornice. For a country look, add another layer of fabric shirred in the center of the cornice.

Creating a country French cornice

When I started working with this Quick-Change Cornice product, my imagination took over. The tuck grooves are deep enough to hold an extra piece of fabric and two lengths of cord-edge trim — and without sewing! Cover the basic cornice as described in the previous section and then just follow these easy steps for the added embellishment used on the great-looking cornice you see in the color section.

To make this cornice, you need the following materials in addition to your Sewing Survival Kit (see Chapter 1):

- ½ yard of home decor fabric to coordinate with the base cornice fabric
- 2 lengths of cord-edge trim the width of the cornice plus 7 inches in a color to coordinate with the fabric
- T-pins (look like a letter "T" and are available in the home decor department of fabric or craft stores)

Follow these steps to create the cornice:

1. **Cut the coordinate fabric in half so that you have two strips that are the width of the fabric by 9 inches long.**

2. **Lay the covered cornice face up on the table or floor.**

   Don't attach the brackets to the cornice until after the embellishments are in place.

3. **Take the first strip of coordinate fabric and poke the top edge into the top tuck groove and the bottom edge into the bottom tuck groove, centering the strip on the face of the cornice.**

   This anchors the strip.

4. **Using both hands, begin scrunching and gathering the long cut edges of the fabric strip, tucking the long edges into the tuck grooves from the center out to one end of the cornice over the returns.**

   The fabric has a three-dimensional shirred look to it.

5. **Take the second strip of coordinate fabric and repeat Steps 3 and 4, scrunching and gathering from the center out to the other end of the cornice.**

6. **Take one length of cord-edge trim and tuck it in the top tuck groove. Take the second length of cord-edge trim and tuck it in the bottom tuck groove.**

Sewing the Easiest Shower Curtain Ever

I know what you're thinking . . . "A shower curtain doesn't go on a window — at least not on any window in my house." In my mind, though, the word "curtain" makes this a perfect warm-up project for making other types of curtains and drapes found in this chapter. You take the same width and length measurements as you do when making a curtain for a window, and you use the same types of fabrics.

Handmade shower curtains look better and cost less than ready-mades, and you can easily create color flow from a bedroom to a nearby bathroom simply by matching or coordinating your fabric choices. Shower curtains aren't lined either, so they're a snap to make.

Shower curtains range in finished sizes from 60 to 80 inches wide by about 70 to 80 inches long. The shower curtain you make in this section is likely to fit most shower and bathtub stalls. You may need to adjust the hem length slightly to fit your stall.

To make this shower curtain, you need your Sewing Survival Kit (which I tell you about in Chapter 1), plus the following items:

✔ 1 square of fabric: One of the simplest fabrics to use is a full-sized unfitted bedsheet; it comes with a ready-made hem! You can also use 2¼ yards of any 60- to 72-inch home decor fabric.

✔ Thread that matches the fabric.

✔ To hang up the curtain: one plastic shower curtain liner, one package of 12 shower curtain rings, and one shower curtain rod.

Follow these steps to create your custom shower curtain:

1. **Cut your fabric.**

   If you're using a sheet with a ready-made hem, cut the sheet 76 inches wide. Measuring from the wide decorative hem-end of the sheet, cut the sheet 74 inches long. This hem is placed at the bottom of the shower curtain. Now you can skip ahead to Step 5.

   If you're using 60- to 72-inch-wide home decor fabric, cut it 80 inches long by the width of the fabric.

2. **Make the doubled lower hem.**

   Fold up, pin, and press a 3-inch hem toward the wrong side of the fabric on the lower edge of the shower curtain. Fold up, pin, and press the hem up another 3 inches so that the hem is doubled.

3. **Set your machine like this:**

   - **Stitch:** Straight
   - **Length:** 3 mm/9 spi
   - **Width:** 0 mm
   - **Foot:** All-purpose

4. **Sewing with the wrong side up, topstitch along the top edge of the hem, backstitching at each end. (See Chapter 5 for more information on topstitching and backstitching.)**

5. **Make the doubled side hems.**

   Fold, pin, and press a 1-inch hem toward the wrong side of the fabric on one side of the shower curtain. Fold, pin, and press the side hem another inch so that the hem is doubled. Repeat for the other side hem of the shower curtain.

6. **Sewing with the wrong side up, topstitch along the hem edge, back-stitching at each end. Repeat for the other side hem.**

7. **Make the heading.**

   At the top of the curtain, fold and press the raw edge under ½ inch. Fold over, press the top to the wrong side another 1½ inches, and pin the heading in place.

8. **Topstitch the heading as you did for the lower and side hems.**

9. **Using your fabric marker or dressmaker's chalk and seam gauge, mark the buttonhole placement, centering one buttonhole on each side hem and then space out the remaining 10 buttonholes across the curtain heading.**

10. **Set your machine like this:**

    - **Stitch:** Zigzag or buttonhole (see your Operating Manual)
    - **Length:** 0.5 mm/fine or 60 spi
    - **Width:** For buttonholes
    - **Foot:** Buttonhole

11. **Make ½- to ¾-inch buttonholes by following the instructions in your machine's Operating Manual. (See Chapter 9 for the how-to's on buttonholes.)**

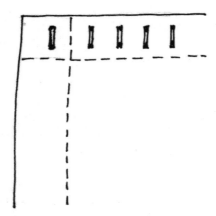

12. **Press the shower curtain and hang it up with the plastic liner and rings.**

Making a Shirred and Bloused Topper

A shirred and bloused topper makes a great finishing touch for a shower curtain (see the color pages). The topper fits from wall to wall over the tub. To create this topper, you need your Sewing Survival Kit (which I tell you about in Chapter 1), plus the following items:

- ✔ 1⅓ yards of home decor fabric
- ✔ Thread that matches the fabric
- ✔ 2 thin tension rods for hanging up the topper

Just follow these steps to make the topper:

1. **Cut the fabric in half from selvage to selvage so that you have two pieces that measure the width of the fabric by 24 inches.**

2. **Set your machine like this:**
   - **Stitch:** Straight
   - **Length:** 3 mm/9 spi
   - **Width:** 0 mm
   - **Foot:** All-purpose

3. Seam the two fabric pieces together at one selvage so that you have a long, thin 24-inch-wide strip.

4. Fold over one short side of the strip, making a 1-inch hem. Pin, and press the selvage edge under, toward the wrong side of the fabric.

5. Sewing with the wrong side up, topstitch, guiding ¾ inch from the side hem edge and backstitching at each end. Repeat for the other short side hem of the topper strip.

6. Make a casing on both long edges of the fabric strip.

   These casings are what the rods slide through, creating this shower topper.

   At the top of the strip, fold and press the raw edge under ½ inch. Fold over and press the top of the strip to the wrong side another 1½ inches, and pin the casing in place. Topstitch the casing, sewing 1¼ inches from the folded edge at the top of the strip.

   Repeat to make the casing along the lower edge of the fabric strip.

7. Thread a tension rod into each casing, shirring the fabric onto the rods.

   Because the fabric is about twice the width of the rods, the fabric slides on and gathers to fit the rod, creating the fullness on the topper.

8. Pop the rods up between the walls over the bathtub so that the fabric has some slack between the rods, and slightly blouses over the bottom rod.

Simple Shirred Curtains and Draperies to Fit Any Window

Shirred curtain or drapery panels are made just like a shower curtain, but without the buttonholes. (See the previous section for more information on making a shower curtain.) The other difference is that rather than a flat curtain that's pulled across the width of the tub, a shirred curtain is at least twice as wide as the window and is shirred onto a rod into soft gathers.

To make this shirred curtain, you need your Sewing Survival Kit (which I tell you about in Chapter 1), plus the following items:

✔ Yardage of 60- to 72-inch home decor fabric (see "Determining how much fabric you need" in the next section to calculate the specific yardage)

✔ 1 pocket rod to fit a 1½-inch wide casing

✔ Thread that matches the fabric

Determining how much fabric you need

Follow these steps to determine how much fabric to buy for your curtain:

1. **Measure the width of your window.**

2. **Multiply the window width by 2.**

   For example, if your window is 58 inches wide, then 58 inches × 2 = 116 inches.

3. **Add 4 inches for double side hems.**

4. **Divide the number you get in Step 3 by the width of your fabric.**

   This is the number of panels of fabric you need.

5. **Measure the length of the window from the top of the rod to the floor.**

6. **Add 9 inches for the double hems and the casing.**

7. **Multiply the number you get in Step 6 by the number of panels you need (see Step 4). This is the length of fabric you need in inches.**

8. **Divide the number you get in Step 2 by 36. This is the length of fabric you need in yards.**

Putting the curtain together

Follow these steps to create a wonderfully shirred curtain:

1. **Seam the fabric panels together at the selvages. (See Chapter 6 for more information on seaming.)**

2. **Follow Steps 2 through 6 of the instructions given in the "Sewing the Easiest Shower Curtain Ever" section, earlier in this chapter.**

3. **At the top of the curtain, fold, pin, and press the raw edge under ½ inch.**

4. **To form a 1½-inch casing for the curtain rod, fold down, pin, and press the top of the curtain 1¾ inches across the width of the curtain.**

5. **Sewing at the bottom of the turned edge, topstitch the bottom of the casing, backstitching at both ends.**

6. **Thread the rod into each casing, shirring the fabric onto the rod.**

   Because the fabric is about twice the width of the rods, the fabric slides on and gathers to fit the rod, creating the fullness on the topper.

Making a Shirred and Flipped Panel Window Treatment

A shirred and flipped window treatment (see the color section in this book) works well on windows of just about every size because both the rod and the treatment adjust to fit each window. (You can easily create a coordinated look in a bedroom by choosing fabric for this window treatment that matches the duvet cover; see Chapter 14 for more information on creating a duvet cover.)

One yard each of two companion or coordinating fabrics makes two reversible panels that shirr to about a 24-inch width. For each 24-inch increment in window width, buy another yard each of your companion fabrics.

You need the tools in your Sewing Survival kit, plus the following, to make this window treatment:

- 1 yard each of coordinating fabrics to make 2 panels
- Thread that matches the fabric
- 1 continental rod with a 3-inch drop

Follow these steps to shirr and flip to your heart's content:

1. **Cut each yard into two panels measuring half the width of the fabric and 36 inches long.**

   For example, if you start with a yard of 54-inch-wide fabric, the resulting panel is 27 inches wide by 36 inches long.

2. **Pin two cut companion fabric panels, right sides together. This way, the finished panel is reversible, and both fabrics show when the panel is threaded onto the rod.**

3. **Set your machine like this:**

   - **Stitch:** Straight
   - **Length:** 3 mm/9 spi
   - **Width:** 0 mm
   - **Foot:** All-purpose

4. **Starting in the center of one long side, sew around the four sides of the panel, using a ½-inch seam allowance. Leave a 6-inch opening on one side of the panel so that you can turn it right side out. To prevent the stitches from ripping out, backstitch at both ends of this opening.**

5. Turn the reversible panel right side out by reaching through the opening, grabbing the fabric, and pulling it through the opening.

6. Using the blunt end of your scissors, push the corners out and then press the seams flat and together around all four edges.

   This step takes a little bit of time, but the results are well worth it.

7. Edgestitch the opening closed, backstitching at the beginning and the end. (See Chapter 6 for more information on edgestitching.)

8. On one of the short ends, run a row of stitching parallel to and 2 to 3 inches from the edge, backstitching at the beginning and end. Repeat for the other short end of the panel.

9. Sew another row of stitching 3½ inches below and parallel to the line of stitches you sewed in Step 8, backstitching at both ends. Repeat for the other short end of the reversible panel.

10. Using your seam ripper, carefully remove the stitches at the edge of the panel between the rows of heading and casing stitches that are 3½ inches apart. This is the casing pocket that the rod fits through. Repeat for the other end of the pocket casing.

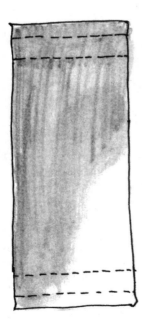

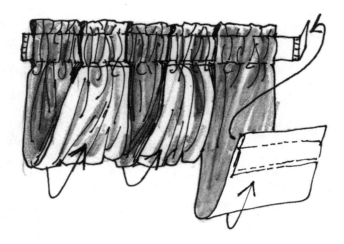

11. Put the panel on the rod through both pocket casings.

Thread the top of the panel onto the rod through the casing and then flip the bottom of the panel up and thread the bottom casing onto the rod. Shirr it to one end, pushing the casing around the return. Repeat for as many panels as you make to fit across your window.

Part V
Alterations and Quick Fixes

The 5th Wave   By Rich Tennant

"The black spots? That's where he has holes in his pants. And he has the nerve to call his felt tip marker a 'sewing' tool."

In this part . . .

You know the old expression "Stuff happens." It happens to your clothes, too. Holes show up in your favorite shirt, and one day, you might try on your lucky pair of pants and discover that they just don't fit like they used to.

When bad stuff happens to your favorite garments, don't throw them away. Read the chapters in this part and give them a second lease on life.

And hey — some of the projects I show you in this part might actually make your garments look better than they did before the bad stuff!

Chapter 17

If It's Too Long, Too Short, Too Tight, or Too Loose

In This Chapter

▶ Lengthening pants and skirts

▶ Shortening things that drag on the floor

▶ Giving yourself some breathing room

▶ Making swimming in your clothes a thing of the past

▶ Creating two fabulous belts to help your clothes fit better

I have the toughest time getting rid of clothes that are still wearable, but I'm also tired of shoving things back into the closet that don't fit right. If you're like me, then you'll like the creative shortcuts I give you for better-fitting clothes in this chapter.

When It's Too Short

 You can reduce shrinkage of most fabrics by not "cooking" washable fabrics in the dryer on the hottest, cotton setting. Fabrics also last longer and don't shrink as much when you dry them on your dryer's perma-press setting.

But what if that information is water under the bridge and your garment is too short to be respectable? Read on to find out what to do.

Cutting off pant legs and rehemming them

You can turn some short pants into shorts by simply cutting off the legs and rehemming them (see Chapter 7 for more information on hemming). Look at the width of the pant legs and imagine them cut off at the length where you normally wear your shorts. Are the pant legs in question full enough for you to cut off? Are they narrow like you like them? The answer really lies in your personal preference. As for the fabrics, stick with woven fabrics such as denim, corduroy, gabardine, or poplin.

Some pant legs just look funny when they're made into shorts, so why not cut them off to a cropped, pedal-pusher length instead (see Figure 17-1) and then rehem them? See the hemming how-to's in Chapter 7.

Figure 17-1:
Pants too long or too short? Make them shorter and rehem them.

Letting down and facing the hem

If your pants or skirt is too short, then the hem allowance may be generous enough to let down and increase the length. Look at the hem allowance on the garment:

- ✔ Is the hem double turned and then stitched?
- ✔ Is the hem allowance a generous 2 inches or more?

If so, you may be able to "let down" the hem and face it. Rip out the hemming stitching and see how much available length you get. With the following technique, you'll get all the length that you can.

If you get enough room from the hem to make a difference, go ahead and buy some *hem facing tape,* which is available in a rainbow of colors from your local fabric store. Try finding a color as close to your fabric as possible. Even though the tape doesn't show, you still want the tape to be as close a color match as possible. Hem facing tapes are also all the same weight because they're made of the same fabric — only the colors are different.

Follow these steps to lengthen your hem by facing it:

1. **Using a steam iron, press over the hem to press out the old hem crease.**

   Sometimes the hem crease won't disappear entirely. You can usually press out a tough crease by sprinkling a half-and-half mixture of white vinegar and water on a press cloth (see Chapter 1), laying the dampened press cloth over the hem crease, and then pressing until the press cloth is dry.

2. **Unfold one edge of the prefolded hem facing and pin the facing edge even to the hem edge, placing the right sides together.**

   The hem facing tape should end up lying on top of the garment fabric.

   Leave the hem tape in one long piece. You cut it off later, after you seam the ends.

3. **Set your machine like this:**

   - **Stitch:** Straight
   - **Length:** Appropriate for the fabric (try some test stitches to find the one that most closely matches the stitch length of the other seamlines)
   - **Width:** 0 mm
   - **Foot:** All-purpose

4. **Sewing with the tape side up, stitch the tape around the hem where the tape is pinned to the edge so that the stitches fall in the fold of the hem tape.**

5. **Stop sewing on the tape about 1 inch from where you started.**

   Don't cut the tape yet. This way, you don't end up cutting the tape off too short. Remove your work and head to the ironing board.

6. **Fold up the faced hem (as you would turn up a normal hem), and using a steam iron, gently press over the hem facing.**

   Press from the wrong side of the garment, using a little steam. This step helps shape the hem facing so that it becomes part of the garment.

7. **Cut off the extra length of hem facing tape, leaving enough length on the short ends for a seam allowance.**

8. **Sew together the short ends of the hem facing tape, press the seam open, and then finish stitching the hem facing to the hem edge.**

9. **Rehem the garment by using one of the hemming methods I describe in Chapter 7.**

Adding a ruffle

My next-door neighbor's child had a favorite jumper. Her torso size hadn't changed, but her legs grew and the jumper was too short. Her mom and I took her to the fabric store where she picked out ¼ yard of a printed fabric she liked, along with a package of yellow rickrack trim. We added a ruffle to lengthen the jumper (see the color section). Between the ruffle and the hem edge, we added the rickrack for color. Rickrack was also added to the side of the front pocket, under the seamline, and at the back of the suspenders. This little jumper looked better after the re-do than it did before, and the little girl got another several months' wear from it.

Review the information in Chapter 8 for the how-to's on gathering — the easy way to make a ruffle.

When It's Too Long

Of course, with pants that are too long you can simply rehem them to the appropriate length (see Chapter 7). But when it comes to sleeves, the following solutions are my favorite ways of solving the too-long problem.

Moving the button over on the sleeve's cuff

A fast way to take care of a too-long sleeve is to move the button over so that the cuff is snug around the wrist. Review the information in Chapter 5 on the ways to sew on a button.

Taking up a tuck in the sleeve

For sleeves that are 1 to 2 inches too long, decide how much the sleeve needs shortening, and then take up the slack by stitching tucks (see Chapter 8 for more information on tucks). Figure 17-2 shows you these horizontal tucks.

To make the tucks, just follow these steps:

1. Decide how much excess fabric you want to put up into the tucks.

Remember that a tuck takes up double its width. For example, a ¼-inch tuck takes up ½ inch of fabric. For heavier fabrics, tucks take up slightly more than double because the turn of the cloth folds over a wider distance.

2. Set your machine like this:

- **Stitch:** Straight
- **Length:** 3 mm/9 spi
- **Width:** 0 mm
- **Foot:** All-purpose

3. Sew the tuck in place, guiding the folded edge along the line on the needle plate.

Guiding the tucks this way helps keep your sewing straight so that the stitches are an even distance from the fold.

4. Repeat the process on both sleeves for as many tucks as you need.

Removing the cuff, shortening the sleeve, and restitching

My husband's arms are shorter than a man's size Large, casual long-sleeved shirt, so I'm constantly shortening shirt sleeves for him. I offered to take up some tucks in his sleeves, as explained in the previous section, but he just wasn't interested.

Thankfully, shortening the sleeves at the cuff is very easy when you follow these steps:

1. **Using a seam ripper, rip off the cuff, carefully cutting the stitches that hold it onto the sleeve.**

   Leave the cuff with the seam allowance pressed toward the inside.

   As a frame of reference, remove one cuff at a time. This way, if you need to check how the shirt manufacturer stitched the cuff on in the first place, you can check the one that hasn't been removed.

2. **Pin the cuff back onto the sleeve so that the finished edge of the cuff is in the desired position.**

   Try on the shirt and bend your arm to be sure that the cuff is positioned in exactly the right spot.

3. **Use your fabric marker and mark along the top of the cuff, establishing the new cuff position.**

4. **Unpin the cuff and cut away the excess sleeve fabric, leaving a ½-inch seam allowance at the bottom of the sleeve, below the cuff placement marks made in Step 3.**

5. **The bottom of the sleeve has fullness that is pleated to fit into the cuff, so repleat the bottom of the sleeve by using the original pleats as a guide.**

   You have to make deeper pleats so that the fullness of the shorter sleeve fits the cuff. After shortening one cuff, repeat Steps 1 through 5 for the other cuff. Double-check that the other sleeve is pleated like the first.

6. **Pin on the cuff so that the seamline is even with the marks you made in Step 3.**

7. **Set your machine like this:**
   - **Stitch:** Straight
   - **Length:** 2.5 to 3 mm/10 to 12 spi
   - **Width:** 0 mm
   - **Foot:** All-purpose

8. **Edgestitch the cuff to the sleeve, guiding the stitches so that they sew over the original stitching line (see Chapter 6 for more on edgestitching). Repeat Steps 6 through 8 for the other sleeve.**

When Pants Don't Fit Well in the Rise

Pants can be too long or too short in the *rise* (the part of the pants between the legs). Before giving them away, try one of these tried-and-true "comfort" alterations.

Lowering the crotch curve

Do you feel like your pants ride up on you every time you move?

Follow these steps to give you a little more room:

1. **Turn the pants inside out, putting one leg into the other.**

   The pants end up looking like they only have one leg.

2. **Slip the pants over the narrow end of the ironing board so that the** *crotch point* **(where all the seams come together) is centered on the board.**

3. **Using a fabric marker, make a mark ¼ inch lower, toward the leg, than the original seamline at the seam intersection.**

4. **Measure 3 to 4 inches up toward the waistband from either side of the new crotch point and draw a new crotch curve by using your fabric marker or dressmaker's chalk, as shown.**

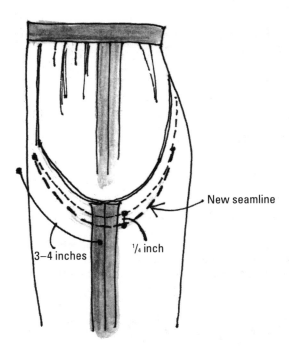

New seamline

3–4 inches   ¼ inch

5. **With a basting-length stitch, restitch the crotch curve on the new line you made in Step 4 (see Chapter 5 for the particulars on machine basting).**

6. **Trim the seam allowance to ⅝ inch and try on your altered pants.**

   If the pants are comfortable, go on to the next step. If you need to lower the crotch another ¼ inch, repeat Steps 1 through 6 until you get a comfortable fit.

7. **Restitch the new crotch curve by using a 2.5 to 3 mm/10 to 12 spi straight stitch.**

If your machine has a stitch called the straight stretch stitch or triple straight stitch that takes two stitches forward and one stitch backward, use it here in the crotch curve. Remember, though, that this stitch is almost impossible to rip out when you make a mistake, so be sure that the pants fit before using it.

Taking in the in-seam

Do you feel like the crotch of your pants hangs just above your knees? Then fix the too-long rise by shortening the crotch depth at the in-seam (the inner leg seam). The following technique shortens the crotch depth while leaving the circumference of the leg intact, which is important when fitting the pants around your thighs.

Just follow these steps:

1. **Turn your pants inside out, holding the crotch seam as shown so that you can pin and take in the inner leg seams.**

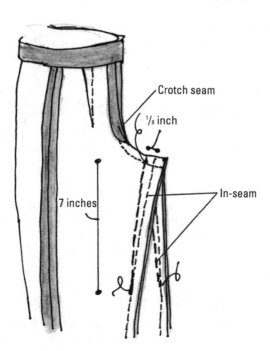

Crotch seam

¹/₈ inch

In-seam

7 inches

This seam is called the *in-seam* because it's on the inside of the leg.

2. **Starting 7 inches down from the crotch seam on one side of the in-seam, sew a gradual row of basting stitches tapering out and up ⅛ inch from the original seamline (see Chapter 5 for more on machine basting).**

3. **Repeat for the other side of the in-seam, sewing from the crotch intersection, tapering the seamline to 7 inches below.**

4. **Put on your altered pants and sit in them.**

   Are they more comfortable? If not, repeat Steps 1 through 3, taking out another ⅛ inch with each row of basting until the pants are comfortable. If so, go on to the next step.

5. **Restitch over the basting stitches by using a 2.5 to 3 mm/10 to 12 spi stitch length and then trim the excess seam allowance to within ¼ inch of the new seamline.**

   If you have several rows of basting stitches, don't forget to remove them.

When It's Too Tight

The tidbits in this section can help you get just a little bit more wear out of your clothes, without forcing you to lose weight or start that exercise program.

Moving the buttons over on a jacket

An easy way to get more room in a jacket is to simply move the buttons over. Moving a button over even ½ inch makes a big difference in the way a garment looks and feels.

Turn a double-breasted jacket into a single-breasted jacket by eliminating one row of buttons and moving the other row so that the buttons and buttonholes are centered (See Figure 17-2). You get the much needed room, and the single-breasted styling is usually more slimming. (See Chapter 5 for more information on sewing buttons by hand and machine.)

Ripping out waistline pleats

I have this jelly roll that "blooms" out below my waistline. I can hide the roll pretty well until I wear pants or a skirt with stitched-down waist pleats (see Chapter 8 for more information on waist pleats). The pleats ride up to my waistline and the waistband usually ends up around my rib cage.

Figure 17-2:
Turning a double-breasted jacket into a single-breasted jacket.

I remedy the situation with my seam ripper by ripping out the stitches that hold the pleats closed. I then can relax, breath easier, and my clothes fit better, too.

When It's Too Loose

Here are a collection of tips and tricks that I use when things are too loose.

Taking in the waistline

This technique works well when taking in casual men's or ladies' slacks that have a front zipper and that don't have the traditional center back seam in the waistband.

Just follow these steps:

1. **Pinch in and pin the necessary amount out of the center back and through the waistband.**

2. **Sew a wider seam allowance at the center back through the waistband so that you're taking in the waistline by the amount you determined in Step 1.**

3. **Starting at the crotch and sewing up through the waistband, edgestitch (see Chapter 6 for more information) next to the seamline, which causes the seam allowance to lay down smoothly and to one side.**

Add elastic inside the waistband

This method is the fastest way to take in a waistband without altering the side seams. You add the elastic to the back-inside of the waistband from side seam to side seam. The waistband not only fits better, it's also really comfortable. *Note:* This technique works for skirts and pants that have a center front zipper.

Just follow these steps:

1. **Rip out the stitches holding the back inside waistband to the garment.**

   Start from 1 inch in front of the side seam on one side to 1 inch in front of the side seam on the other side of the waistband. Leave the stitches intact that hold the front part of the waistband to the waistline of the pants or skirt.

2. **Using elastic that is slightly narrower than the finished width of the waistband, cut a length of elastic that, when stretched 1 inch or so, fits comfortably across the back of the waistline, from one side seam to the other.**

3. **On the inside of the waistband, stitch across the elastic, securing the short ends of the elastic to the back, inside the waistband, so that the ends of the elastic are even with the side seams.**

4. **Pin the back of the waistband to the inside of the garment at the waistline seam and then stitch it back together by hand or by machine, following the original stitches you removed from the waistband.**

   If the waistband wasn't topstitched, then stitch it back together by stitching-in-the-ditch. (See Chapter 5 for more on this wonderful technique.)

Making a Belt That Anyone Can Wear

Adding a belt to your outfit can help take up extra room in a shirt, blouse, or dress, creating a truly quick and easy fix to a fitting issue!

Want a belt that shrinks or grows with you? Then quickly craft this very comfortable belt of a woven cotton belting, which you can see in the color section of this book.

In addition to your Sewing Survival Kit, you need the following materials:

- ✔ 41 inches of 2-inch Guatemalan belting (see the appendix for sources)
- ✔ 2 8-inch loop-side Velcro strips
- ✔ 2 2-inch hook-side Velcro strips
- ✔ Thread to match the belting
- ✔ Fabric glue, such as Cool Gloo or FABRI-TAC
- ✔ FrayCheck

To create the belt, follow these steps:

1. **Dribble a bead of FrayCheck on each end of the belting to prevent the ends from fraying.**

   Set the belting aside to dry for about 5 minutes.

2. **Fold, press, and pin small tucks at each end, on the outside of the belting.**

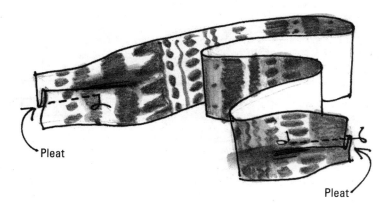

Pleat

Pleat

3. **Set your machine like this:**
   - **Stitch:** Straight
   - **Length:** 3.5 mm/7 spi
   - **Width:** 0 mm
   - **Foot:** All-purpose

4. **Pin the two short strips of hook-side Velcro over the tucks on the outside of the belting and sew the Velcro in place around all four sides.**

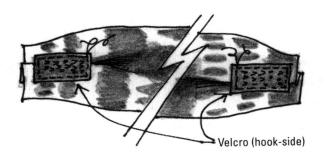

Velcro (hook-side)

5. **Centering the two, long, loop-side strips of Velcro, place and glue them 4 inches in from each end and on the inside (or the other side) of the belting strip.**

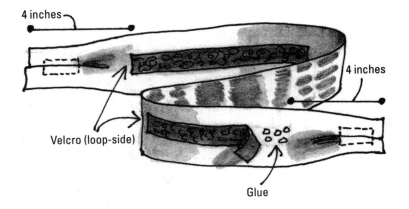

4 inches

4 inches

Velcro (loop-side)

Glue

You glue the long strips so that stitches won't show through to the outside of the belt.

6. **Let the glue dry as directed by the manufacturer (usually at least 24 hours for a permanent bond) before using the belt.**

Creating a Stitch-Sampler Belt

The inspiration for this project came from a beaded belt I saw in a mail-order catalog. Instead of beads, I used different-colored decorative stitches. Instead of satin, I used denim, which makes the belt great for everyday wear. I love these colorful stitches on denim, and I know that you will, too.

To make this project, you need your Sewing Survival Kit (see Chapter 1) plus the following materials:

- ✔ Threads in red, yellow, orange, kelly green, light blue, royal blue, and light purple
- ✔ Black bobbin embroidery or darning thread
- ✔ Tear-away stabilizer (available through your local fabric store or sewing machine dealer)
- ✔ #90/14 HS Stretch sewing machine needles (see the Cheat Sheet in the front of this book)
- ✔ ¼ yard denim
- ✔ 4 inches of Velcro (both hook and loop sides)

Follow these steps to make this great-looking belt (which you can see in the color section of this book):

1. **Preshrink the denim (see Chapter 2 for the scoop on preshrinking).**

2. **Cut the denim into two long strips, 4 inches by the width of the fabric.**

   You embroider one strip and use the other as the backing.

3. **Fold one denim strip in half the short way, gently finger-pressing the strip to mark the center.**

   Using your dressmaker's chalk, draw a line 10½ inches to the right of the center fold. Repeat by drawing a line 10½ inches to the left of the center fold.

   Because you don't want to decorate the belt any more than necessary, the decorative stitching is centered on the strip between the chalk marks.

4. **Using your dressmaker's chalk, mark off lines and gentle curves, as shown in the color section of this book.**

   These lines are stitched with yellow thread and designate where the decorative stitches are grouped.

5. **Set your machine like this:**

   - **Stitch:** Zigzag

   - **Length:** 0.5 to 0.8 mm/fine or 60 spi

   - **Width:** 2.5 to 3 mm

   - **Foot:** Embroidery

   - **Needle:** #90/14 HS Stretch

   - **Thread:** Needle — yellow rayon embroidery; bobbin — black darning

6. **On a denim scrap, place a piece of tear-away stabilizer under a single layer of denim and stitch out several decorative stitches. (Tear-away stablilizer looks like interfacing and is placed under the fabric to prevent the stitches from puckering. It is removed after sewing is complete.)**

   Experiment with the stitch lengths, the stitch widths, making notes of which stitches and stitch settings you like best. Practice pivoting a decorative stitch at a corner — some stitches are easier to pivot than others.

7. **After you complete the trial run of your stitches, decide which ones to use in your project and make a list of the colors you want to use and the various stitch widths and lengths you've selected.**

   A sample list for a project like the belt in the color pages may look like the following:

   - **Yellow:** Zigzag stitch set on a 0.5 length and 2.5-mm width

   - **Orange:** Cross stitch (see your Operating Manual for settings)

   - **Light blue:** Zigzag stitch set on a 0.5 length and 2.5-mm width

   - **Light purple:** Lattice (see your Operating Manual for settings)

   - **Royal blue:** Zigzag stitch set on a 0.5 length and 2.5-mm width

   - **Kelly green:** Zigzag stitch set on a 0.5 length and 2.5-mm width

   - **Red:** Zigzag stitch set on a 0.5 length and 5-mm width

8. **Sew the decorative stitches, using one color at a time until all the decorative stitching is complete.**

   Starting with the light colors, work your way stitch-by-stitch to the darker colors. Sew one row next to the first, sewing a presser-foot width away.

9. **Remove the tear-away stabilizer by pulling it off the back of the fabric, tearing it away from the stitches.**

10. Shape the belt.

Because the decoration is centered on the denim strip, you want the stitched section to be the focal point. However, denim is stiff; if the belt were the same width all the way around, you wouldn't be able to breathe or sit comfortably. So, cut the belt into shape, narrowing the ends to 2 inches and so that there are 3 to 4 inches of overlap on both ends.

11. Cut the denim backing, cutting it the same size and shape as the shaped belt.

12. Set your machine like this:

- **Stitch:** Zigzag
- **Length:** 4 mm/6 spi
- **Width:** 3 to 4 mm
- **Foot:** Embroidery
- **Needle:** #90/14 HS Stretch
- **Thread:** Needle — red rayon embroidery; bobbin — red rayon embroidery

13. Pin and baste the belt and backing together (see Chapter 5 for more on basting).

Baste these two pieces together with a wide zigzag stitch, guiding the fabric under the foot so that the needle catches the fabric on the left and swings off the raw edge at the right.

When sewing long lengths together, as in this belt project, the fabric shifts easily. Prevent shifting by pinning the fabric together first. Grasp the fabric edge in front and behind the needle, take a few stitches, stop, and then reposition your hands. Remember to pull out the pins before sewing over them. Don't help the fabric along — just guide it straight. If you pull on the fabric as you sew, the fabric may stretch out of shape.

14. Set your machine like this:

- **Stitch:** Zigzag
- **Length:** 0.5 to 0.8 mm/fine or 60 spi
- **Width:** 5 to 6 mm
- **Foot:** Embroidery
- **Needle:** #90/14 HS Stretch
- **Thread:** Needle — red rayon embroidery; bobbin — red rayon embroidery

15. **Starting at one end, and with the embroidered side up, stitch over the basting stitches, sewing around the outside edge of the belt.**

    Guide the fabric under the foot so that the needle catches the fabric on the left and swings off the edge on the right. Pull the threads to the back of the belt and tie them off, putting a drop of FrayCheck on the knot.

16. **Set your machine like this:**

    - **Stitch:** Straight
    - **Length:** 3 to 3.5 mm/7 to 9 spi
    - **Width:** 0 mm
    - **Foot:** Embroidery
    - **Needle:** #90/14 HS Stretch
    - **Thread:** Needle and bobbin — all-purpose sewing in blue to match the denim

17. **Stitch the hook side of the Velcro on the underlap by sewing around all four sides; stitch the loop side of the Velcro on the overlap by sewing around all four sides.**

Chapter 18

Making Repairs on the Run

· ·

In This Chapter

▶ Repairing a seam

▶ Patching things up the easy way

▶ Mending tears

▶ Replacing zippers

· ·

*I*n this chapter, I share some great shortcuts for painlessly cutting the repair pile down to size in a hurry. If you're looking for information on the most basic (and common) repair of all — sewing on a new button — then turn to Chapter 5.

Assembling Your Quick-Fix Tools

To be prepared for any sewing emergency, always keep your Sewing Survival Kit fully stocked. (See Chapter 1 for a list of all the tools your kit should include.) You use essentially the same tools for repairs and fixes as you use for regular sewing.

Repairing a Seam

If you have a simple ripped seam, where the stitches in a seam are ripped or broken, your repair job is an easy one. (If the fabric has deteriorated, pulled away from the stitches, or is totally obliterated at or around the seam allowance, see the next section, "Patching Holes and Rips," for more information.) Just follow these steps to repair a simple ripped seam:

1. **Turn the item inside out so that you can easily access the seam allowances.**

2. **Remove the broken and ripped stitches.**

3. **Pin the seam allowances back together into their original position to hold them in place as you sew.**

4. **Start sewing over the intact seam stitching ½ inch from the split and keep stitching ½ inch over the intact seam on the other side of the split. Backstitch at the beginning and end of the repairing stitches.**

Patching Holes and Rips

My brother is a commercial salmon fisherman in Alaska. Before he was married, I would visit and he'd have a pile of mending waiting for me. Talk about holes! He had so many holes in his shirt sleeves that he cut the sleeves off long-sleeved shirts to avoid getting holes in the elbows!

Even if you don't give your clothes quite the workout that a fisherman does, you may find holes in your clothes and other sewing projects from time to time.

The amazing Quick-Fixes Sew-Vival Kit

Even though I have an entire room devoted to sewing stuff, I keep a wonderful little clothing care and repair kit, called the Quick-Fixes Sew-Vival Kit, in my nightstand where I know I can always find it in a hurry. The Quick-Fixes Sew-Vival Kit contains the following helpful tools and accessories, among others (See the appendix for sourcing information):

✔ **Ribbon thread braid:** A colorful braid made of 363 separate stands of thread in 28 different colors. Simply pull out the thread in the color you need from the braid — no tangling — and it's good-quality thread, too.

✔ **Self-threading hand needles:** These needles have a notch in the top, which means no more threading those pesky little needle eyes. (See Chapter 5 for more information on self-threading needles).

✔ **Emergency shirt buttons:** These no-sew replacement shirt buttons poke through the fabric in an instant.

✔ **Safety pins and straight pins:** You can't have enough of these for little emergencies.

✔ **Collar extender:** This tool for the "mature" neck extends the collar band another ¾ inch.

✔ **Res-Q-Tape:** This sticky double-faced tape helps hold things in place. (See Chapter 7 for more on using Res-Q-Tape.)

✔ **Folding scissors:** Use them for cutting threads and Res-Q-Tape.

✔ **Snag repair tool:** Helps in pulling snags through to the wrong side of the fabric easily and invisibly.

Patching holes with decorative patches

I find the following technique to be the very best way to patch the holes. You can use this method to patch over holes in elbows, knees, or anywhere that holes find their way into a piece of fabric.

Patches can be large or small and arranged artfully to cover other messes besides holes, as shown on the shirts in the color pages. Small pocket patches arranged in a collage (see Chapter 11 for more on sewing pockets) cover an indelible ink stain. A larger, diamond-shaped patch covers tea stains on the front of the poet blouse, shown in the color section of this book.

Just follow these steps:

1. **Find a fabric similar to the garment you're patching.**

   If possible, steal fabric by stitching a pocket shut that doesn't get a lot of use, and cutting away the fabric from underneath. If you can't find a matching fabric, find one that's close.

   I save worn-out jeans, so I have a plentiful supply of used denim for patching.

2. **Cut out a patch ½ to ¾ inch larger than the hole, all the way around. The patch can be any shape you like.**

   Before cutting the patch to size, inspect the fabric around the hole. You may decide that you need a bigger patch to cover any frays in the area.

   Iron-on patches are also available for patching and can be used to patch a hole. However, experience has taught me that, after a little washing and wearing, the adhesive quits, and you have a patch that's coming off. If you're using iron-on patches, also stitch them on.

3. **Pin the patch in place, centering it over the hole so that the right side of the patch fabric is up.**

   Because the patch is larger than the hole it's covering, pin around the edges, pinning through the patch and the garment underneath.

4. **Set your sewing machine like this:**

   - **Stitch:** Three-step zigzag
   - **Length:** 0.5 to 0.8 mm/fine setting or 60 spi
   - **Width:** 5 mm to the widest width
   - **Foot:** Embroidery
   - **Needle:** #90/14 HJ denim or jeans (for heavy fabrics); #80/12H Universal for everything else

5. **Place the garment and patch under the foot, right side up.**

   The patch should be under the foot so that the edge is slightly to the right of the needle.

6. **Start sewing so that, when the needle travels to the right, the last stitch formed is on the outside edge of the patch.**

   Remember to pull out the pins before sewing over them.

7. **If the patch is a circle, sew all the way around it. If the patch is a rectangle or square, sew to the corner and pivot.**

   Sew to the corner, stopping with the needle in the far right side of the stitch. Doing so positions the patch so that it's double-stitched and reinforced in the corner. Lift the foot, pivot 90 degrees, lower the foot, and sew the second side of the patch, again stopping with the needle in the far right side of the stitch and pivoting. Continue like this until the patch is sewn on. Pull the threads to the back of the fabric and tie them off. (See Chapter 6 for more information on tying off threads.)

Patching with appliqués

Sometimes you can get creative by making or purchasing a ready-made appliqué and using it as a patch in low-stress areas. Before doing that, though, consider where the appliqué falls on the garment and decide whether it makes sense to have it there. Appliqués aren't strong enough for patching knees, elbows, and other high-wear areas.

Sometimes you can disguise your appliqués and make them look like decorations. I've patched a hole with an appliqué and then placed another appliqué or two on the garment in other places so that the appliqués looked like they were on the garment all along.

Appliqués make short work of repairing holes. Just follow these steps to patch with an appliqué:

1. **Pin the appliqué over the hole so that it stays in place as you sew.**

   If the appliqué is too thick to pin through, glue it into place by using your fabric glue stick.

2. **Using thread that matches the appliqué, straight stitch at the appliqué inside the satin-stitched edge. (See Chapter 5 for more information on these two stitches.)**

3. **Pull the threads to the wrong side and tie them off.**

Mending Tears on Woven Fabric

The goal in mending a tear on woven fabric is to have the repair be flat and as invisible as possible. You accomplish this by using the three-step zigzag stitch and some lightweight fusible interfacing. (See Chapter 2 for more information on interfacing.)

If you're lucky enough to find a lightweight darning or embroidery thread through your local sewing machine dealer in the color that matches your garment, use it in the needle and on the bobbin. This finer weight of thread comes in a limited color range, so you may need to suffer through with regular, all-purpose thread. The finer thread is still very strong when sewn with the three-step zigzag stitch, and because it's lightweight, it creates a nearly invisible mend.

To mend tears on woven fabric, just follow these steps:

1. **Cut a ½-inch-wide strip of lightweight fusible interfacing the length of the tear plus 1 inch.**

   For example, if the tear is 5 inches long, the strip of interfacing would be ½ inch wide and 6 inches long.

2. **Trim off the loose threads from the tear.**

3. **Fuse the interfacing to the back of the tear, following the manufacturer's instructions.**

   Lay the repair on the ironing board. Push the raw edges of the tear together and place the interfacing over the tear and fuse it.

4. **Set your machine like this:**

   - **Stitch:** Three-step zigzag
   - **Length:** 0.5 to 0.8 mm/fine setting or 60 spi
   - **Width:** 5 to 7 mm
   - **Foot:** Embroidery

5. **Starting at one end ½ inch before the tear and with the right side of the fabric up, lower the foot, centering it over the tear.**

6. **Sew so that the stitches go back and forth over the tear.**

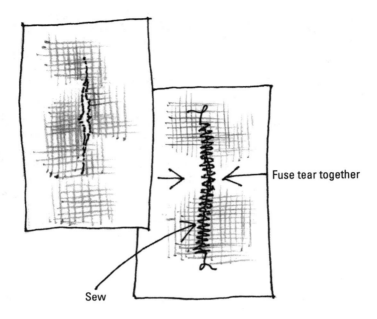

Fuse tear together

Sew

If the tear is wider than the stitch width, stop with the needle in the fabric, pivot 180 degrees, and stitch another row of mending stitches slightly over but next to the first.

7. **Pull the threads to the back and tie them off.**

Replacing Zippers (It's Easier Than You Think)

It really is. The reason is that the fabric is already shaped, pressed, and stitched with the original zipper, so it's all figured out for you. All you do is rip out the old zipper and then slip in and stitch the new one.

Replacing a fly-front zipper

I bet you have a pair of pants, jeans, shorts, or skirt in the repair pile badly in need of a zipper replacement. Just follow these instructions.

It's often much easier replacing a zipper that's longer than the opening. (It doesn't matter how much longer because it is eventually cut to fit.) No, you don't squeeze it in to make it fit. You can stitch in the longer zipper without having to maneuver the presser foot around the pull. Just unzip the zipper and cut off the excess length at the top to make the zipper fit the opening.

1. **Remove the old zipper by ripping out the topstitching and other stitching that attaches the zipper to the garment (see Chapter 5 for more on topstitching and see Chapter 6 for more on ripping).**

   Unzip and remove the old zipper by carefully ripping out the stitches with a sharp pair of embroidery scissors or a seam ripper.

   Take notes or make sketches of how the zipper was installed. They come in handy when you're putting everything back together.

   You will have to rip back the waistband just far enough to remove the old zipper.

2. **Mark the original topstitching line with tape.**

3. **Set your machine like this:**
   - **Stitch:** Straight
   - **Length:** 2.5 to 3 mm/10 to 12 spi
   - **Width:** 0 mm
   - **Foot:** Zipper

4. **Open the fly-front facing extension. With the right sides together, either pin or hand-baste the zipper so that the left edge of the zipper tape is even with the left edge of the facing extension.**

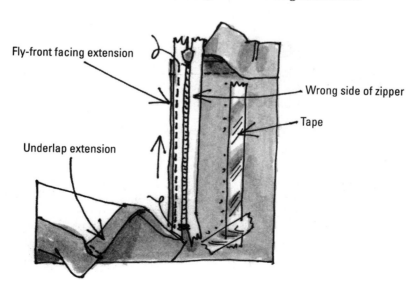

Fly-front facing extension

Wrong side of zipper

Tape

Underlap extension

5. Sewing from the bottom of the zipper tape, stitch up all the way along the left edge of the zipper tape.

6. Unzip the zipper. Pin the other side of the zipper so that the zipper tape is sandwiched between the underlap and the underlap extension and the fold is next to the zipper teeth.

7. Unzip the zipper and check that the zipper and the fly front are smooth. When everything is smooth, unzip the zipper again and stitch the other side of the zipper, sewing close to the teeth.

8. Set your machine like this:

   - **Stitch:** Straight
   - **Length:** 2.5 to 3 mm/10 to 12 spi
   - **Width:** 0 mm
   - **Foot:** All-purpose

9. Restitch the underlap side of the zipper to the waistband.

Underlap extension

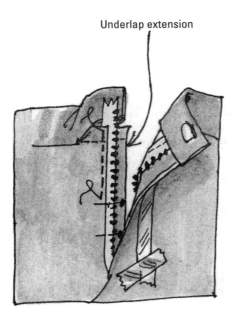

10. Unzip the zipper, cut off the excess zipper tape, tuck the underlap end of the zipper under the waistband, and restitch.

11. Guiding the needle next to the transparent tape, topstitch the fly front. Sew the top of the zipper opening to one side of the waistband. Restitch the other side of the waistband to the opening by stitching-in-the-ditch (see Chapter 5 for the how-to's of stitching-in-the-ditch).

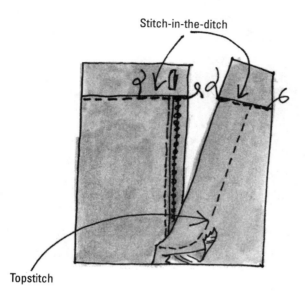

Stitch-in-the-ditch

Topstitch

Replacing a separating zipper

Use this easy procedure to replace an ailing zipper with one that can hold things together:

1. Buy a replacement zipper the same length as the zipper opening.

2. Rip out the stitches of the old zipper carefully, using sharp embroidery scissors or a seam ripper.

3. Separate the replacement zipper.

4. Open the lining so that it's flat.

5. Pin the first side of the zipper to the lining with the right sides together so that the zipper pull faces to the outside.

Lining

6. **Set your machine like this:**

   - **Stitch:** Straight
   - **Length:** 3 to 3.5 mm/10 to 12 spi
   - **Width:** 0 mm
   - **Foot:** Zipper

When repairing zippers in a leather, suede, or pigskin jacket, use a leather machine needle (available through your local sewing machine dealer) and set your stitch length so that the stitches land in the exact same holes as the original topstitching — otherwise the stitches perforate and tear the leather.

7. **Stitch the first side of the zipper, sewing through one layer of the lining.**

   Guide the foot so that you're sewing down the center of the zipper tape.

8. **Pin the jacket front opening over the first side of the zipper, pinning through all the fabric layers.**

9. **Topstitch over the original topstitching line.**

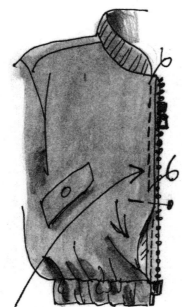

Stitch on original stitching line

10. **Sew the second side of the replacement zipper to the front jacket opening.**

    Sew on the second side of the zipper. Align the jacket lining, and pin and sew as explained in Steps 3 through 5.

Part VI
The Part of Tens

The 5th Wave   By Rich Tennant

"I'm not sure who put the tattoo memory card in my sewing machine, but that's why my pillows are embroidered in serpents coiled around a dagger."

In this part . . .

For your sewing pleasure, Chapter 19 of this book includes ten projects you can make in just hours (some of them less than that!). Any of the projects in this chapter will convince your friends and family that you have truly mastered your sewing machine.

I also include two chapters packed with hints and tips to help keep your sewing smooth.

Chapter 19

Ten Easy Projects

*F*abric touches almost everything in a person's daily life. Children cuddle up with pillows and soft toys and dress up in costumes for fun. People wear clothing to be comfortable, to stay warm, and to be fashionable. People also appreciate and admire handmade heirlooms.

So with all that's included in this world I call "sewing," I hope that you find a project or two in this chapter that you like. Preview these and many other projects found throughout the book (you can see pictures of them in the color section of this book) for inspiration. Then, when you finish your projects, wear them with pride, play in them, admire your work, and hand them down to your loved ones.

Sewing Fast with Place Mats

Want to amaze your friends and family with your creative talents? Then turn everyday place mats into a one-of-a-kind vest or jacket and take just about an hour to complete it. Finished sides and edges add to the overall garment design, while the back and front of the mats completely line the projects, making them reversible. Whether you're tall, short, thin, chunky, old, or young, this fashion accessory is a welcome and novel addition to any wardrobe.

As you prepare to make these place mat fashions, keep the following pointers in mind:

- ✔ **Choose all-cotton place mats:** I used rectangular mats measuring about 12 by 18 inches to make the vest and jacket you see in the color pages of this book, but you can make this project with oval-shaped mats, too.

- ✔ **Choose soft and pliable place mats:** If they're too stiff, you'll look like a scarecrow because you won't be able to put your arms down to your sides.

- ✔ **Pick mats with two good-looking sides:** Both the front and the back of the place mat will show in the finished project. Decide which side of the mat you want as the right side by holding it up to your chin and letting the "lapel" fold over at the center front (see Figure 19-1).

- ✔ **Preshrink cotton mats before putting your creation together:** Simply wash, dry, and press the mats the way you plan to take care of the finished project.

- ✔ **Use a zipper foot for fabric bound edges:** Stitching next to fabric bound edges of a place mat is easier when you use a zipper foot. The foot has a single, narrow toe and adjusts to either side of the needle for the most accurate stitching. For other types of mats, an all-purpose foot works just fine.

Figure 19-1:
Choosing the best-looking side of a place mat.

The place mat vest

This vest looks great with jeans or over a turtleneck or a summer dress. Besides making a great fashion accessory, you also see how to sew on buttons for further embellishment.

To make this project, you need the following materials in addition to your Sewing Survival Kit described in Chapter 1:

- ✔ 4 cotton place mats
- ✔ Thread to match the mats
- ✔ 2 buttons of a color, shape, and size that complements the place mats
- ✔ Pearl cotton or embroidery floss in a color that complements the colors in the mats
- ✔ 1 tapestry or large-eye hand needle

Follow these steps to make the place mat vest:

1. **On a table, turn two place mats vertically, overlapping and pinning them together ¼ inch at the top and 4 inches at the bottom.**

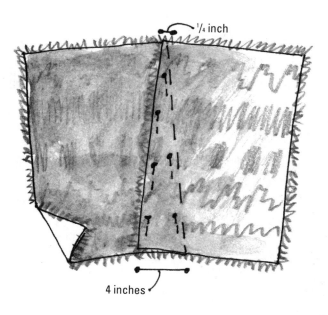

¼ inch

4 inches

Remember, the sides of the mats you want to show are facing out. This part is the center back and may be adjusted out or in, as needed, before you start sewing.

2. **Overlap and pin two more mats at the shoulders about ½ inch, stopping 5 to 6 inches from center front.**

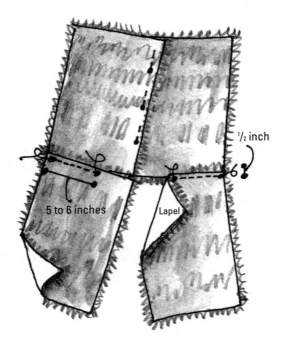

Doing so allows the mats to fall open at the neckline, creating lapels.

3. **Place the long sides of the mats together, pinning from the bottom up 6 to 7 inches.**

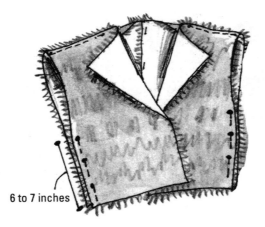

This step creates the side seams. The spaces left open should be large enough to comfortably fit your arms. Overlap the seams for mats with fabric-bound or hemmed edges. Place seams with wrong sides together for mats with fringed edges.

4. **Try on the vest and adjust it to fit.**

   If the vest is too big, overlap the mats at the center back a little more, and then pinch in and pin a tuck or pleat on both sides of the overlap until you like how the garment fits (see Chapter 8 for more information on tucks and pleats). If the vest is too small, narrow the overlap at the center back.

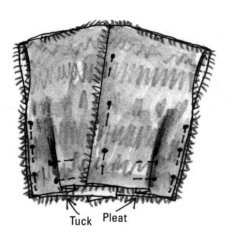

Tuck   Pleat

5. **Set your machine like this:**
   - **Stitch:** Straight
   - **Length:** 3 mm/9 spi
   - **Width:** 0 mm
   - **Foot:** All-purpose

6. **Unpin the side seams so that the vest is flat and pinned together only at the shoulder seams and center back overlap.**

   Doing so makes the actual sewing easier.

7. **Stitch the center back overlap and the overlap at both shoulders.**

   Sew each overlap by guiding a presser-foot-width away from the edge of the place mats. Backstitch at the beginning and end of each line of stitching.

8. **Re-pin the side seams together (refer to Step 3) and then double-check the fit by trying on the vest.**

   If the vest is too boxy, make larger side seams. If it's too skimpy, make smaller side seams.

9. **Stitch the side seams, backstitching at the top and bottom of each seam.**

10. **Turn back and gently press the lapels and armholes.**

11. **Using the tapestry or large-eye hand needle and the pearl cotton or embroidery floss as the thread, secure the armhole cuffs in place at the shoulder seam by sewing on a button, which holds the cuff in place.**

    See Chapter 5 for more information on sewing on buttons.

The place mat jacket

Simply add two more place mats to the place mat vest (see the preceding section) to create sleeves for this clever jacket.

To make this project, you need the following materials in addition to your Sewing Survival Kit, which I tell you about in Chapter 1:

- 6 cotton place mats (I used ones that already had the hand blanket stitching around the edges)
- Thread to match the mat
- (Optional) 3 buttons in a contrasting color
- (Optional) Pearl cotton or embroidery floss in a color that complements the place mats
- 1 tapestry hand needle

Follow these steps to make the place mat jacket:

1. **Follow Steps 1 to 7 for the place mat vest.**

2. **Open the vest flat, center the long sides of two more mats over each shoulder seam, and pin the two new mats to the jacket, overlapping the long sides ½ inch.**

   These two mats (I call them *sleeve mats*) create the sleeves.

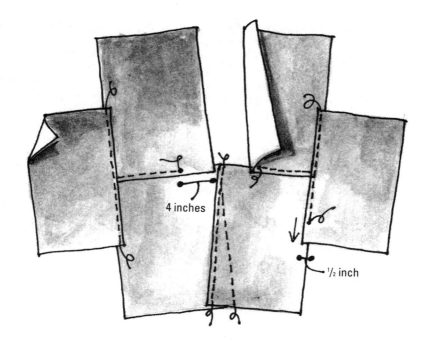

3. **Sew the sleeve mats onto the body of the jacket along the long edges, as shown in the preceding figure.**

4. **Place, pin, and sew the jacket side seams (right sides together and backstitching at both ends of the seam).**

5. **Place and pin the long, free edges of the sleeve mats, right sides together, to complete the sleeves.**

   Make sure to pin the underarm seams up to the edge of the mats that you're using for the sleeves.

6. **Sew the underarm seams the length of the sleeve mats, backstitching at both ends of each seam.**

7. **Place, pin, and sew the jacket side seams, right sides together, backstiching at both ends of each seam.**

   The jacket has an "air hole" where the sleeves and side seams come together under the arm.

8. **Turn back and gently press the lapels and cuffs.**

To create the embellished look of the jacket you see in the color pages of this book, you need to do a little hand stitching. Using a single strand of #8 pearl cotton or embroidery floss, decorate the lapels and the overlap at the center back with small, hand running stitches (see Chapter 5 for more information on hand running stitches). Then attach three large contrasting buttons to the lapels for a unique look.

Making Costumes for Dress-Up and Play

These next four projects are real crowd-pleasers for the little ones in your family and neighborhood. And kids love them even if they don't turn out just perfect. So cut your teeth by making these costumes. Then when you're ready to tackle something more challenging, you'll have a little more sewing experience and a lot more confidence.

The princess skirt

This tulle princess skirt makes a welcome addition to any dress-up box. Have your little princess wear it over leotard and tights, and she can also become a bride or the Good Witch of Oz.

To make this project, you need the following materials in addition to your Sewing Survival Kit, which I tell you about in Chapter 1:

- ✔ 3 yards of 72-inch-wide bridal tulle
- ✔ 3 yards of 1-inch satin ribbon
- ✔ Thread to match the fabric
- ✔ A large safety or bobby pin

Follow these steps to make the princess skirt:

1. **Open the tulle flat and refold it.**

    Fold the cut edges so that they meet in the center. Fold the tulle in half again, this time the long way so that you have four layers of tulle, with the long fold at the top. Press the long folded edge.

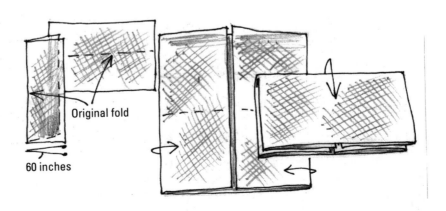

Original fold

60 inches

2. **Set your machine like this:**

   - **Stitch:** Straight
   - **Length:** 2 to 2.5 mm/10 to 12 spi
   - **Width:** 0 mm
   - **Foot:** All-purpose

3. **Edgestitch ⅛ inch from the top fold of the tulle, backstitching to secure the stitches.**

   See Chapter 6 for more information on edgestitching.

4. **Sew a second row of stitching 1¾ inch from the first, creating a casing for the ribbon to slide through.**

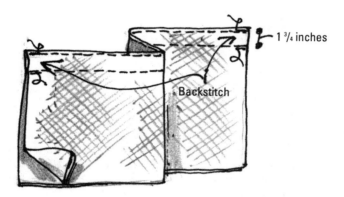

Backstitch · 1 ¾ inches

5. **Thread the ribbon through the casing.**

   To make the ribbon threading easier, attach a large safety pin to the end of the ribbon, or cut a slit in the end of the ribbon and slide the bobby pin into the slit. Pull the ribbon through the casing by working the safety pin or bobby pin down the length of the casing.

6. **Pin and stitch through the ribbon and casing at the center back so that the ribbon won't inadvertently slide out while you finish up the skirt (and when your little princess is paying with it).**

7. **Shirr up the tulle, sliding it down the ribbon until the waistline of the skirt is shirred into soft gathers and the skirt fits comfortably around the waist.**

8. **Pin and stitch through the ribbon and casing again, just to each side of the center back, backstitching to secure the stitches.**

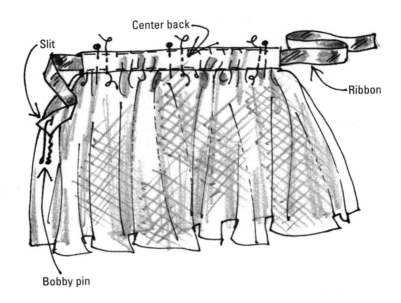

Center back

Slit

Ribbon

Bobby pin

The princess cape or overskirt

This project has an adjustable ribbon, so your princess can wear it over her shoulders as a cape or at the waistline as an overskirt with the tulle princess skirt (see the preceding section).

To make this project, you need the following materials in addition to your Sewing Survival Kit (see Chapter 1):

- ✔ 1 yard lace, approximately 36 to 45 inches wide
- ✔ 2½ yards of 1-inch satin ribbon
- ✔ Thread to match the fabric
- ✔ A large safety or bobby pin

Follow these steps to make the princess cape or overskirt:

1. **Cut two strips of lace, each 15 inches by the width of the lace from edge to edge.**

   You end up with two pieces of lace that are 15 inches by the width of the lace.

   Instead of cutting straight across the lace, find the lace's design and follow it, cutting the lace apart through the fine netting.

2. **Overlap two ends of the lace strips so that the design of the lace from the top layer matches the design of the lace from the bottom layer.**

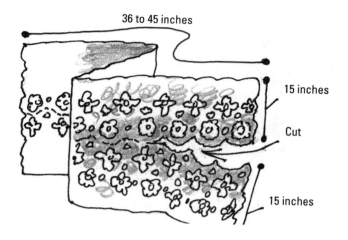

You can have as little as ¼-inch overlap. Pin the lace together.

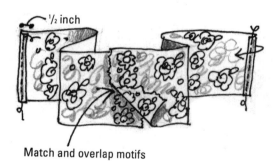

Match and overlap motifs

The wrong side of the top layer touches the right side of the bottom layer.

3. **Set your machine like this:**

   - **Stitch:** Zigzag
   - **Length:** 2 to 2.5 mm/10 to 12 spi
   - **Width:** 2 mm
   - **Foot:** All-purpose

4. **Sew the lace together over the boldest part of the lace design.**

   Pull threads to one side of the lace and tie them off (see Chapter 6 for more on tying off threads).

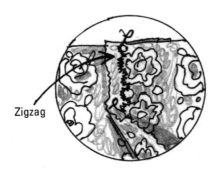

Zigzag

5. **Carefully trim away excess lace from both the top and bottom layers, up to the stitch.**

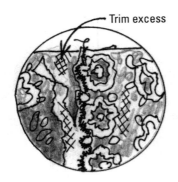

Trim excess

The seam should be almost invisible.

6. **Set your machine like this:**

   - **Stitch:** Straight
   - **Length:** 2 to 2.5 mm/10 to 12 spi
   - **Width:** 0 mm
   - **Foot:** All-purpose

7. **Press and stitch ½-inch hems on the two short sides of the lace.**

   See Chapter 7 for more information on hems.

8. **Fold down one edge of the lace 3 inches; press and edgestitch the folded-down edge.**

   See Chapter 6 for more information on edgestitching.

9. **Sew a second row of stitching 1¼ inches from the first, creating a casing for the ribbon to slide through.**

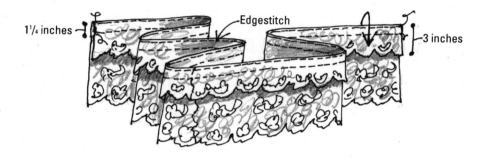

1¼ inches Edgestitch 3 inches

10. **Thread the ribbon through the casing.**

    See Step 5 in "The princess skirt" section, earlier in this chapter, for a tip on ribbon threading.

11. **Pin and stitch through the ribbon and casing at the center back so that the ribbon won't inadvertently slide out while you finish up the skirt (and while your little darling is playing in it).**

12. **Shirr up the lace, sliding it down the ribbon.**

    This cape is shirred into soft gathers so that it fits comfortably around either the shoulders or the waist.

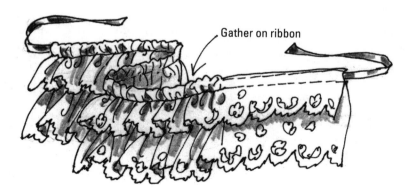

Gather on ribbon

13. Pin and stitch through the ribbon and casing again, just to each side of center back, backstitching to secure the stitches.

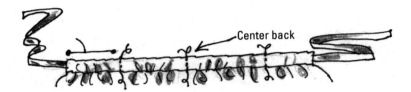

This step keeps the shirring cinched in and around most of the overskirt or cape, prevents the ribbon from coming out of the casing, and provides some growing room for your little princess.

The bride's veil

You can combine this veil with the princess skirt and overskirt to make the prettiest bride costume on the block.

To make this project, you need the following materials in addition to your Sewing Survival Kit, which I describe in Chapter 1:

- ⅔ yard lace, 36 to 45 inches wide
- 1 yard of 72-inch-wide bridal tulle
- Thread to match the fabric
- 1 silk floral stem to create the headpiece
- Wire cutters
- 2 small, clear hair combs (½ inch by 1 inch)
- 1 tapestry hand needle
- 12 inches of elastic cord
- Cool Gloo or a hot glue gun

Follow these steps to make the bride's veil:

1. **Fold the bridal tulle so that the sides are folded toward the center.**

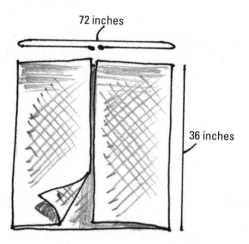

72 inches

36 inches

2. **Cut one piece of lace 36 inches wide by 24 inches long, cutting the lace by following the design and cutting through the fine netting.**

   See Step 1 in "The princess cape or overskirt" in this chapter for tips on following the design in lace.

3. **Set your machine like this:**

   - **Stitch:** Straight
   - **Length:** 2 to 2.5 mm/10 to 12 spi
   - **Width:** 0 mm
   - **Foot:** All-purpose

4. **Place the lace over the tulle so that the right side of the lace is up, and then pin the lace and tulle together, 3 inches from the top edge.**

   Remember, the lace and the folded tulle are the same size.

5. **Sew one row of stitching 3 inches from the top edge, backstitching at each end; then sew a second row of stitching 4 inches from the top edge, also securing the stitches with backstitching.**

   This step creates a casing for the headpiece.

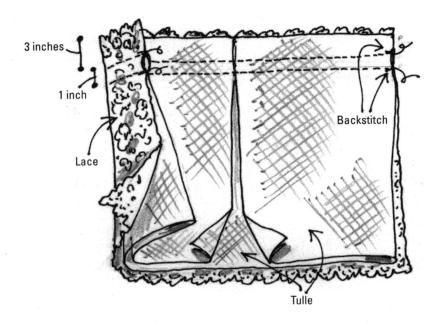

3 inches

1 inch

Lace

Backstitch

Tulle

6. **Using your tape measure, take a quick head measurement of your little princess and write it down.**

   This measurement is the finished size of the floral headpiece.

7. **Cut off the excess floral stem with the wire cutters so that when shaped into a circle, the floral stem fits around her head, with 1 inch of overlap.**

8. **Thread the end of the silk floral stem through the veil casing.**

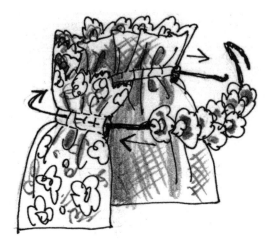

You may have to cut off some of the leaves so that the veil slides up to the base of the flowers. If you cut off leaves, set them aside. You use them later.

9. **Shape the floral stem into a circle and tie the stem end. Secure the ends together by using a hand needle, thread, and glue.**

   Wrap the end of the stem overlap by using the needle and thread. Then, to secure the thread wrap, drop a little glue on the ends and let the glue dry, following the manufacturer's instructions.

10. **Glue extra leaves and flowers to the stem, artfully covering the spot where the two ends join and overlap.**

11. **Sew a comb on either side of the headpiece, attaching them with elastic cord and a large-eyed, tapestry hand needle.**

    • Thread the needle with a length of elastic cord.

    • Position one comb on each side of the headpiece at the temples.

    • Slip the needle through one end of the first comb, threading it through a tooth.

    • Tie the cord in a knot securing it around the floral stem.

    • Repeat for the other end of the comb.

    • Repeat for the second comb.

The superhero cape

This cape transformed our son from a mild-mannered four-year-old into Batman, Superman, Zorro, The Devil, Dracula, a bullfighter, or anyone else his imagination could dream up. In fact, for about two years, the only time he wasn't wearing his cape was when he was sleeping. I made it washable and reversible — black on one side, red on the other — so that his identity could change instantly.

To make this project, you need the following materials in addition to your Sewing Survival Kit (see Chapter 1):

- 2 yards of 45-inch-wide, lightweight polyester lining or satin-type fabric in black
- 2 yards of 45-inch-wide, lightweight polyester lining or satin-type fabric in red
- Thread to match the fabric
- 2 yards of 1-inch grosgrain ribbon

✔ ¼ yard fusible interfacing (see Chapter 2 for information about interfacing)

✔ Tissue paper or pattern tracing material

✔ 42- to 45-inch kite string

Before you begin creating the cape, you need to photocopy the pattern piece for the collar (see Figure 19-2), enlarging it four times the original size.

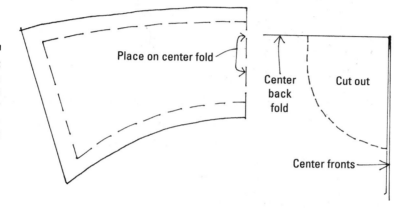

Figure 19-2: This pattern piece is quarter scale, so enlarge it four times the original size.

Place on center fold

Center back fold

Cut out

Center fronts

Follow these steps to make the superhero cape:

1. **Unfold and then refold the black fabric and pin it together so that it's 45 inches wide and 1 yard long.**

2. **Tie the dressmaker's chalk to the end of the string.**

   The string should measure 36 inches from the chalk point to the end of the string.

3. **Draw a hemline on the black fabric.**

   Hold the string in the upper-right corner and use the string and chalk like a compass, marking the outside edge of the cape.

4. **In the upper-right corner of the folded black fabric, use your measuring tape and dressmaker's chalk and mark the rounded neckline, following the dimensions shown in the following figure.**

   Cut out the neckline by cutting on the chalk line.

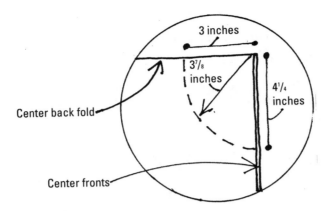

5. Cut out the cape, cutting along the chalk line you made in Step 3.

6. Repeat Steps 1 through 5 for the red fabric.

7. Cut out one collar pattern each of the interfacing, red fabric, and black fabric.

8. Fuse the interfacing onto the black fabric, following the manufacturer's instructions.

   See Chapter 2 for tips on working with interfacing.

9. Set your machine like this:

   • **Stitch:** Straight

   • **Length:** 2.5 to 3 mm/10 to 13 spi

   • **Width:** 0 mm

   • **Foot:** All-purpose

10. Using a ⅝-inch seam allowance and with right sides together, pin and stitch the red and black cape pieces together, leaving the neck edge open.

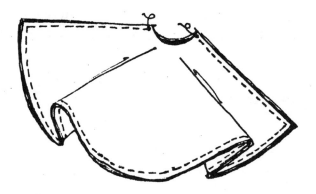

11. **Notch the curved seam allowance every inch or so, so that the seam allowance is smooth when the cape is turned and pressed.**

    See Chapter 6 for more information on notching a seam allowance.

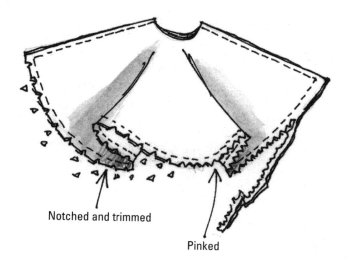

Notched and trimmed

Pinked

12. **Trim the curved seam to ¼ inch.**

    Notching and trimming the seam allowance of an outside curve ensures that the curved edge is smooth when turned right side out. When using pinking shears (see Chapter 6), you trim and notch the seam allowance simultaneously.

13. **Press the seams open and then closed and toward the red side of the fabric.**

14. **Trim the seam allowance close to the seamline in the corners.**

   See Chapter 6 for more information on seaming and trimming away the bulk at the corners.

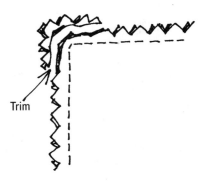

Trim

   Trimming eliminates unnecessary bulk from the seam allowances so that the corners look sharp when the cape is turned right side out.

15. **Using red thread, understitch the seam allowance toward the red side (see Chapter 6 for the how-to's on understitching).**

   Understitching allows the fabric to turn more easily, and the edges are smooth and crisp after pressing. Note that you can't get all the way into the corners, so understitch as far as you can, stop, and then pick up understitching at the other side of the corner. Pull the threads to the inside of the cape and tie them off (see Chapter 6 for hints on tying off threads).

16. **Turn the cape right side out, gently pushing out the corners with curved-bladed scissors or a point turner.**

   Press along the understitched edges.

17. **Staystitch the neck edge ½ inch from the cut edge (see Chapter 6 for tips on staystitching).**

   Clip the neck edge to about ⅛ inch from the row of staystitching.

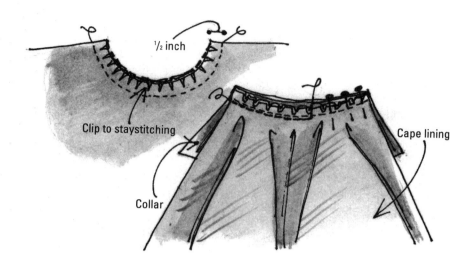

1/2 inch

Clip to staystitching

Collar

Cape lining

18. **Make the collar the same way as the cape — but much smaller of course — by following Steps 9 through 16.**

19. **Place and pin the collar to the neck edge of the cape, putting the right sides together.**

If you want the red side of the collar to show when the black side is being worn, place the red side of the collar to the black side of the cape. If you want the black side of the collar to show when the black side of the cape is being worn, place the black side of the collar to the black side of the cape.

20. **Stitch the collar to the cape by using a ⅝-inch seam allowance. Backstitch at both ends of the seam.**

21. **Fold the ribbon in half the short way so that you make a crease in the middle of the ribbon, and then mark the center of the neck edge, using a pin or dressmaker's chalk.**

Place and pin the ribbon into the inside of the neck edge over the seam allowance, matching the center marks.

22. **Stitch the ribbon to the neckline, sewing it onto the seamline.**

23. Sew a second row of stitching next to and ⅜ inch away from the first. Backstitch at both ends of the stitching lines and then press.

Creating a Fleece Scarf, Hat, and Jacket Ensemble

Ploarfleece is a warm, versatile fabric that's easy to work with. These easy fleece scarf, hat, and jacket projects give you a great introduction to this magical fabric.

The do's and don'ts of working with fleece

Here are a few general tips to help you work well with fleece:

✔ **Know the right from wrong side of the fleece:** As fleece wears, the color ages differently on the right and the wrong sides of the fabric. Here's an easy way to figure it out which sides are which: When stretched on the selvage, fleece curls to the **right** side; when stretched across the grain, it curls to the **wrong** side (see Figure 19-3).

✔ **After cutting out your pattern, mark the wrong side of the fabric by using a dressmaker's pencil or chalk:** Mark the center front with a single hash mark and the center back with a double hash mark.

✔ **Mark notches with a chalk pencil instead of clipping into the seam allowance.**

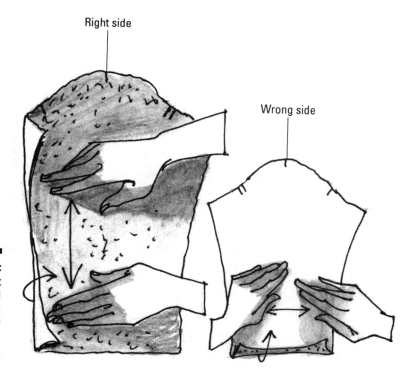

Right side

Wrong side

Figure 19-3:
Figuring out the right and wrong sides of a piece of fleece.

✔ **Wash your finished project by turning it inside out:** Use lukewarm water, the gentle wash cycle, and powdered detergent. Liquid detergents can damage the chemical finish on the lighter-weight fleeces, impairing its moisture-wicking capabilities.

✔ **Don't prewash fleece:** Fleece is usually made of polyester or a polyester blend that doesn't shrink, and the colors don't fade.

✔ **Don't press the fleece after you sew seams:** If you feel that a pesky seam needs shaping, set the iron for "steam" and hold it 3 to 4 inches above the seamline, letting the steam penetrate the fibers. Then finger-press the seam in shape by holding and patting your hand over it until the fabric cools. Placing a hot iron directly on the fabric crushes the nap and can melt the fibers. For the most part, put your iron away for fleece projects.

The fleece scarf

You can make this scarf plain (without the reverse appliqués) or fancy (with the reverse appliqués). It's sure to be a hit for you or someone else on your gift list.

To make this project, you need the following materials in addition to your Sewing Survival Kit (see Chapter 1):

✔ ¼ yard red fleece (54 to 60 inches wide)

✔ Embroidery scissors

✔ Thread to match the fabric

✔ (Optional) For the appliques you see in the color pages of this book, two fleece bands, 3 inches by 9 inches, in sunshine yellow and turquoise

✔ (Optional) Sulky Sticky Adhesive Tear-Away Stabilizer

Follow these steps to make the fleece scarf:

1. **Cut the scarf 30 to 60 inches long by 9 inches wide.**

2. **On each short end of the scarf, mark a line 3 inches from the edge with disappearing dressmaker's chalk.**

Folk art reverse appliqué

Want to know how I made those great appliques that you see in the color pages of this book? Simple: Cut shapes out of coordinating Polarfleece and edgestitch them on to the scarf, hat, or jacket. (See Chapter 6 for more information on edgestitching.)

3. **Starting in the center of one short edge, use your shears and cut straight up to the marked line.**

   Continue cutting each remaining section in half until you have the desired amount of fringe. Repeat for the other short edge of the scarf.

   You're done, unless you want to decorate your scarf with some appliques. See the sidebar "Folk art reverse appliqué" in this chapter for more information.

The wacky hat

If you've been on the ski slopes lately, you may have noticed innovative fashions emerging from those wild and wacky snowboarders. I love their inventive head gear and thought you might, too, so here's a mild version.

To make this project, you need the following materials in addition to your Sewing Survival Kit (see Chapter 1):

- 1 hat pattern (most pattern companies make a simple pattern for the hat you see in the color section of this book)
- ½ yard of red fleece
- ½ yard of turquoise fleece
- ⅛ yard sunshine yellow fleece for cuff bands
- Red thread

Follow these steps to make the wacky hat:

1. **Find the hat pattern piece.**

   If the pattern calls for a turned back cuff, eliminate it by folding back the pattern tissue to the foldline.

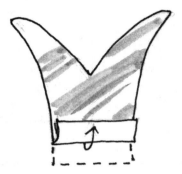

2. **Cut one pattern piece from the red fleece and one from the turquoise fleece.**

3. **Cut two bands of yellow fleece the width of the hat by 3 inches long.**

   These bands are the cuff of the hat.

4. **Edgestitch the yellow fleece bands to the bottom of each hat piece and to the right side of the fabric.**

   See Chapter 6 for the tips and tricks of edgestitching.

5. **Cut one strip of fleece, 6 inches by ½ inch, from each of the three colors.**

6. **Cut the 6-inch fleece strips in half, grouping them together into two groups so that each group has one 3-inch red, one 3-inch yellow, and one 3-inch turquoise strip.**

7. **Place and pin each group of strips on the right sides of the pointed ends of the hat so that the short ends of the strip ends are inside the ⅝-inch seam allowance and the long ends are toward the center of the hat.**

8. **Pin and sew the hat, right sides together, curving the stitching line at the points.**

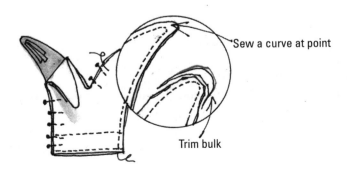

Sew a curve at point

Trim bulk

Trim back the bulk of the fabric at the curves (see Chapter 6 for more on trimming away bulk from the seam allowance).

You catch the strips in the seam allowance as you sew over them.

9. **Turn the hat right side out and marvel at your creation.**

The fleece jacket

Polarfleece is one of the most user-friendly fabrics to work with. The fabric is soft, warm, cuddly, and wears like iron. After you make this jacket, you'll want to sew with fleece again and again.

To make this project, you need the following materials in addition to your Sewing Survival Kit (see Chapter 1):

- 1 fleece jacket pattern with side seams, set-in or raglan sleeves, and pockets, and without a collar or hood (most pattern companies make a simple pattern for the fleece jacket you see in the color section of this book)

- Red fleece yardage as specified on the pattern

- Thread to match the fabric

- #20 long, prong-style sport snaps, SnapSetter Tool and Adapter by The Snap Source (available through your local sewing machine dealer), or buttons specified on the back of the pattern envelope

- Woven, nonfusible interfacing for behind the snaps

- 4.0 twin needles for your sewing machine (available from your local sewing machine dealer)

To color block a jacket like you see in the color section, subtract ¾ yard from the fabric specified on the back of the pattern envelope. Buy ¾ yard of a turquoise fleece. Also, buy another ¼ yard of sunshine yellow fleece for accents. Note that all seam allowances in this project are ⅝ inch unless otherwise stated.

Follow these steps to make the fleece jacket:

1. **Except for the pockets and sleeves, cut out the fleece jacket by following the suggested layout on the pattern guide sheet.**

2. **Cut out the sleeves from the turquoise fabric by following the pattern layout.**

3. **Cut out the pocket pattern pieces from the turquoise fabric, eliminating the seam allowance and the hem at the top of the pocket.**

4. Cut two yellow fleece strips, 2 inches by the width of the top of the pocket, and then pin each strip to the top edge of each pocket.

5. Edgestitch at the top edge and the bottom edge of each yellow strip to the top of each pocket.

6. Using the disappearing dressmaker's chalk, mark the notches, pocket placement, button, and buttonhole placement on both jacket fronts.

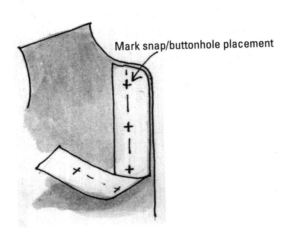

Mark snap/buttonhole placement

7. Place the pockets on the jacket front and edgestitch, backstitching at each corner.

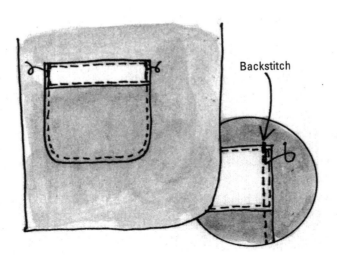

Backstitch

8. Cut eight yellow fleece strips 1½ by 2½ inches.

This jacket doesn't have a *front facing* (a second layer of fabric) on the front of the jacket to support the wear and tear of buttonholes or snaps. So you sew these fleece strips on later as a second fabric layer to fortify the areas under the buttons and buttonholes or snaps.

9. Cut eight 1½ inch squares of woven, nonfusible interfacing.

10. Place a square of interfacing, centering it under each yellow fleece strip.

Position and pin each interfaced strip to the wrong side of the jacket front so that one short end of each strip is ⅝ inch in from the cut edges at each of the button and buttonhole markings.

11. Edgestitch around three sides of the fleece strips on the inside of the jacket fronts.

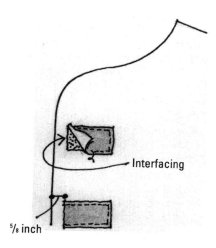

Interfacing

⅝ inch

12. Sew a ⅝-inch seam at the shoulder seams at the ⅝-inch seamline.

13. Placing right sides together, pin and stitch the sleeves into the armholes.

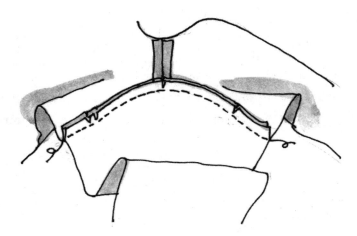

14. **Placing right sides together, pin and stitch the side seams together starting at the hem edge of the jacket and sewing up through the underarm seams.**

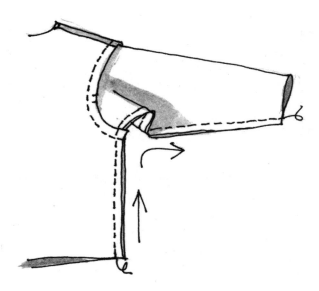

15. **Using a long basting stitch, stitch ⅝ inch from the cut edge of the jacket opening, all the way around the cut edge.**

16. **Run a second row of basting stitches at the curved edges and then gently pull up the bobbin thread.**

    Doing so pulls the longer outside edges of the curve into shape, allowing you to turn and topstitch the edge more easily later.

17. **Fold and pin the seam allowance at the ⅝-inch stitching line you made in Step 15, all the way around the jacket.**

18. **Pin up sleeve hems to the desired length.**

19. **Put 4-mm twin needles into your machine and thread the machine for twin needle sewing (see your Operating Manual).**

    If your machine can't use twin needles, then simply use a single needle instead.

20. **Twin-needle topstitch around the edge of the jacket and the sleeve hems.**

21. **Set your machine like this:**

    - **Stitch:** Straight
    - **Length:** 4 mm/6 spi
    - **Width:** 0 mm
    - **Foot:** Embroidery

22. **Topstitch around the edge of the jacket, guiding the foot ½ inch from the folded edge.**

    See Chapter 5 for information on topstitching.

23. **Apply the sport snaps by following the manufacturer's instructions or sew in your buttonholes and sew on your buttons by following your machine's Operating Manual.**

Making Father Time

Father Time is an heirloom you'll cherish for years to come. Start this breathtaking project by using a few basic hand and machine sewing skills, and then put him together with a little bit of crafting for a one-of-a-kind project you can make to suit any home decor. This project may take longer to complete than the other projects in this chapter, so make it easy on yourself by tackling only one element at a time.

To make this project, you need the following materials in addition to your Sewing Survival Kit (see Chapter 1):

- ¾ yard burgundy velvet or velour
- 1 yard taupe moiré
- Thread to match the fabric
- 2¼ yards brush decorator trim
- 3 yards barberpole cord-edge decorator trim to match brush trim
- 1 porcelain face and hands (available at your local craft store)
- 12 inches curly wool
- 1 wooden base (available at your local craft store)
- 15 to 20 inches ⅜-inch wooden dowel
- 15-inch length of fine gauge coat hanger wire
- ¼ yard of batting
- 1 yard of twine
- Cool Gloo or a hot glue gun and glue sticks

If you don't live near a craft store or can't find the components to make Father Time, Bon Coeur, a craft supply and home decor company out of Scottsdale, Arizona, has a wonderful kit designed by talented designer and crafter Pattie Lloyd. This kit has everything you need, including the porcelain head and hands, dowel, base, batting, wire, twine, and pattern for the robe, gown, and hat. You can even get a matching kit with a sleigh, cushions, and sack to match (see the color section). Available with or without fabric and decorator trim, these kits save a good deal of running-around time. See the appendix to find out where to get these kits.

Before you begin creating Father Time, you need to photocopy and enlarge the pattern pieces for the gown, robe, and hat, shown in Figure 19-4, at your local copy center. Enlarge them by 400 percent.

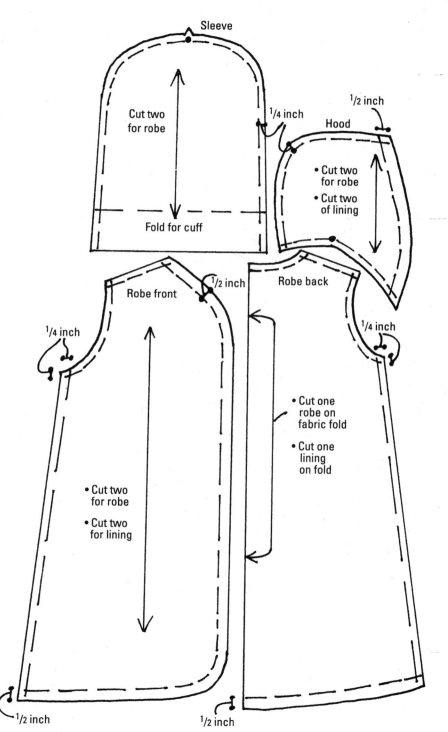

Sleeve

Cut two
for robe

Fold for cuff

¹/₄ inch

¹/₂ inch

Hood

• Cut two
  for robe

• Cut two
  of lining

¹/₂ inch

Robe back

Robe front

¹/₄ inch

• Cut one
  robe on
  fabric fold

• Cut one
  lining
  on fold

¹/₄ inch

• Cut two
  for robe

• Cut two
  for lining

¹/₂ inch

¹/₂ inch

Figure 19-4:
This pattern
is quarter
scale, so
enlarge
each
pattern
piece four
times the
original size
(see next
page for
more pat-
tern pieces).

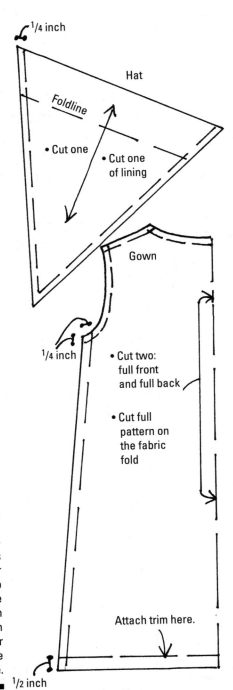

¹/4 inch

Hat

Foldline

• Cut one

• Cut one
of lining

Gown

¹/4 inch

• Cut two:
full front
and full back

• Cut full
pattern on
the fabric
fold

Figure 19-4:
This pattern
(continued
from previ-
ous page) is
quarter
scale, so
enlarge
each
pattern
piece four
times the
original size.

Attach trim here.

¹/2 inch

Then cut out the pieces, following the pattern layout shown in Figure 19-5. (See Chapter 4 for more information on cutting out pattern pieces).

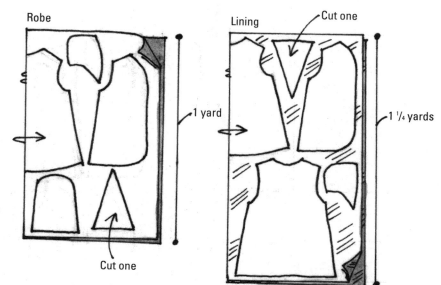

Robe

Lining

Cut one

1 yard

1 ¼ yards

Figure 19-5:
The pattern
layout for
Father Time.

Cut one

The robe is made of velvet, which has a nap, so remember to cut out all velvet pattern pieces in the same direction.

Making the gown

Follow these steps to construct Father Time's gown:

1. **Placing right sides together, pin and stitch the gown together at the shoulder and side seams.**

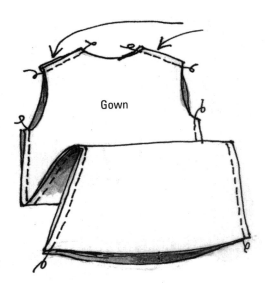

Gown

2. **Set your machine like this:**

   - **Stitch:** Straight
   - **Length:** 3 mm/9 spi
   - **Width:** 6 mm
   - **Foot:** All-purpose

3. **Decide which side of the gown is the front (they're both the same) and then press the seams to one side toward the front.**

4. **Using the barberpole cord-edge decorator trim, measure and cut the trim to fit around the hem edge of the gown.**

   Before cutting the trim to length, tape over the section that will be cut, and then cut through the taped cord. This way, the cording doesn't separate and unwind and is much easier to work with.

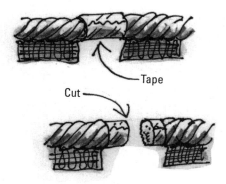

Tape

Cut

You use the rest of this cord as a belt, so set it aside for now.

5. **Pin the cord-edge trim to the hem edge of the gown and, using your zipper foot and a 3 mm/9 spi stitch length, sew trim to the hem edge, sewing as close to the cord as possible.**

The zipper foot allows you to get the needle close to the cord edge.

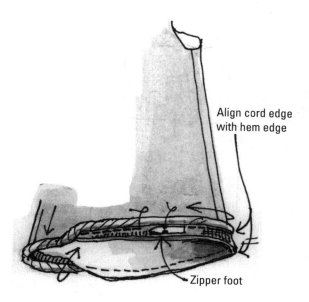

Align cord edge
with hem edge

Zipper foot

At the cord ends, either overlap the cord or untwist a few strands, and then overlap the twists so that the cord plies line up and the cut ends extend into the seam allowance.

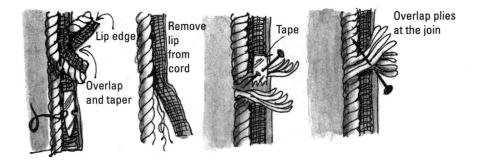

6. **Turn under the hem allowance at the cord and press the hem into place.**

7. **Cut a length of cord-edge trim 30 inches long, remembering to tape the section that is cut through (see the tip in Step 4 in this section).**

8. **Remove the lip edge from this cord-edge trim by loosening a few stitches far enough so that you can get a good grip; holding the cord side with one hand, and the lip edge with the other, pull quickly and hard to break the stitches and remove the lip edge from the cord.**

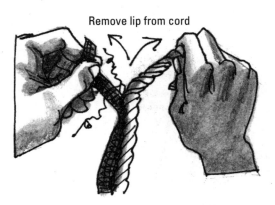

Remove lip from cord

Don't worry — this treatment won't hurt the cording at all.

9. **Remove the tape and fray out 1 inch at each end of the cord.**

Using a few unraveled threads still attached to the cording, tie a knot. Drop a dot of glue on the knot and set it aside to dry.

Knot and glue

Making the robe

Follow these steps to make Father Time's nifty robe:

1. **Pin the shoulder seams, right sides together.**

2. **Set your machine like this:**

   - **Stitch:** Straight
   - **Length:** 3 mm/9 spi
   - **Width:** 6 mm
   - **Foot:** All-purpose

3. **Press the seams to one side.**

   When pressing velvet or velour, you don't want to crush the nap or create shine on the right side of the fabric by overpressing. To prevent this problem, place a large scrap piece of velvet on the ironing board, nap (fuzzy) side up. Place the robe, wrong side up, so that the nap of the robe is against the nap of the velvet scrap on the board. Place a press cloth over the robe and then gently press with very little pressure, letting a little steam penetrate the fabric. Allow the fabric to dry for a permanent press.

4. **Match the center notches of the sleeves to each shoulder seam, and then stitch the sleeves into the robe, using a ¼-inch seam allowance.**

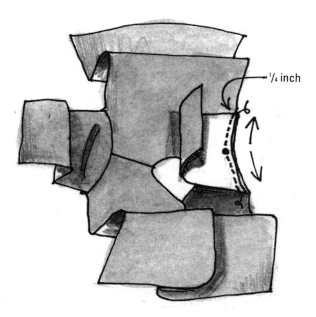

¼ inch

5. **Press the sleeve seams toward the neck edge and from the wrong side.**

6. **Pin the robe, right sides together, at the side and underarm seams.**

   Sew ¼ inch seams, starting from the bottom and sewing up and including the underarm seams. Press the seams toward the front.

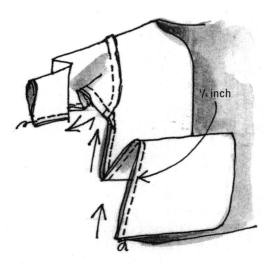

7. **Pin the hood, right sides together.**

   Sew a ¼-inch seam allowance. Press the seam from the wrong side, flat and together.

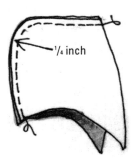

8. **Pin the hood to the robe, right sides together, at the neck edge.**

   Using a ¼ inch seam allowance, sew the hood to the robe. Gently press the seam toward the robe, and then set the robe aside.

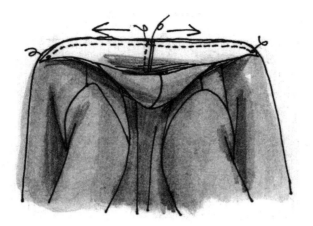

9. **Pin the front and back lining, right sides together.**

   Sew the shoulder and side seams, using a ¼ inch seam allowance. Press the seams toward the front of the lining.

10. **Follow Steps 7 and 8 to make and stitch the hood lining into neck edge of the robe lining.**

   You sandwich and sew brush decorator fringe between the lining and robe fabrics. Please read Steps 11 through 17 before actually doing them to avoid mistakes.

11. **Lay the robe on the table, right side up.**

12. **Attach the brush fringe decorator trim.**

   Starting at the center back, pin the trim along the outside edge, aligning the lip edge with the cut edge of the robe. Be sure that the fringe side, secured with a chain stitch, faces toward the center of the robe. Overlap trim ends about ½ inch.

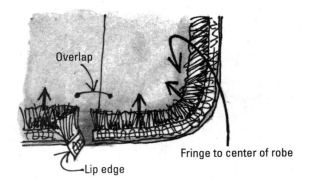

Overlap

Fringe to center of robe

Lip edge

 Do not remove the chain stitch from the edge of the fringe until after you finish the project. This chain stitch keeps the fringe from tangling while you're working with it.

13. Pin the robe and the lining, right sides together, pinning the lining on top of the fringe.

If you've pinned everything together correctly, you won't see any fringe poking out.

14. **Set your machine like this:**
    - **Stitch:** Straight
    - **Length:** 3 mm/9 spi
    - **Width:** 0 mm
    - **Foot:** Zipper

15. **Sew the robe and lining together, using a ½-inch seam allowance all the way around the outside edge.**

16. **Clip the inside curves and notch the outside curves of the seam allowance every inch or so (see Chapter 6 for more information on clipping seams).**

    This way, when you turn the robe right side out, the clipped seams lie smoothly around the curves.

17. **Turn the robe right side out and press.**

    Carefully reach in and pull the robe through one of the armholes in the lining. The sleeves have a raw edge that is finished after you dress Father Time.

18. **From the lining side, gently press along the outside edges of the robe.**

Making his hat

Even Father Time needs a topper to keep his head warm on a frosty holiday evening. Here's how you make his hat:

1. **Pin and stitch the velvet hat together, using a ¼-inch seam allowance.**

   Repeat for the moiré hat lining.

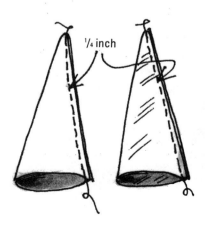
¼ inch

2. **Turn the velvet hat right side out.**

3. **Insert the hat lining inside the velvet hat, putting the wrong sides together.**

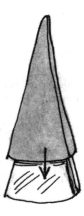

4. **Fold up the bottom of the hat about 1 inch so that the lining shows on the outside of the hat like a cuff.**

   Fold the lining over again just a little bit, to hide the raw edges.

5. **Glue or hand-stitch a little barberpole cord-edge trim at the top and around the folded cuff edge.**

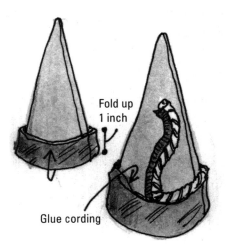

Fold up
1 inch

Glue cording

Assembling Father Time

Putting Father Time together is as easy as following these steps:

1. **Unbraid the curly wool for the beard, hair, mustache, and eyebrows by removing the two braiding strings.**

2. **Stretch the curly wool strand straight and cut the following pieces:**

   - 7 3½-inch lengths for his beard
   - 7 2½-inch lengths for his hair
   - 1 1-inch length for the eyebrows and mustache

   Hold one end of the cut strand of curly wool between your thumb and index finger and spread it to a width of about ½ inch. Do the same to all but the 1-inch curly wool lengths before gluing them to the head in the next step.

3. **Starting at the center of his porcelain chin, glue the first 3½-inch length of curly wool to his chin.**

   Glue the remaining wool lengths on either side of the first, spacing them evenly and working from the center, out and across his face, until he has a beard up to his ears.

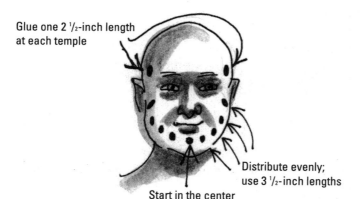

Glue one 2 ½-inch length at each temple

Distribute evenly; use 3 ½-inch lengths

Start in the center

4. **With the front of his head facing you, glue one 2½-inch length of curly wool at each temple.**

   Turn his head over. Starting at the center back and working from the center out, glue the remaining shorter wool lengths, spacing them evenly across the back of his head.

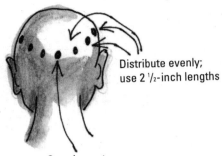

Distribute evenly;
use 2 ½-inch lengths

Start in center

5. **Separate 15 to 20 individual strands from the 1-inch piece of wool.**

Center and glue a 1-inch strand under his nose. Repeat for each eyebrow. Trim the mustache and eyebrows so that they look in proportion to his face.

Use several short lengths of curly wool

1-inch lengths of curly wool

6. **Fluff out the beard and hair by pulling apart each length of curly wool.**

After you fluff out all the lengths, run a line of glue along the chin and jaw line and then press down the beard (a little glue goes a long way here, so don't overdo it). Repeat at the back of his head. Press his hair down just above the neck.

Making his body

Follow these steps to make Father Time's body:

1. **Bend the 15-inch wire 1 inch at each end; find the center of the wire, lay the dowel on the center of the wire (twisting it around the dowel twice), and then position it 4 inches from the top.**

   Heavily glue the wire in place. Let the glue dry and add more as needed, securing his arms.

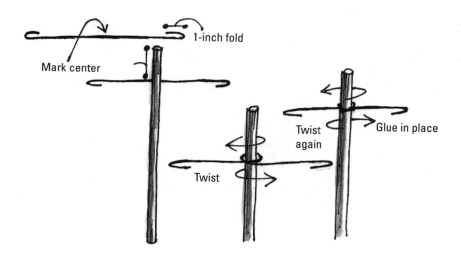

2. **Put the dowel in the base, but don't glue it.**

   You may or may not want to permanently glue the dowel to the wooden base. Some folks like to keep the base unglued to make for easy storage. If you don't glue in the dowel, use a hunk of floral clay in the hole of the base so that Father Time won't fall over during your holiday festivities.

3. **Fill up each hand halfway with glue, place each hand over the folded wire ends, and let the glue dry.**

   The thumbs need to be facing up, so figure out what arm each hand goes on before gluing.

   If you're using hot glue, the glue heats up the porcelain and can really burn you if you're not careful.

4. Make his chest and tummy.

Use the batting that's cut into a long, 4-inch-wide strip, and twine. Starting in the front, wrap the batting up and around the top of the dowel, creating his shoulders. Continue wrapping the batting around once or twice in the chest area and around the mid-section. Glue the end of the batting in place and tie the twine around his arms and torso, adding stability to the chest and tummy area.

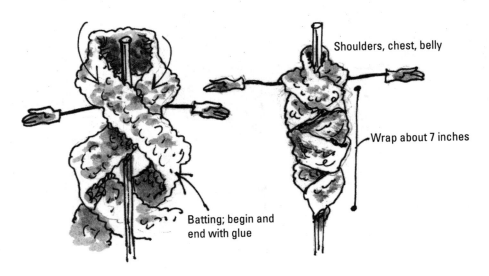

Shoulders, chest, belly

Wrap about 7 inches

Batting; begin and end with glue

5. Glue a small piece of batting, 1 to 2 inches square, on top of the dowel.

This piece goes up into his head and keeps it from wobbling.

Dressing Father Time

Follow these steps to get Father Time ready to see the world:

1. Scrunch in the neckline of the gown, snugging it up to the batting and around the dowel.

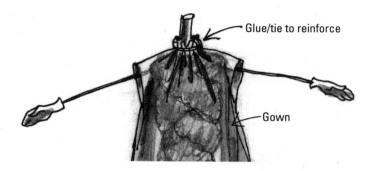

Check that the gown is long enough to cover the wooden base after you tie the belt around his waist. If the gown is too short, cut off a little of the dowel. Glue the neck edge of the gown to the batting and then tie a piece of twine around the neckline to keep everything stable.

2. **Wrap the belt around Father Time's waist and tie a simple square knot.**

3. **Turn the head over and fill it with about 4 or 5 squirts of Cool Gloo or hot glue; then set the head on top of the batting-covered dowel and let the glue dry.**

   Don't forget to be very careful when working with hot glue.

4. **Dress Father Time in his robe.**

   Bend his arms toward the front. His sleeves extend over his thumbs, so adjust the sleeve length by turning under the excess fabric.

   Glue the barberpole cord-edge trim so that the cord is around the inside edge of each sleeve. The cording joins at the bottom of the sleeve, so it won't show.

5. **Set the hat on his head, tucking the point down over one shoulder or around his head like a turban.**

   Once you like how it looks, glue the hat in place.

Sewing Bravo Bear

This bear is fun to make and gives you a chance to try several techniques applicable to other types of sewing projects. When you finish, you have something with personality.

To make this project, you need the following materials in addition to your Sewing Survival Kit (see Chapter 1):

- ¾ yard of 60-inch-wide woven fabric
- Thread to match the fabric
- 1 black felt square (approximately 8½ by 11 inches)
- 1 beige felt scrap about 2 inches square
- 2 yards decorator braid with a lip edge
- 2 half-inch black ball buttons
- ⅛ yard of 45-or 60-inch-wide coordinate fabric for the tie
- 1 bag of polyester stuffing
- 1 wooden spoon with a smooth handle
- Fabric glue stick

If you don't live near a fabric store or don't want to run all over town to find the components to make Bravo Bear, Bon Coeur, a craft supply and home decor company out of Scottsdale, Arizona, has an adorable kit designed by talented designer and crafter Pattie Lloyd. The kit has everything you need, including the fabric, pattern, trim, buttons, stuffing, and fabric for the tie.

Before you begin creating Bravo Bear, you need to photocopy and enlarge the pattern pieces, shown in Figure 19-6, at your local copy center. Enlarge them by 400 percent.

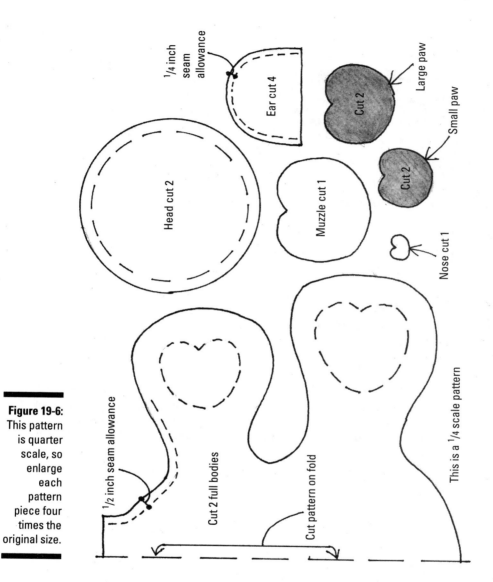

Figure 19-6: This pattern is quarter scale, so enlarge each pattern piece four times the original size.

¹/₄ inch seam allowance

Ear cut 4

Large paw

Cut 2

Small paw

Cut 2

Head cut 2

Muzzle cut 1

Nose cut 1

¹/₂ inch seam allowance

Cut 2 full bodies

Cut pattern on fold

This is a ¹/₄ scale pattern

Cut out the pieces, following the pattern layout shown in Figure 19-7. (See Chapter 4 for more information on cutting out pattern pieces.)

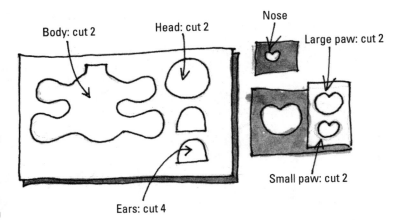

Figure 19-7:
The pattern
layout for
Bravo Bear.

Body: cut 2

Head: cut 2

Nose

Large paw: cut 2

Small paw: cut 2

Ears: cut 4

Then follow these steps to put Bravo Bear together:

1. **Set your machine like this:**
   - **Stitch:** Zigzag
   - **Length:** 0.5 to 0.75 mm/fine or 60 spi
   - **Width:** 4 to 6 mm
   - **Foot:** Embroidery

2. **Using the thread that matches the bear fabric and the embroidery foot, sew a row of satin stitches down the center of the black felt muzzle, starting and stopping about 1 inch from the top and ½ inch from the bottom.**

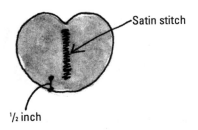

Satin stitch

½ inch

3. **Glue-stick the nose onto the muzzle.**

4. **Using a 2.5 mm/13 spi straight stitch and an embroidery foot, edgestitch the nose onto the muzzle.**

   Lift the foot and pivot frequently to follow the shape of the nose. Pull threads to the back of the muzzle and tie them off (see Chapter 6).

   Glue-stick, then edgestitch

   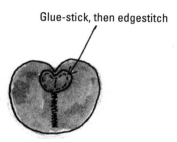

5. **Glue-stick the muzzle to the right side of one head circle so that the muzzle is slightly lower than dead center.**

   Tuck the lip edge of the trim under the felt muzzle, starting and stopping the ends at the top, notched side of the muzzle. Pin the muzzle and the trim in place.

   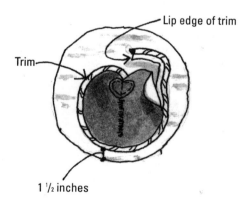

   Lip edge of trim

   Trim

   1 ½ inches

6. **Sew the muzzle to the head circle, using a zipper foot, far-left needle position (if possible), and a 3 mm/9 spi straight stitch.**

   Pull loose threads to the back and tie them off (see Chapter 6).

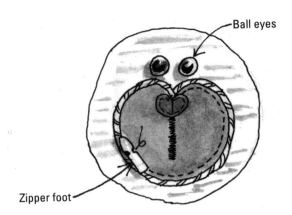

Ball eyes

Zipper foot

7. **Using a double thread, hand sew the button eyes in place, just above the muzzle.**

   Chapter 5 has more information on sewing on buttons.

8. **Pin the head circles together, right sides together.**

   Using the embroidery foot and a 3 mm/9 spi straight stitch, sew the circles together, using a ½-inch seam allowance. Start and stop at the upper-right side, leaving a 2-inch opening to turn the head through.

Notch the seam allowance just shy of the seamline (see Chapter 6), or trim the seam allowance to ¼ inch with pinking shears.

Don't trim away the seam allowance at the opening where you turn the head through. If you do, hand sewing is much harder later.

9. **Turn the head right side out, carefully reaching in and pulling the fabric through the opening.**

10. **Using an easy slipstitch (see Chapter 5), close the top of the head, turning in and stitching the seam allowance closed.**

    One of the ears will go here, so these hand stitches won't show.

11. **Pin the ears with right sides together. Use a ¼-inch seam allowance and stitch them together.**

    Clip into the seam allowance just shy of the seamline every ½ inch, or trim the seam allowance with the pinking shears to notch the curve (see Chapter 6 for information on notching seams). Turn the ears right side out and press them.

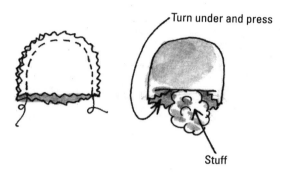

Turn under and press

Stuff

12. **Turn under the raw edges of each ear ¼ inch and press.**

    Slightly stuff each ear, and then pin on and hand-stitch each ear to the bear's head, using even slipstitches (see Chapter 5).

Making Bravo's body

Follow these steps to make the bear's body:

1. **Using one of the body pieces, glue-stick and sew each paw and trim in place as you did for the muzzle in Steps 5 and 6 in the previous section.**

    The small paws go on the front legs, and the large paws go on the hind legs.

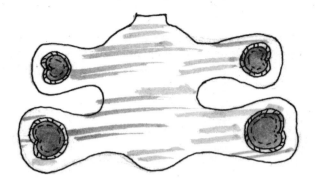

Starting and stopping the trim at the notch-part of each paw is much easier.

2. **Pin and sew the body pieces, right sides together, using a ½-inch seam allowance.**

   Notch just shy of the seamline at the corners. Notch or trim the outside curves by using the pinking shears.

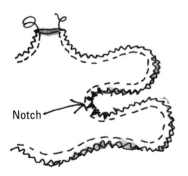

Notch

3. **Turn the body right side out through the neck opening.**

   Gently press the seamline flat and together.

4. **Stuff the front and hind legs.**

   Using the polyester batting, stuff your bear's front and hind legs, pushing the stuffing in place with the handle of your wooden spoon. Use a long straight stitch (4 mm length or 6 spi) and stitch the joint lines.

5. Stuff and close the body.

Fold the raw neck edge toward the inside ½ inch and press. Finish stuffing the body up to the neckline. Close the opening by hand or with machine stitching.

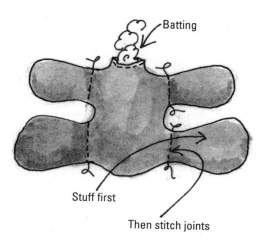

Batting

Stuff first

Then stitch joints

6. Pin and then hand sew the neck to the center back of the head, using double thread and even slipstitches (see Chapter 5).

Making his tie

Follow these steps to put the finishing touch on Bravo — his tie:

1. **Fold the tie fabric in half the long way and sew it together, using a straight stitch and a ⅝-inch seam allowance.**

2. **Center the seam down the length of the tie and press the seam open.**

   Stitch one end of the tie closed, using a ½-inch seam allowance. Turn and press a ½-inch hem on the open end of the tie.

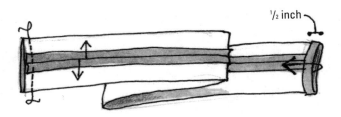

½ inch

3. **Turn the tie right side out through the open end and topstitch the opening closed.**

   Topstitch the other short end of the tie to match the first.

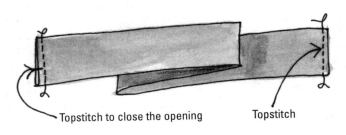

Topstitch to close the opening   Topstitch

4. **Put the tie around the bear's neck and tie a bow (see the color section in this book).**

Chapter 20

Ten Mistakes Beginners Often Make

*W*hile putting the information together for this chapter, I remembered the stumbling blocks I had when I first started sewing and those that my beginning students experienced. This chapter alerts you to ten of the most common sewing mistakes and pitfalls. I hope that you take my advice, read the recommended information, and have a wonderful sewing experience.

Attempting a Project beyond Your Skill Level

I like challenges as much as the next guy, but when it comes to sewing, there's a fine line between challenging and frustrating. The bottom line for your first project: Don't even think about making a suit jacket with notched lapels out of an uneven wool plaid. That's a recipe for disaster. You'll probably waste your time and money — and you may never wear the thing after it's done. You may never even sew again.

Instead, look for projects with few seams, such as the easy envelope pillow in Chapter 15 or the place mat vest project in Chapter 19. Both projects have just a few seams and don't need a lot of fitting; you can sit down, have fun, and make each one in a couple hours or less.

Also know that the first time you make something, you'll be on a learning curve, and the result probably won't be perfect. In fact, you may never wear the garment. That's okay. Your skills improve with every project, and you will get better. After you've mastered the basics, you can move on to more challenging projects that have a little bit more style.

Choosing Difficult Fabrics to Work With

Don't choose fabrics that are too heavy, are too fine, must be pattern-matched (such as plaids, stripes, and 1-inch gingham checks), or are too expensive (with the proviso that using the best fabrics you can afford adds to the tactile experience of sewing). Read the information on fabrics and fibers in Chapter 2 and choose those that work with your lifestyle, personal style, and comfort requirements.

Also stay away from lightweight slippery fabrics such as polyester faille, silk crepe or charmeuse, acetate linings, and the entire category of microfibers. These fabrics scoot around during cutting, attract static electricity, are slippery when they are pinned together, and require special handling during sewing and pressing.

Because of the nap or the fuzzy texture, fabrics such as corduroy and velvet are also challenging because you can lay out and cut the pattern pieces only in one direction. You need to take extra care during pressing so that you don't crush the nap. So I suggest that when you're ready to make a project out of a napped fabric, choose a fabric such as Polarfleece and try a project or two from Chapter 19. Then, when you have a little more experience, go on to the corduroys and velvets.

Cotton poplin, chambray, and sweatshirt fleece are very easy fabrics for beginners to work with.

Choosing an Unflattering Style

As much as we all want to look like the models in the pattern and mail-order catalogs, remember to choose clothing styles that look good on you when you shop for ready-to-wear. Chances are that if elastic-waist, pull-on pants from your local department store don't look good on you, elastic-waist, pull-on pants that you make for yourself won't look good on you either. Check out Chapter 4 to help you determine your figure type.

Using the Wrong Fabric for the Pattern

If the pattern says "For Knits Only" and you decide to use a woven poplin because it's a perfect color, the project won't fit. Knits stretch and contribute to the overall fit of the garment. So read the back of the pattern envelope and choose from the list of recommended fabrics.

Laying Out the Fabric Incorrectly

Have you ever had your pants legs twist uncomfortably around your legs while walking? And perhaps this same pair of pants makes you look bow-legged even when you carefully press the creases. Chances are good that the fabric was cut off-grain.

Before cutting, lay out the pattern as your pattern guide sheet instructions recommend, and read Chapter 4. Then remember the old adage: "Measure twice and cut once." You'll avoid costly mistakes.

Neglecting to Use Interfacing

I remember my mom complaining about using interfacing in projects. "After all, it really doesn't show, you know," she'd say, "and I don't want to spend the money on it." We agreed to disagree.

Interfacing is a layer of fabric that gives body and oomph to collars, cuffs, and front plackets. It doesn't show on the outside of the garment, but it makes a world of difference in the final look of the project. My feeling is that if I'm spending my time and effort making something, I want it to look as professional as possible. Interfacing helps me do that.

See Chapter 2's information about interfacing and plan on using it in your next project. You'll love the results.

Failing to Press as You Sew

I remember one of my favorite college professors at the State University of New York's Fashion Institute of Technology (FIT for short) telling me to "have a love affair with your iron." I never really thought too much about the value of pressing garments-in-progress until he said it, but he's right. When you press a project after each seam, you're shaping a flat, shapeless piece of fabric into something that fits the forms and curves of whatever is under it — almost like pressing the fabric into submission. See Chapter 5's section on pressing and have a love affair with your iron when you sew.

Using an Old, Beat-Up Sewing Machine

I work with a friend who used to sew and has an "oldie but moldy" sewing machine. It has been hidden away in the garage, never seeing the light of day for the last 10 to 15 years. Every so often I'll hear her say, "I think I'll dig out the machine and start sewing again." She never does, and I can only imagine how well it works after all this time in retirement.

When I sew, part of the joy for me is sitting down in front of the machine, knowing that it works perfectly every time. So, instead of borrowing Grandma's old clunker, get a sewing machine that's in good working order by

- ✔ Renting or borrowing a machine from your local dealer.
- ✔ Taking a sewing class.
- ✔ Buying a new or reconditioned machine.

No, you don't have to buy one of those $4,000 do-everything models. You need just one that provides good, reliable service. Then, when you're ready, trade up to a better model as your skills improve and as your budget permits.

When you use a machine that's in good working order, you also need to maintain it to keep it that way. See the section in Chapter 1 about sewing machine care and then treat yours with the TLC it deserves.

Neglecting to Use a New Needle on Every Project

I once met a woman who complained about her needle unthreading each time she sewed. I asked her to bring the machine to me so that I could diagnose the problem. When she did, I discovered she'd worn the needle down to the eye! No wonder she was having trouble. We put in a new needle, and the machine worked perfectly again.

I worked with another woman who was having a terrible time with skipped stitches (where the line of stitching had two or three short stitches followed by one long stitch, which wasn't supposed to happen). I suggested that she change the needle. She pulled a different one out of her pincushion and put it in the machine. Again, she experienced the same problem. This result happened two more times in the same afternoon. She was ready to take the machine to the local service center until I insisted that she use a brand-new needle from the package — no more skipped stitches.

Even though the needle looks perfect to the naked eye, the point bends, contracts burrs, and just plain wears out with use, like a razor blade. So change your needle and throw it away after each project.

Refusing to Cut Yourself Some Slack

Remember when you first learned how to ride a bike? You weren't perfect, were you? I spent my first bike-riding summer with scabs on both knees until I figured out what I was doing.

Sewing is like anything new. You can't be perfect from the get-go, so cut yourself some slack. If you can live with a sewing mistake, don't rip it out.

Chapter 21

Ten Sewing Fundamentals to Remember

In This Chapter

▶ Making your sewing easier

▶ Getting more pleasure out of sewing by remembering some basic rules

*I*n this chapter, I give you some tips that I wish someone had given me when I first started sewing. Post these hints on a bulletin board in front of you when you sew, or write them on stick-on notes and stick them on your sewing machine.

Buy the Best Fabric You Can Afford

Sewing is a tactile craft. For me, one of the pleasures of sewing is working with the best fabric I can afford. Better fabrics are easier to work with; are woven, knitted, or printed on grain; and usually produce a better end product. (See Chapter 4 for more information about grain.)

I also don't waste my valuable sewing time working with poor-quality fabric because it probably won't hold up with a lot of washing and wearing. What makes a good quality fabric? Several things, but the most important are the following:

✔ **Check the fiber content.** Reread the information in Chapter 2 about fabrics and fiber content, and then preshrink the fabric. If the fabric looks like a droopy dishrag just by preshrinking it, chances are the fabric will look like a dishrag when the project is finished. So return the fabric to the store before putting your time into it.

✔ **"Hand" or feel the fabric.** Take a corner in your hand and crush it and see what it does. Do the wrinkles stay in? Drape a length around your arm or neck. Does it drape in smooth folds, or does it bend in stiff creases?

✔ **Consider what you pay per yard.** Although there are always exceptions, I've discovered that you usually get what you pay for when it comes to fabric.

When making a garment, I usually buy the yardage recommended on the back of the pattern envelope because the pattern companies are generous with their recommendations. When it comes to home decor projects, though, I usually buy fabric for one more pattern repeat than I think I need (see Chapter 4 for determining the pattern repeat in a fabric).

Know Your Fabric Terminology

Fabrics have selvages, a crosswise grain, a lengthwise grain, and a bias. You need to know what these terms mean in order to understand the pattern layout and cutting instructions, the basic project construction, how to buy the proper amount of fabric, and how to plan your project. I give you a handy run-down in the following list:

✔ **Selvages:** These are the finished edges of the fabric. Selvages run the length of the fabric.

✔ **Crosswise grain:** The width of the fabric, perpendicular to the selvages.

✔ **Lengthwise grain:** The length of the fabric from one cut end to the other cut end, parallel to the selvages.

✔ **Bias:** The 45-degree angle between the crosswise grain and the lengthwise grain.

See Chapter 4 for more details on each of these terms.

Know the Difference between Right and Wrong

After presenting a two-hour seminar to beginning sewers, a guy stood up in the back of the room and said (with the most perplexed expression on his face), "What's all this about the right and the wrong sides? I think it would be better if you said the top and the bottom or the front and the back. I don't get it."

This experience reminded me never to skip over the basics with someone new to the craft. The following list gives you the lowdown on the right and wrong sides:

> ✔ **The right side of the fabric:** The pretty side that faces to the outside of the project and usually has the brightest colors and more defined textures.

> ✔ **The wrong side of the fabric:** The side that faces to the inside of the project where the seams are.

For more information on fibers and fabrics, see Chapter 2.

Place Right Sides Together

When sewing, place the right sides of the fabric together to make a seam. This is as basic to sewing as the needle and thread. In other words, place the right side of one piece of fabric against the right side of another piece of fabric (usually matching the notches along the seamline). See Chapter 6 for more information on making perfect seams.

Put Your Foot Down before Sewing

The presser foot, that is. The presser foot firmly holds the fabric under the needle. Without the presser foot, the fabric just flops around, and you can't sew straight. When the foot is lowered onto the fabric, the upper thread tension also engages so that the stitches form properly. Use these handy tips to know when to put your foot down:

> ✔ Lower the foot when you start to sew.

> ✔ Raise the foot to remove your work after you finish sewing.

Remember that your sewing machine comes with several different presser feet designed for different uses. Review your machine's Operating Manual and Chapter 1 to find out the benefits of sewing with your feet.

Stop and Start Sewing the Right Way

I can't think of anything more frustrating than getting ready to sew a nice long seam, stomping on the foot pedal, and having the needle come unthreaded. The following tips help you stop and start sewing the right way to avoid this problem:

✔ Stop sewing at the end of the stitch cycle. If you don't, the take-up lever pulls out a length of thread for the next stitch and unthreads the needle. By stopping when the needle is out of the fabric and the take-up lever is at the highest position, you eliminate the problem. Newer sewing machine models have this feature built in. See Chapter 5 for more information on taking the first stitch.

✔ When stitching a corner, stop with the needle in the dead-lowest position before pivoting at the corner to avoid a skipped stitch.

Righty, Tighty; Lefty, Loosey

This little rhyme refers to the tension knobs on your sewing machine and serger.

Turning the tension dials to the right makes them tight. Turning them to the left makes them loose — this trick works with pickle and peanut butter jars, too. (You can find more about balancing thread tensions in Chapter 1.)

Test-Stitch First

When sewing, you want the seams and buttonholes to turn out as flat and as good-looking as possible so that, when they're pressed, you aren't fighting with them.

The best way to make sure that the seamlines will behave is to test the stitch you intend to use for the seam on a scrap piece of fabric before you sew the real thing. This rule works with not only the straight stitch but also all the other stitches available on your sewing machine and serger.

Use the following guidelines to help you adjust the stitch length as necessary:

✔ **If your fabric puckers, shorten the stitch length.** Shortening the stitch length puts more thread into the stitch so that the fabric is freed up and goes back to its original shape.

✔ **If your fabric waves out of shape, lengthen the stitch.** Lengthening the stitch removes thread from the stitch so that the fabric relaxes into its original position.

See Chapter 5 for more of the particulars on taking the first stitch.

Sew from Bottoms Up

Here are a couple of hard and fast rules that work for vertical seams and horizontal seams, and they apply to any project:

✔ When you sew a vertical seam (like a side seam on a skirt or a pair of pants), sew from the hem edge up to the waistline.

✔ When you sew a horizontal seam (like a shoulder seam or a collar), sew from the outside edges toward the center.

Press Seams Flat and Together — Then Open or to One Side

Proper pressing technique transforms homemade projects into custom-made masterpieces. Your project's instructions may tell you to press in any of the following ways:

✔ **Press the seam flat and together:** Press the iron over the seamline from the wrong side of the fabric. Doing so sets or "blends" the stitches in the fabric. Then position the iron so that you press the seam allowance together from the seamline out toward the edge.

✔ **Press the seam open.** Press a ⅝-inch seam from the wrong side of the fabric so that one seam allowance falls to the right and the other seam allowance falls to the left. The seamline itself ends up centered between the seam allowances.

✔ **Press the seam to one side.** Press a ¼-inch seam from the wrong side of the fabric, pressing it to one side or the other so the crack of the seam faces to the back of the project.

For more information about the art of pressing, see Chapter 5.

Clip with Your Scissors' Tips

Don't cut a hole in your project where you don't want one! Any time you cut from an edge into a seam allowance (for example, when you clip or notch a curve — see Chapter 6 for info on clipping and notching) and toward a seamline, use the very tips of your scissors or shears. This way, you won't accidentally cut into the seamline.

Appendix

Sewing Resources

Sewing Organizations

American Sewing Association
1375 Broadway
New York, NY 10018
Phone: 212-302-2150
Fax: 212-391-8009
E-mail: ahsca@aol.com

American Sewing Guild
P. O. Box 8476
Medford, OR 97504
Phone: 541-772-4059
Fax: 541-770-7041

Sewing Publications

Butterick Pattern Magazine
161 6th Avenue
New York, NY 10013
Phone: 212-620-2500
Fax: 212-620-2746

Creative Machine Newsletter
P. O. Box 2634
Menlo Park, CA 94026-2634
Phone: 650-366-4440
Fax: 650-366-4455

McCall's Patterns Magazine
11 Penn Plaza
New York, NY 10001
Phone: 212-465-6800
Fax: 212-465-6814

Sew News
741 Corporate Circle, Suite A
Golden, CO 80401
Phone: 303-278-1010
Fax: 303-277-0370
E-mail: sewnews@sewnews.com

Simplicity Pattern Magazine
2 Park Avenue, 12th Floor
New York, NY 10016
Phone: 212-372-0500
Fax: 212-372-0628
E-mail:
info@simplicitypatt.com
Web site:
www.simplicitypatt.com

Sewing Machine Companies

BabyLock, USA
P. O. Box 730
Fenton, MO 63026
Phone: 800-422-2952
Web site:
www.babylock.com

Bernina of America, Inc
3500 Thayer Court
Aurora, IL 60504-6182
Phone: 630-978-2500
Fax: 630-978-8214
Web site:
www.berninausa.com

Brother International
200 Cottontail Lane
Somerset, NJ 08875
Phone: 908-356-8880
Fax: 908-469-1783

Elna, USA
1760 Gilsinn Lane
Fenton, MO 63026
Phone: 800-848-ELNA

Necchi/Allyn International
1075 Santa Fe Drive
Denver, CO 80204
Phone: 800-525-9987
Fax: 303-825-5078

Pfaff American Sales Corp.
610 Winters Avenue
Paramus, NJ 07653
Phone: 201-262-7211
Fax: 201-262-0696
Web site: www.pfaff.com

Riccar America
1800 East Walnut
Fullerton, CA 92831
Phone: 800 995-9110
Fax: 714-525-3200

Singer Sewing Company
4500 Singer Rd.
Murfreesboro, TN 37129
Phone: 800-877-7762
Fax: 615-893-2830

Viking Sewing Machines, Inc.
31000 Viking Parkway
Westlake, OH 44145
Phone: 800-541-3357
Fax: 440-847-0001

Pattern Companies

Burda Patterns, Inc.
1831-B W. Oak Parkway
Marietta, GA 30062
Phone: 800-241-6887
Fax: 770-423-9103

Kwik Sew Pattern Company, Inc.
3000 Washington Avenue North
Minneapolis, MN 55411-1699
Phone: 800-328-3953
Fax: 612-521-1662

McCall Pattern Company
11 Penn Plaza
New York, NY 10001
Phone: 212-465-6800
Fax: 212-465-6814

Simplicity Pattern Company, Inc.
2 Park Avenue, 12th Floor
New York, NY 10016
Phone: 888-588-2700
Fax: 212-372-0628
E-mail:
info@simplicity.com
Web site:
www.simplicity.com

Stretch & Sew, Inc.
P. O. Box 25306
Tempe, AZ 85285
Phone: 800-547-7717

Vogue/Butterick
161 6th Avenue
New York, NY 10013
Phone: 212-620-2500
Fax: 212-620-2746

Notion Companies

Belva Barrick of Arizona
(Makers of The Seam Stick)
5643 West Townley Avenue
Glendale, AZ 85302
Phone: 602-934-8459

Bond America
(Makers of Cool Gloo)
178 Maple Street
Glen Falls, NY 12801-3735
Phone: 800-862-5348
Fax: 518-798-2269
E-mail: bond.america@
connect2.org

Creative Feet
(Makers of piping foot and
other creative presser feet)
8933 East Larado Drive
Prescott Valley, AZ 86314
Phone: 800-776-6938
Fax: 520-775-4250
Web site:
www.creativefeet.com

**Fiskars Manufacturing
Corporation**
(Makers of scissors, shears,
rotary cutters)
P. O. Box 8027
Wausau, WI 54402-8027
Phone: 800-950-0203
Fax: 715-848-5528

Gingher, Inc
(Makers of scissors, shears,
pinking shears)
P. O. Box 8865
Greensboro, NC 27419
Phone: 336-292-6237
Fax: 336-292-6250

Mundial
(Makers of scissors and shears)
50 Kerry Place
Norwood, MA 01062
Phone: 781-762-8310
Fax: 781-762-0364

Prym/Dritz Corporation
(Makers of sewing notions and
home decor trims)
P. O. Box 5028
Spartanburg, SC 29304
Phone: 800-845-4948
Fax: 800-574-3847

The Snap Source
(Makers of sport snaps and
snap tools)
P. O. Box 99733
Troy, MI 48099-9733
Phone: 800-725-4600
Fax: 248-280-1140
E-mail: SnapSource@aol.com

Wm. E. Wright, LP
(Makers of trims and tapes for
fashion sewing and home decor)
85 South Street
West Warren, MA 01092
Phone: 413-436-7732

Notion Mail Order Companies

Nancy's Notions
P. O. Box 683
Beaver Dam, WI 53916
Phone: 800-833-0690
Fax: 800-255-8119
E-mail: nzieman@aol.com
Web site:
www.nancysnotions.com

Clotilde, Inc.
Box 3000
Louisiana, MO 63353-3000
Phone: 800-772-2891
Fax: 800-863-3191
E-mail:
clotilde@ix.netcom.com
Web site: www.clotilde.com

Interfacing Companies

Freudenberg Non-Wovens
(Makers of Pellon Interfacings)
3440 Industrial Drive
Durham, NC 27704
Phone: 919-620-3916
Fax: 919-620-3945

HTC - Handler Textile Corporation
24 Empire Boulevard
Moonachie, NJ 07074
Phone: 201-272-2000
Fax: 201-272-2035

Thread Companies

Coats & Clark
Consumer Service
P. O. Box 12229
Greenville, SC 29612
Phone: 800-648-1417
Web site:
www.coatsandclark.com

Gutermann of America
P. O. Box 7387
Charlotte, NC 28217
Phone: 704-525-7068
Fax: 704-525-7071
E-mail: wroberts@aol.com

Sulky of America, Inc.
3113 Broadpoint Drive
Harbor Heights, FL 33983
Phone: 800-874-4115
Fax: 941-743-4634
Web site: www.sulky.com

Kits

Bon Coeur It's Kits
(Makers of Father Time and Bravo
Bear Kits, Quick-Change Window
System, Quick-Fix Sew-Vival Kits)
15100 North 78th Way, Suite 101
Scottsdale, AZ 85260
Phone: 877-400-6560

Global Village Imports
(Makers of Guatemalan belts)
3439 N.E. Sandy Blvd. #263
Portland, OR 97232-1959
Phone: 503-236-9245
Fax: 503-233-0827
Web site:
www.globalfabric.com/gvi

Index

Notes

Notes

Notes

Notes

Notes

Notes

Notes

Notes

Notes

WWW.DUMMIES.COM

IDG BOOKS WORLDWIDE BOOK REGISTRATION

Register This Book and Win!

We want to hear from you!

Visit **http://my2cents.dummies.com** to register this book and tell us how you liked it!

- Get entered in our monthly prize giveaway.

- Give us feedback about this book — tell us what you like best, what you like least, or maybe what you'd like to ask the author and us to change!

- Let us know any other *...For Dummies*® topics that interest you.

Your feedback helps us determine what books to publish, tells us what coverage to add as we revise our books, and lets us know whether we're meeting your needs as a *...For Dummies* reader. You're our most valuable resource, and what you have to say is important to us!

Not on the Web yet? It's easy to get started with *Dummies 101*®: *The Internet For Windows*® *98* or *The Internet For Dummies*®, 6th Edition, at local retailers everywhere.

Or let us know what you think by sending us a letter at the following address:

...For Dummies Book Registration
Dummies Press
7260 Shadeland Station, Suite 100
Indianapolis, IN 46256-3945
Fax 317-596-5498

BESTSELLING BOOK SERIES FROM IDG